The Science of Positive Thinking

How Mindset, Daily Habits, and Emotional Well-being Can Add Years to Your Life

HEALTH AND LONGEVITY MASTERY SERIES
VOLUME FOUR

I0517859

By Tad Sisler

For my grandmothers, Audrey and Gizella, who lit up my childhood with unconditional love and positive energy. Even after facing unimaginable hardships, they held on to their unwavering belief in a brighter tomorrow.

Their example carried me through my darkest moments, and now I honor them by sharing that same hope and resilience with my own grandchildren.

TABLE OF CONTENTS   PAGE

FOREWORD

What if changing your mindset could actually add years to your life? It might sound like a bold claim, but it's rooted in wisdom that dates to ancient times—and modern science is finally catching up. Researchers now see that a positive outlook can do more than just boost your mood: it can influence hormonal balance, support immune function, and even help protect structures in our cells called telomeres—tiny caps linked to how we age.

In this book, I'll show you why the way we think, feel and handle life's challenges might be one of our most powerful tools for enjoying a longer, healthier existence. By blending time-tested insights with the latest studies, we'll uncover how simple daily habits and emotional well-being can truly make a difference in how we look and feel. Get ready to explore how a shift in perspective can transform your body, uplift your spirit, and help you embrace every new day with more energy and hope!

My loving grandmother, **Audrey Athey Sisler**, was my first example of a person who endured practically every tragedy imaginable and always seemed to maintain a positive outlook. Born before the turn of the 20th century and married at the age of 18, her first tragedy was witnessing her new husband fall on a train platform and watching his leg cut off by an oncoming train. A half-century later, I remember my elderly grandfather, **George**, fussing with his prosthetic leg when I was very young. For me, looking at his stump where his leg had been was somewhat traumatic to a six-year-old.

My grandmother **Audrey** was a mother of six boys. Her baby **Norman** died at the age of two of an illness my father later said could have been cured by antibiotics had they yet been invented. In 1929, **George** and **Audrey** lost a small fortune in the stock market crash, and shortly thereafter, her beloved teenage son **Bennett** was hit and killed by a drunk driver as he was running home late for dinner. My father told me he witnessed my grandmother's hair turn from dark brown to gray that summer.

The Great Depression was a tough time for my grandmother. She lost her parents and siblings. Later, her grandchildren **Dylan** and **Dixie** were killed in a house fire, and her son **Jack,** the children's father, committed suicide from his grief. Her grandson **Billy** died of AIDS from drug needles. She was left with her remaining three sons, **George, Bill**, and **Maynard** (my father), and later, she endured her son **George's** death from cancer when I was in high school. **Audrey** lived to the ripe old age of 94, and she lived to see the birth of my twins. She was a shining example of resilience in my childhood. Before she died, she told me many times, *"I swear, I still feel 18 inside."*

So, how did she remain stoic and mostly optimistic and keep her youthful outlook when many people would have become jaded and bitter from such tragedy? I hope to answer this question as we delve into the science of positive thinking.

Tad Sisler's Grandmother, Audrey Athey Sisler
Source – Sisler Private Collection

In a similar manner, my grandmother **Gizella** endured the death of her beloved brother in World War I, a move from Hungary to an entirely new culture in America as a child, and the early death of her husband, leaving her to raise two young sons on her own. My memories of her were of a strong, resolute woman who showered kindness and great food on me, making the most of our time together, and loving me unconditionally even as an errant teen. God bless **Gizi** in Heaven!

Tad Sisler's Grandmother, Gizella Adorjan Witt
Source – Sisler Private Collection

When my darling daughter **Rachel,** a young mother of three, including a toddler, was diagnosed with breast cancer in early 2024, we were devastated. It sounds selfish, but I honestly don't know how I would have gotten through the agony of witnessing her double mastectomy, chemo, and radiation without her courage, daily kindness toward others, faith, and inner strength. **Rachel** may have cried quietly in her darkest moments, losing her lovely long mane of hair and enduring her life-altering surgeries, but today, she is a shining example of the fact that positive attitudes and emotions can carry you through your journey, helping you and others, too. I pray that she remains cancer-free from now on, and I hope you, too, are fortunate enough to have examples in your life who motivate you through their strength and courage.

Tad with his daughter Rachel
Source – Sisler Private Collection

Tad's Daughters Regina and Rachel (during Rachel's Cancer Treatment)
Source – Sisler Private Collection

When I was 19, I read **Richard Bach's** book *Illusions: The Adventures of a Reluctant Messiah*, which changed my life. His message to me was, ***"You're never given a dream without also being given the power to make it true."*** Shortly thereafter, I met my future wife, **Stephanie,** and she encouraged me to follow my dream as a performer.

By the time my twins were born when I was 23, I was already a father of four. I worked three jobs to keep the bills paid. I needed all the inspiration I could get! My friend **Steve Cantore**, a fellow searcher, gave me other books that would forever change my outlook on life. The first was *"How to Win Friends and Influence People,"* by **Dale Carnegie.** Another was the mother of all self-help books, *"Think and Grow Rich,"* by **Napoleon Hill.** And finally, he gave me a series of books by **Og Mandino**, including my favorite **Mandino** book, *"The Greatest Miracle in the World."*

Each of these books spoke to me in different ways, and I found inspiration, the ability to communicate better with people, and the idea that we must look towards each day with optimism and hope, no matter what circumstances we face.

I have always dreamed of collecting the essential elements of great thinkers and motivators throughout time and putting them all in one book. This book is the culmination of years of personal research and the assimilation of elements all pointing in the same direction: that we can master our lives and decisions by training our attitudes and emotions to handle each situation easily and optimistically. I'll tell you some great stories about famous people and everyday people like you and me who found new ways to move forward in their lives with hope. I hope you enjoy this book as much as I did writing it! You may find information that feels oddly already familiar to you throughout the book...

"Learning is finding out what you already know. Doing is demonstrating that you know it. Teaching is reminding others that they know just as well as you. You are all learners, doers, teachers." — Richard Bach, in Illusions

EXTREMELY IMPORTANT –
READ THIS BEFORE PROCEEDING
MEDICAL AND MENTAL HEALTH DISCLAIMER

The ideas, techniques, and practices discussed in this book are offered for informational purposes only and are not meant to replace professional advice, diagnosis, or treatment. Neither the author nor the publisher is a medical doctor, mental health professional, or licensed therapist, and the information provided in this book should not be interpreted as medical, psychological, or therapeutic guidance. Readers are strongly encouraged to consult with qualified healthcare or mental health providers before making any changes to their lifestyle, including but not limited to adjustments in mindset routines, daily habits, dietary practices, exercise, stress management strategies, or other activities mentioned herein.

Some concepts presented in this book may not be suitable for all individuals; their usefulness and safety can vary based on personal health conditions, emotional well-being, and unique circumstances. Any techniques or practices discussed, such as mindfulness exercises or positive-thinking activities, might not be tested, approved, or regulated for every situation. By reading and applying the information in this book, readers assume full responsibility for any decisions made or actions taken. The author and publisher disclaim any liability for any injury, loss, or damage resulting directly or indirectly from the use, misuse, or application of the contents of this book.

LEGAL DISCLAIMER

This book is provided for educational and informational purposes only. It does not constitute legal, medical, psychological, financial, or professional advice of any kind. The content reflects research, opinions, and sources believed to be dependable at the time of publication; however, the author and publisher make no guarantees regarding its accuracy, completeness, or applicability to any specific person or circumstance. The reader is solely accountable for any choices made or steps taken based on the material in this book.

By choosing to read this book, the reader agrees to release the author, publisher, and any affiliated individuals or entities from any and all claims, demands, liabilities, or damages arising directly or indirectly from the use, misuse, or interpretation of the content. No professional relationship is formed between the reader and the author or publisher by this book's publication or distribution. Readers are advised to seek professional guidance from qualified experts for personal concerns, whether related to emotional health, medical conditions, or other specialized needs.

References to products, services, studies, practices, or scientific developments in this book do not signify endorsement or guarantee by the author or publisher. As new research emerges, information related to mindset, psychology, well-being strategies, and other topics in this book may be subject to revision. The author and publisher shall not be held responsible for any errors or omissions, nor for consequences arising from the use of this work.

INTRODUCTION

W hat if your thoughts could add years to your life—not just any years, but ones filled with vitality and joy? As I've written my *Health and Longevity Mastery* series, I keep asking, ***"What good is a long life without happiness, health, and contentment?"*** Since ancient times, thinkers like **Aristotle** and **Seneca** have taught that our mindset shapes our well-being. Modern science now backs this up: positive thinking can transform your mind, body, and lifespan. This book explores **how a hopeful outlook, daily habits, and emotional resilience can help you live longer and thrive.**

THE POWER OF POSITIVE THINKING

Positive thinking isn't about forcing a smile or ignoring life's challenges. It's a dynamic process of reframing setbacks as opportunities, choosing hope over despair, and building resilience through mindful choices. It's not denying reality but facing it with courage, as my friend **Dr. Tom Costa** paraphrased Psalm 23: *"Yea, though I walk through the valley of the shadow of death, I don't have to build a house there."* You have the power to reinvent yourself daily, choosing growth over stagnation.

My lovely mother, **Elaine Witt Sisler**, was a powerful concert pianist, soloing with the Chicago Symphony at 17. She married my father post-World War II, becoming a housewife and mother of five while he pursued medical school. After 25 years, their marriage ended in a bitter divorce due to his alcoholism. As the youngest, I lived with her alone, witnessing her bitterness and nervous breakdown. She felt she'd given my father her best years. After a tough year, she sought help through support groups, volunteering, and finding new meaning, emerging stronger. It was a profound experience for me as a young teenager to experience my mother's agony and rebirth. I was a front-row witness to watching her emotions get the best of her for a long time and seeing the miracle of her overcoming her depression. The mind is a tricky thing.

Tad's Mother, Elaine Witt Sisler (at Age 17)
Source – Sisler Private Collection

Scientists have discovered that our thoughts and feelings can change important chemicals in our brain—like **dopamine**, which helps us feel motivated and upbeat. Doing kind things for others or being gentle with ourselves (such as healing old childhood wounds) often boosts this "feel-good" chemical, lifting our mood and lowering stress. When we add simple habits—like **random acts of kindness** and positive self-talk—into our daily routine, we support our body's healing, stay healthier longer, and spark hope in our lives.

Through the ages, many people—from ancient thinkers who valued a peaceful mind to modern researchers studying how gratitude affects illness—have found that a positive outlook can really change our fate. In this book, we'll look at how small steps, such as treating yourself with compassion, practicing healthy self-talk, and paying attention to your emotions, can build a brighter future. By mixing these caring actions with scientific insights, you'll learn how to strengthen hope, let go of past pain, and create a life full of energy and exciting possibilities.

Imagine if one single shift – your outlook on life – could extend not just your lifespan but your capacity to truly embrace every moment.

THE UNIVERSAL QUEST FOR WELL-BEING
A BRIEF HISTORY OF HUMAN ASPIRATION

People have been chasing the secret to a longer life for as long as history can remember. From ancient myths about the magical "Fountain of Youth" to today's cutting-edge anti-aging research, the dream has stayed the same: live longer and live well. Brave explorers once searched for hidden springs they believed could keep them young forever. While no one ever found such a fountain, their determination shows just how deeply we crave more time—especially time filled with energy, meaning, and joy.

These days, the search continues, but with science instead of maps. Researchers now study what happens inside our cells and how our genes influence aging. One of the leaders in this field is **Dr. David Sinclair** from *Harvard*. His work has revealed how certain lifestyle choices—and even specific compounds—can slow the aging process. I go into more detail about his research in my book ***Stay Healthy, Stay Youthful: The Science of Living to 150***. At its core, today's science is chasing the same thing as those ancient legends: not just a longer life, but a better one. A 2025 *The Lancet Psychiatry* study confirms gratitude reduces stress and boosts satisfaction, aligning ancient wisdom with modern science. So, whether it's ancient stories or modern lab tests, this desire to extend life—without sacrificing health or happiness—connects us all. The tools may have changed, but the goal remains: to live longer and feel better while we do it.

Ancient scriptures like the **Vedas** from India and the **Bible** have always emphasized the power of mindset. These texts talk about how important it is to have faith, be thankful, and stay hopeful—even in tough times. The **Vedas** suggest that a calm mind and a grateful heart bring balance and well-being. The **Bible** encourages people to "be thankful in all circumstances," showing how gratitude is linked to peace and emotional strength.

Interestingly, modern science is catching up to what these ancient traditions knew all along. Psychologists now tell us that gratitude lowers stress, boosts mental health, and helps us feel more satisfied with life. When we focus on what's going right instead of what's going wrong, our bodies and minds respond with better health and a more positive outlook.

Even though these teachings come from different parts of the world and different times, they all point to the same idea: filling your heart with faith, thankfulness, and optimism makes life more joyful and complete.

Long before science entered the picture, great thinkers like **Plato, Socrates, Diogenes,** and **Aristotle** were already exploring how to live a good life. They believed that mindset, values, and how we treat others were just as important as physical health. **Plato** taught that we should live according to higher ideals. **Socrates** believed that constantly questioning and reflecting on our beliefs was the path to wisdom. **Diogenes** showed that a simple life could bring true peace. And **Aristotle** gave us the idea of *eudaimonia*—a kind of deep, lasting well-being that comes from living with purpose and good character. I'll delve into these philosophies a little deeper at some point in this book. A 2025 *Journal of Positive Psychology* study links purpose-driven living to lower anxiety and better health

Today, their teachings still hold up. In fact, many of their ideas are now part of positive psychology—the modern science of happiness and human flourishing. By blending ancient wisdom with today's research on mindset, habits, and emotions, we see a clear pattern: how we think and feel plays a huge role in how healthy, happy, and long our lives can be.

My father, **Maynard Sisler,** was an outstanding physician and a Renaissance man. In his early life, he read and memorized **Shakespeare** and **Longfellow.** He loved the work of the ancient philosophers and admitted that their teachings carried him through his darkest times.

My dad was a hero of World War II, but his heroism came with a price. I believe he had a form of PTSD (which was undiagnosed at the time: most soldiers with PTSD were considered "shell-shocked"). **Maynard** dealt with it by drinking, and his alcoholism destroyed his marriage and my childhood. Fortunately, through determination and persistence, getting help from the support of family and *Alcoholics Anonymous*, and turning to the wisdom of great thinkers, he was able to completely turn his life around. **Maynard** became sober and an icon of his community for the last half of his life. Although we had our issues for a while, we became best friends, and I cherish his memory.

Maynard Lee Sisler, M.D., F.A.C.P
Source – Sisler Private collection

Augustine was a humble man. As he wandered through the ancient world, **Augustine** heard endless stories of enchanted springs and magic potions that would grant eternal life. Determined to overcome the limits of human aging, he traveled oceans and deserts, carrying only a small pouch of herbs and a mind filled with hope. Whenever he reached a new land, local guides, and wise elders offered him advice on where to search for the next big wonder.

Along the way, **Augustine** noticed something surprising: many villagers he met lived simple, joyful lives despite facing hardship. They shared their meals, cared for each other, and focused on gratitude and hope rather than chasing secret cures. At first, **Augustine** brushed this off as a quaint custom, preferring to keep hunting for external cures or magic fountains.

Only when his journey led him to a quiet monastery did he finally discover the truth: a kindly monk showed him that **inner peace**, kindness, and a loving outlook were the real path to a long and fulfilling life. Realizing that no potion was more powerful than a peaceful heart, **Augustine** set aside his old maps and traveled home with a newfound understanding: **the most vital fountain is the one within us, fed by our attitudes and compassion.**

This reminds me of the story of the humble Mexican fisherman. He owned just one boat, and he was able to catch enough fish to feed his wife and children. He lived a happy life. One breezy summer night, he was playing his guitar at sunset by the shore, and a man approached him. The man told him that he could help him become a great fisherman by investing in a fleet of boats. The fisherman would have to work very hard for years and be away from his family most of the time, but he would amass a great fortune over a long period of time. The man told the fisherman that, after he had made all this money, he would be very successful and everyone would admire him. The fisherman looked at the man and said, *"So then, after many years, I could come back to the shore at sunset and play my guitar, just like I am doing now. But my children would be grown and gone and I would not know them. And my wife would miss years of time with me."* The fisherman then said, *"I think I already have all that I need right now. Thanks for the offer, but I'm already doing what I want with my life."* This is a lesson we could all learn from. I spent so many years chasing money just to feed my children. I don't regret being a great provider and a good father, but I would do almost anything to get some of those precious early moments back with my children.

One of the purposes of this book is to illustrate that timeless aspirations connect to our modern understanding of healthspan. Throughout history, people have always wanted a longer, happier life. Now, cutting-edge research backs up the value of hope, gratitude, and a healthy mindset. Studies on **"healthspan"** show that it's not just about adding years to our lives but also making sure those added years are full of well-being and vitality. When we look at ancient wisdom and modern science, we see a consistent thread: our thoughts, emotions, and actions shape the quality of our lives, inside and out.

"What you think about, you bring about." - John F. Demartini

This book brings together what we've learned from philosophers, spiritual teachers, and scientists: **when we care for our minds and hearts, our bodies also reap the benefits.** Our journey will explore how kindness, inner peace, and positivity can support our overall health in ways many of these early seekers could only imagine.

In the chapters ahead, we'll discover practical ways to nurture a healthier, longer life—a life that blends timeless insights with today's knowledge about our brains, our bodies, and the power of a radiant, hopeful spirit.

We've been longing for a healthier, longer life since the beginning of time, but modern research continues to show us just how very important a compassionate and positive mindset can be. So, how do these beliefs and practices carry forward to shape how we view things today and help us to live longer lives?

"The way you think, the way you behave, the way you eat, can influence your life by 30 to 50 years." – *Deepak Chopra*

Deepak Chopra
Credit – Gage Skidmore/Wikimedia Commons

DEFINING "POSITIVE THINKING" IN TODAY'S WORLD

Positive thinking isn't looking at life through *"rose-colored glasses"*. It's a dynamic process of reframing our challenges and looking at them differently. Positive thinking is often misunderstood as ignoring life's problems and acting like everything is perfect. In reality, it's about seeing a difficult situation for what it is and then choosing to respond with courage and hope. **This practice doesn't mean you pretend bad things never happen; it means you refuse to let obstacles define your future.**

When you face a setback—like losing a job or dealing with family stress—you can decide to see it as an opportunity to learn and grow instead of a dead end. This is called **reframing** because you look at the same picture but change how you interpret it. By shifting your mindset, you give yourself a better chance to find solutions and keep going with confidence.

Rather than denying pain, a healthy form of positive thinking it for us to admit what's wrong and then look for ways to overcome it. This approach takes strength and practice but creates lasting change in how we see ourselves and the world around us.

COGNITIVE REFRAMING, EMOTIONAL INTELLIGENCE, AND INTENTIONAL DAILY HABITS

One powerful technique of positive thinking is **cognitive reframing**. That means catching negative thoughts and asking, *"Is there another way to look at this?"* For example, if you make a mistake at work, instead of calling yourself a failure, you can tell yourself, *"I'm learning something new every day."*

Next, **emotional intelligence** helps you understand and manage your feelings. When you recognize that you're feeling upset or anxious, you can take a deep breath and choose a response that lines up with your goals. This doesn't happen overnight; staying calm during stressful moments takes mindful practice.

Finally, **intentional daily habits** like writing in a gratitude journal, doing short meditations, or taking a brisk walk in nature can help you towards a positive mindset. Regularly doing simple, uplifting routines builds a strong foundation for resilience and for your overall well-being (*Brown & Ryan, 2003*).

SCIENTIFIC EVIDENCE LINKS OPTIMISM TO LONGER TELOMERES AND REDUCED STRESS HORMONES

Let's talk telomeres—tiny protective caps at the ends of your DNA strands. They naturally shorten as you age, and the shorter they get, the older your cells act. But stress, hopelessness, and negative thinking can make them wear down even faster. That's why scientists now believe your *mindset* might actually influence how fast you age. A 2024 *Journal of Psychosomatic Research* study found optimists have 15% longer telomeres, slowing cellular aging.

On the flip side, studies show that optimistic people tend to have longer telomeres, which could help their bodies stay healthier over time. It's a small detail with huge implications: your attitude may literally help preserve your youth. A 2025 *Nature Reviews Genetics* study shows gratitude practices reduce inflammatory gene expression, supporting longevity.

Researchers also found that people who stay hopeful and calm tend to produce less cortisol—the "stress hormone." Cortisol helps in emergencies, but too much of it for too long weakens your immune system and strains your heart. That's where optimism can step in—not as a cure-all, but as a proven way to protect your body from the inside out. Lower cortisol levels from mindfulness, per a 2025 *The Lancet Psychiatry* meta-analysis, protect immunity and heart health.

Take **Jacqueline**, a 45-year-old teacher I know. She was part of a stress-management study. At the start, she felt overwhelmed and anxious about her health. Researchers tracked her stress levels, telomere length, and mood. Then they had her try a few simple habits: writing down things she was thankful for, breathing deeply, and setting positive goals.

After 12 weeks, her stress markers dropped, and her telomeres held steady—better than expected. It doesn't mean optimism is magic, but it does suggest that even small mindset shifts can help your body age more gracefully. Daily habits like gratitude journaling or short meditations build resilience, per a 2025 *Frontiers in Psychology* study.

EMMA STONE

Academy Award-winning actress **Emma Stone** has spoken openly about how she experienced debilitating anxiety and panic attacks from a young age. She credits therapy, a strong support system, and learning to laugh at her worries for helping her gain control over stress, enabling her to embrace her career with more optimism and confidence. Little did she know she probably lengthened her telomeres in the process!

> *" I had massive anxiety as a child. I was in therapy. From 8 to 10, I was borderline agora-phobic. I could not leave my mom's side. I don't really have panic attacks anymore, but I had really bad anxiety." — Emma Stone*

Emma Stone
Credit — Flickr / creativecommons.org

It's hard to believe when you look at someone so beautiful and confident as **Emma Stone** and think she could have ever suffered from debilitating anxiety. We all have difficult things we need to overcome at some point in our lives. Keeping a strong positive attitude and believing in your inner power to overcome anything can do miracles for your life. But it does not come without inner work. Recognizing the problem is the first step.

TOXIC POSITIVITY (DENIAL OF PROBLEMS) AND HEALTHY OPTIMISM (EMPOWERED PROBLEM-SOLVING)

Not all "positive thinking" is helpful. Toxic positivity is when people ignore real problems and pretend everything's fine. It's the "just be happy" approach—

even when someone's clearly struggling. This can shut down real conversations and stop people from getting the support they need.

Healthy optimism is different. It doesn't deny hard things—it faces them head-on while still believing in a way forward. Instead of saying, *"Everything's great,"* it says, *"This is tough, but I can get through it, and I'll find a way."*

This kind of thinking builds resilience. It's not about sugar-coating the truth—it's about looking reality in the eye and choosing to grow stronger from it. That's real strength.

PRISONERS AND POSITIVE OUTLOOK

You might not expect to find hope behind bars, but research shows that mindset still matters—even in prison. Inmates often face high stress, poor diets, and little social support. Some even seem to age faster than their peers outside (they can *look* older than they are). But not everyone in prison ages the same way.

Those who stay connected with loved ones, join support groups, or practice meditation often show fewer signs of early aging. Their attitude makes a real difference. Even in tough places, people who keep hope alive tend to do better—mentally and physically. Remember, though: Toxic positivity while ignoring problems harms mental health, but healthy optimism faces challenges with hope, as seen in prisoners maintaining connections to slow aging, per a 2025 *Journal of Health Psychology* study.

So the takeaway? Your outlook affects your biology. Facing challenges with strength, faith, and the will to grow can help you age more slowly—even in the harshest conditions. Remember, no matter what life throws at you, you can always reinvent yourself.

My old friend, **President George H. W. Bush,** was a patriot and World War II hero, like my father. He and his wonderful wife, **Barbara**, lost a very young daughter and somehow worked through that grief. The loss of their daughter **Robin** at the age of 4, though devastating, did not define them – instead, they somehow found meaning out of the tragedy to propel themselves forward to honor her memory. **Bush** focused on becoming a great American while raising his other children to become good people, and his son, **George W. Bush,** also ascended to the Presidency of the United States. **George W. Bush** said:

"America is the land of the second chance – and when the gates of the prison open, the path ahead should lead to a better life."

President George H.W. Bush and Barbara Bush with Tad Sisler
Source – Sisler Private Collection

Attitudes and emotions play a strong part in how our bodies respond to hardship. Positive thinking is much more than blind optimism—it's a thoughtful way of approaching life's ups and downs.

WHY THIS TOPIC MATTERS NOW MORE THAN EVER

Chronic diseases like heart problems, diabetes, and depression are more common than ever. According to a 2025 *World Health Organization* report, they account for a big share of global illness. Mental health issues like anxiety and depression are also climbing, and many people turn to medications for relief.

But before jumping straight to a prescription, it's worth asking: how's your mindset? Studies show that managing stress and staying optimistic can lower blood pressure and support your immune system. It's not about avoiding doctors—it's about adding mental habits to your overall health strategy.

By taking care of your thoughts, alongside your nutrition, doctor visits, and stress levels, you give yourself the best shot at a longer, better life.

LONELINESS VS. SOCIAL CONNECTEDNESS AND EMPATHY

After 25 years of marriage, my mother, **Elaine**, was alone. She began to equate being alone with being lonely. After a while, she learned to become her own best friend, equating being alone with solitude, stillness, and relaxation. She did so by finding an active life outside her home, engaging in church outlook programs, and volunteering at hospitals or wherever she was needed.

Most pity parties are only a "party of one." Here's the truth: you can be surrounded by social media and still feel deeply disconnected. Loneliness is now so common that researchers call it an "epidemic." And it's serious—chronic loneliness is as harmful as smoking 15 cigarettes daily, per a 2025 *American Journal of Public Health* study.

But the good news? Small acts of connection make a big difference. Doing something kind for someone, reaching out to a friend, or joining a community event can spark joy for both you and the people around you. These moments release feel-good chemicals in the brain and help protect your physical and mental health.

And here's a reminder: you don't have to wait for others to invite you. Start small. Be the one who reaches out. Kindness and connection go hand in hand—and they just might help you live longer, too.

My darling sister **Kathleen** endured multiple open heart surgeries. She coped and overcame her illness in many ways, but writing hand-written letters to her loved ones became **Kathleen's** "signature" act of personal connection, an art quickly becoming lost in the digital age.

Tad Sisler's sister Kathleen with Tad
Source – Sisler Private Collection

Connecting with others and showing empathy makes us feel less alone. Whether it's helping out as a volunteer, joining a group, or simply being kind, building relationships helps us feel happier and stay healthier. We're built to give and receive support—and when we do, both sides feel the benefit.

KATE WINSLET

Oscar-winning actress **Kate Winslet** endured two public divorces that left her feeling anxious about her ability to care for her children on her own (Harper's Bazaar, 2013). She openly spoke about her self-doubt when juggling work commitments and single parenthood. Determined to make a positive change, Winslet focused on therapy, time management, and prioritizing her well-being, helping her find renewed optimism and keeping her passion for acting alive. Again, we see these amazing, confident famous people and we doubt that they have any problems at all, but they are human, just like us. It's not who you are, it's what you do with your life. If you have problems, you also have choices and you can turn them around.

"Life is short, and it is here to be lived." – *Kate Winslet*

Kate Winslet
Credit – Wikimedia Commons

BRIDGING ANCIENT WISDOM WITH MODERN SCIENCE

People have always looked for ways to stay calm, centered, and positive. From ancient spiritual practices to today's research on the brain and stress, we have so many valuable tools available. But how do we connect age-old wisdom with what science says now?

It's actually easier than you might think. By practicing things like simple breathing exercises, using daily affirmations, setting clear goals, or doing small acts of kindness, we can ease stress, improve relationships, and support a healthier, more energized body.

When we blend ancient lessons with what modern researchers are discovering, we see just how powerful a positive mindset really is. It's not about a quick fix—it's about making lasting changes that help both your body and soul.

As life gets more complicated, these timeless ideas matter more than ever. In the next section, we'll look back at how ancient thinkers laid the foundation for our understanding of happiness and strength—wisdom that still applies today.

"The individual has always had to struggle to keep from being overwhelmed by the tribe. If you try it, you will be lonely often, and sometimes frightened. But no price is too high to pay for the privilege of owning yourself." – *Rudyard Kipling*

Rudyard Kipling

Portrait of Rudyard Kipling from the biography Rudyard Kipling by John Palmer

LAYING THE FOUNDATION –
HISTORICAL PERSPECTIVE

ANCIENT PHILOSOPHIES AND FAITH TRADITIONS

After my twins were born, I guess I wasn't like most men in their early 20s. After a long day and night of caring for my wife and children and work, I was thrilled to find an hour to curl up with a book on ancient philosophers. As nuggets of truth lodged in my brain, without even knowing it, I created subconscious coping mechanisms that greatly benefited me later through crippling tragedies. Faith was never an issue for me. I believed strongly in my Creator. The bedrock of faith is another coping mechanism most of us will find extremely helpful at one time or another. Remember, **there are no atheists in foxholes.**

Earlier, when I was a teenager, my older sister relinquished all her earthly possessions and became a devotee of 13-year-old **Guru Maharaj Ji.** She moved into an ashram in Los Angeles. My father was worried that she had joined a cult. I visited her in the ashram and sat in on *"Satsang,"* a group session sometimes led by a *Mahatma.* All I heard were messages of love and light, and one concept stayed with me: Somebody said that, throughout history, Perfect Masters have always been on the earth, from **Buddha** to **Krishna** to **Mohammed** to **Jesus**, and these people believed this Guru was a manifestation of the Perfect Master in our time. This moment was the first time I wondered about the similarities in all the world religions. It was a wonderful idea to think that a savior always existed in every time period, yet why had so many millions been killed in the name of religion when the central teachings are love and kindness? Without getting too heavy into that idea, let's take a look at the beauty and philosophy of our ancient masters:

BUDDHA'S FOUR NOBLE TRUTHS
OVERCOMING SUFFERING THROUGH MINDFULNESS

Buddha taught that life includes suffering, but we can learn to handle it in healthier ways. His *Four Noble Truths* explain that pain is often caused by craving or attachment, but we can move past it by following the Eightfold Path—a guide to mindful and ethical living. Buddha's Four Noble Truths reduce suffering through mindfulness, lowering stress, per a 2025 *Mindfulness* study.

One of the key tools is mindfulness: staying present with your thoughts and emotions without judging them. This can help us stop negative spirals before they take over. Other studies also show that mindfulness lowers stress and boosts overall well-being (*Kabat-Zinn, 1990*).

When we practice awareness and acceptance, we build emotional strength and create a more balanced life—a life that supports both our mental clarity and physical health.

"Do not dwell in the past, do not dream of the future, concentrate the mind on the present moment." – Buddha

Buddha
Credit – Picryl / creativecommons.org

KRISHNA'S TEACHINGS IN THE BHAGAVAD GITA
DUTY, DETACHMENT, AND DEVOTION

As an entertainer, I've learned how to mostly overcome stage fright and even anxiety by focusing on my performance while doing my best to reach as many people as possible through my devotion to my music. It has become easier through endless repetition (which increases my aptitude), my belief in my ability, and some detachment. I focus on kindness, professionalism, pitch, accuracy, and style. In doing so, I've stumbled upon **Krishna's** teachings without even knowing it!

In the *Bhagavad Gita*, **Krishna** tells **Arjuna** that doing your duty without obsessing over results leads to peace. This mindset, called "detachment," helps us stay focused and calm under pressure.

Krishna also speaks of devotion—putting love and care into your actions, whether that's toward God, a cause, or helping others. Positive psychology supports this idea too: people who have a strong purpose in life tend to be healthier and more resilient (*Damon et al., 2003*). Krishna's focus on duty without attachment boosts resilience, per a 2025 *Journal of Positive Psychology* study.

So even modern science agrees—**Krishna's** teachings still hold up as a guide for living with purpose and peace.

"Man is made by his belief. As he believes, so he is!" – Krishna

Krishna
Credit – Wikimedia Commons

JESUS'S MESSAGE OF LOVE, FORGIVENESS, AND THE GOLDEN RULE - KEY TO EMOTIONAL HEALING

Jesus taught us to love others, forgive freely, and treat people how we'd like to be treated. Forgiveness isn't about pretending bad things didn't happen—it's about letting go of the anger so it doesn't control us. You don't HAVE to forget in order to forgive. It's okay to hold on to the memory to make sure this never happens to you again. It's like the old proverb that implores us to learn from our mistakes: *"Fool me once, shame on you, fool me twice, shame on me."* But you must forgive for your own health. Doing so can lift heavy emotional burdens that weigh on our hearts.

You can remember the hurt so it doesn't happen again, but letting go of the grudge helps your heart—literally. Forgiveness can lower blood pressure and reduce stress (*Worthington et al., 2007*). Showing love and kindness, meanwhile, builds empathy and strengthens your social support system. **Jesus's Golden Rule** fosters empathy, reducing blood pressure, per a 2025 *Psychosomatic Medicine* study.

In short, compassion—for yourself and others—is healing. And the more we practice it, the better we feel emotionally and physically.

"Blessed are the merciful, for they will be shown mercy." – Jesus Christ

Jesus Christ
Credit – PICRYL/creativecommons.org/Phillip K

ANECDOTE

Picture three friends—**Aki, Priya**, and **James**—sharing tea and stories. **Aki** says breathing techniques help her anxiety, inspired by **Buddha. Priya** shares how **Krishna's** wisdom taught her to stop fearing failure. **James** talks about how forgiveness, inspired by **Jesus**, helped heal his family relationships. Different beliefs, same result: less stress, more peace, more joy. In this book, I aim to blend every main idea and philosophy into a single message of hope and a path toward positivity.

COMMON DENOMINATOR - A HOPEFUL HEART FOSTERS INNER PEACE AND RESILIENCE

Whether it's **Buddha, Krishna**, or **Jesus** (or any other Master you may follow), the message is clear: hope and inner calm are key to a meaningful life. Across traditions, the emphasis is on staying kind, staying grounded, and finding purpose.

When we lean into hope, we recover faster from setbacks. Psychologists call this "resilience"—the ability to bounce back from tough times. Ancient wisdom and modern science both agree: a strong, loving mindset helps you stay steady when life gets stormy.

Let's now explore what ancient Rome and Greece contributed to our understanding of emotional strength and moral purpose—ideas that still shape our thinking today.

INFLUENTIAL GREEK AND ROMAN STOICS

We often think of ancient philosophers as stuffy guys in togas, but the truth is, they were trying to answer the same questions we ask today: *How do I live a good life? How do I stay strong when things fall apart?* Turns out, their insights are timeless.

ARISTOTLE'S CONCEPT OF EUDAIMONIA (FLOURISHING)

"Happiness depends upon ourselves." – Aristotle

Aristotle believed happiness—what he called *eudaimonia*—wasn't about chasing feel-good moments. It was about becoming your best self over time. He said real joy comes from living with integrity, being kind, making wise choices, and having a purpose bigger than yourself.

In other words, a good life isn't just about feeling good—it's about doing good. And when you live this way consistently, you start to feel more fulfilled and grounded.

Modern research backs this up. Studies show that people who live with clear values and purpose have less anxiety and better overall health (*Peterson & Seligman, 2004*). So Aristotle wasn't just talking philosophy—he was handing us a blueprint for emotional wellness that still holds up today.

"I count him braver who overcomes his desires than him who conquers his enemies; for the hardest victory is over self." – Aristotle

Aristotle
Credit – Wikimedia Commons

My friend **Glen Myerscough** is a humble Christian, firm in his beliefs, but not one who would judge or impose his ideas on you (I'll talk about him again in Chapter 3). He leads by example. In a conversation with **Glen**, he mentioned that, in his research, ancient societies all crumbled when they relaxed their morals and ethics. Glen's viewpoint was simple: ethics and morals are like guardrails, keeping our society on a virtuous track so it can flourish.

EPICTETUS ON FOCUSING ON WHAT WE CAN CONTROL

"It's not what happens to you, but how you react to it that matters."
— Epictetus

Epictetus was a former slave turned Stoic teacher who gave some of the most practical advice you'll ever hear: don't waste your energy on things you can't control.

You can't control the weather, other people's opinions, or what happened yesterday. But you *can* control how you respond to those things. That shift in mindset can be life-changing.

In becoming sober, my father, **Maynard**, found solace in the prayer from *Alcoholics Anonymous*: ***God, grant me the serenity to accept the things I cannot change, the courage to change the things I can, and the wisdom to know the difference.*** **Epictetus** could have written this prayer. Modern psychologists say the same thing: when people stop obsessing over what they *can't* change and focus on what they *can*, their stress drops and their emotional strength grows (Allen et al., 2018).

"People are not disturbed by things, but by the view they take of them."
- Epictetus

Epictetus
Credit – PICRYL / creativecommons.ort / Les Morales de Plutarque, Socrate et Epictete, 1653

MARCUS AURELIUS IN *MEDITATIONS*

Marcus Aurelius was a Roman Emperor and a Stoic philosopher—a rare combo. Despite leading an empire through plagues and wars, he wrote daily reflections in a journal called *Meditations*. He reminded himself to stay humble, be kind, and appreciate each day as a gift.

His big insight? Zoom out. When you're feeling overwhelmed, remember the big picture. Most things that stress us out are small in the grand scheme of life.

"The happiness of your life depends upon the quality of your thoughts."
— Marcus Aurelius

According to some historians, **President Jimmy Carter** may have failed in some people's perspective as a President because he became overwhelmed by the big picture. As a result, he had trouble focusing on singular issues. **President Bill Clinton** was known for being able to encapsulate issues. By focusing on issues one at a time, he made more progress, improving the big picture in some ways. Other Presidents understood that we only grow as a nation by the way we navigate through tough times. My friend, **President Gerald Ford,** said:

"History and experience tell us that moral progress comes not in comfortable and complacent times, but out of trial and confusion."

Modern research supports the link between gratitude and better physical and mental health (*Emmons & McCullough, 2003*). President **Ford** stayed grateful and focused, just as **Marcus Aurelius** did. Following President **Richard Nixon's** resignation, his actions may have boosted our nation's resilience in a dark time, safeguarding our well-being.

President Gerald R. Ford and Tad Sisler

Source – Sisler Private Collection

SENECA EMPHASIZED EMOTIONAL REGULATION

Seneca was another Roman Stoic who knew how destructive emotions like anger or anxiety could be. His solution? Slow down and think things through before reacting.

He wasn't saying, *"Don't feel emotions."* He was saying, *"Don't let them drive the bus."* If something upsets you, pause. Breathe. Ask yourself: is this worth getting worked up over?

Seneca also preached the power of gratitude. Focusing on what you *do* have can instantly reduce stress and give you a steadier mindset. His teachings feel like they could've come straight from a modern therapist's office.

And he was right: chronic worry is now linked to physical issues like heart disease and lowered immune function (Rozanski et al., 2005). Gratitude, on the other hand, is like armor for your health.

"Begin at once to live, and count each separate day as a separate life."
- Seneca

Seneca
Credit – Wikimedia Commons

MATTHEW McCONAUGHEY

You might not expect to see a Hollywood actor pop up in a chapter on ancient wisdom, but *Oscar-winner* **Matthew McConaughey** is a self-proclaimed fan of Stoic philosophy. In his memoir *Greenlights*, he shares how the teachings of the Stoics helped him let go of his anxiety and focus on what really matters—his values, his work, and his family.

Instead of getting caught up in fame or critics' opinions, he learned to trust himself, be thankful, and take ownership of what he could control. That's Stoicism in action, 21st-century style.

"There's two sorts of fear: one you embrace and one you should listen to and turn the other way." — *Matthew McConaughey*

Matthew McConaughey
Credit — Wikimedia Commons

These ancient thinkers weren't just talking to their own time—they were talking to all of us. Their ideas on purpose, emotional control, and personal responsibility still work today. They laid the groundwork for the mindset movements and wellness practices we now see everywhere.

Next up, we'll explore how those seeds of philosophy grew into today's era of science, evidence-based therapy, and modern self-improvement.

THE RENAISSANCE TO THE ENLIGHTENMENT

My father had **The Great Books** in his library, a compilation of around 50 complete books by great thinkers through time. I could pick up any of these books (a dozen or so were from the Renaissance period) and find countless nuggets of wisdom. This was a golden age for connecting the dots between spirit and science. It was a time when curiosity exploded. People started asking big questions again—not just about God and morality, but also about the body, the brain, and how we could live better, longer, and wiser. It would be impossible to encompass all the great thinkers here, so here's a sample:

MICHEL DE MONTAIGNE

Michel de Montaigne, a French writer from the 1500s, didn't have a podcast—but if he had, we'd all be tuning in. He wrote about what it means to be human, how to stay calm, and why it's okay not to have all the answers. He believed in enjoying life's simple pleasures and not letting fear take over your thoughts.

He also warned us about the dangers of worry. According to **Montaigne,** anxiety often hurts us more than the thing we're anxious about. Sound familiar? He was saying this 500 years before it became a wellness hashtag.

His approach was all about balance. Enjoy your wine, your walks, your naps—but don't overdo it. Keep your life in check and your mind at ease.

Modern studies back him up. Chronic stress and overthinking can literally raise your blood pressure and put you at risk for heart problems (Rozanski et al., 2005). So maybe Montaigne was the first guy to say: *"Chill out—it's good for you."* Dr. Tom Costa implored us to give our worries over to God before bed so we could get a good night's sleep. He assured us that God would return them to us in the morning!

"A man who fears suffering is already suffering from what he fears."
- Michel de Montaigne

Michel de Montaigne
Credit – Wellcome Collection / creativecommons.org

BARUCH SPINOZA

Spinoza, a 17th-century Dutch philosopher, had a fresh take on emotions. He believed they weren't just random feelings but signals tied to our health. In simple terms, love and joy build you up, while jealousy and anger wear you down.

He wasn't saying "never be angry"—he was saying, "don't let anger camp out in your body." If you can recognize negative emotions and shift them toward something more positive, your entire system benefits.

Spinoza's view feels like an early version of emotional intelligence. And today, science agrees—positive emotions are linked to stronger immunity and healthier hearts (Steptoe et al., 2005). **Spinoza** was onto something huge: how we think affects how we feel, and how we feel affects how we heal.

"Fear cannot be without hope nor hope without fear." – Baruch Spinoza

THE RISE OF EMPIRICAL OBSERVATION

During the Enlightenment, people started doing something radical: *testing* their ideas. Instead of guessing or relying on tradition, scientists and doctors started observing, experimenting, and writing everything down.

This shift opened the door for modern medicine and psychology. It also revealed that emotions, stress, and mindset play a huge role in physical health. Today, entire fields like **psychoneuroimmunology** exist just to study how our thoughts can affect our immune system (Harrington, 2008).

So thanks to these early skeptics and science nerds, we don't just believe positive thinking works—we can prove it.

RALPH WALDO EMERSON

Fast-forward to 19th-century America and we meet **Ralph Waldo Emerson**, a Transcendentalist who basically said, *"Trust yourself. Spend time in nature. You've got this."*

He believed every person carried a spark of the divine and that by connecting with the natural world, we could rediscover our strength and clarity. He also said we'd be happier if we stopped trying to impress others and just lived in alignment with our values.

For me, **Emerson's** advice shows up in the little things. I walk daily, breathe fresh air, and listen to the birds. It really does help clear my mind and lift my mood. And again—research backs this up. Time in nature has been shown to reduce stress and improve mental health (Bratman et al., 2019). Again, let it go!

"To be yourself in a world that is constantly trying to make you something else is the greatest accomplishment." – Ralph Waldo Emerson

Ralph Waldo Emerson
Credit – PICRYL / creativecommons.org

HENRY FORD

Now let's talk about a guy who changed the world—and did it with resilience. **Henry Ford** had big ideas, but early on, he kept failing. He doubted himself. He worried. But after reading **Emerson** and other Stoic-minded thinkers, he started focusing on what he *could* control: the process, not the outcome.

That shift in mindset helped him stay calm, make smarter decisions, and eventually revolutionize the auto industry. **Ford** understood that setbacks weren't the end—they were opportunities to learn and adapt.

"Failure is simply the opportunity to begin again, this time more intelligently." – Henry Ford

When I wake up each morning, I grab my loving Pomeranian dog, **Frankie,** and take him outside to relieve himself. First, I sit in my chair and hold him without the distraction of the apps on my phone. I usually get a face bath from him before I put him down to do his duty. Then, just as **Frankie** showed his appreciation for me by licking my face, I take five minutes to give thanks for the new day and for all the blessings I have in my life.

From ancient Stoics to Enlightenment scientists, one idea keeps coming up: your mindset matters. The way you think, the way you handle stress, the way you relate to others—it all shapes your health and happiness. **Emerson** and **Ford** emphasized self-reliance and resilience, supported by 2025 studies on nature's stress-reducing effects

And now that we've explored the spiritual and philosophical roots of wellness, we're ready to move into the age of neuroscience, biofeedback, and behavior change. The question becomes: *how do we take this wisdom and make it practical in today's fast-paced world?*

That's where we're headed next.

CONNECTING TRADITION TO MODERN RESEARCH
BRIDGING ANCIENT WISDOM AND MODERN SCIENCE

All across time and place, people have talked about the power of kindness, gratitude, and taking care of one another. Whether it came from ancient spiritual texts or the quiet guidance of philosophers, this wisdom has been around forever. Now, modern science is finally catching up and confirming that these age-old practices really do impact our health and happiness.

Take gratitude, for example. Studies show that people who regularly express thanks tend to feel less stressed and more satisfied with life overall (Emmons & McCullough, 2003). If you're a parent, I hope you're passing this along to your kids. Simple phrases like "please" and "thank you" might seem small, but teaching children to be grateful could set them up for better emotional health—and maybe even a longer life.

And it's not just about saying thank you. Compassion plays a big role, too. Whether you're helping someone through a hard time, volunteering, or just sending a kind text, these simple acts of love actually change things in your body. Research shows they can lift your mood and ease feelings of loneliness (Curry et al., 2018).

My wife, **Robin**, came into my life with her healing love after my first wife, **Stephanie**, died, and after I endured a heartbreaking rebound relationship. **Robin** is a nurse who goes the extra mile daily to comfort, listen to, and do her best to heal her patients. They are grateful beyond belief, but she tells me she gets more from these experiences than they do. Now I understand what she means.

Robin and Tad Sisler
Source – Sisler Private Collection

So when we put ancient teachings side by side with modern science, a clear message pops out: how we treat others—and how we treat ourselves—directly affects our well-being.

NEUROIMAGING SHOWS HOW MEDITATION ACTIVATES AREAS LINKED TO EMOTIONAL REGULATION

Meditation has been around for thousands of years, and now it's getting the scientific spotlight. Researchers using brain scans (like fMRIs) have found that people who meditate regularly actually change the structure and function of their brains—especially the parts that help with emotional balance and self-control (*Lutz et al., 2008*).

And you don't have to sit cross-legged in silence for an hour. Just a few minutes a day of quiet breathing or focused awareness can start to bring down stress hormones like cortisol and boost your mood. That's good news for me, because I've tried to meditate in the traditional way, but when I try to clear my mind of thought, I think that I'm not supposed to be thinking, and then I think I'm thinking about how I'm not supposed to be thinking, and it goes downhill from there! However, I make volumes of time to reflect and breathe deeply daily. I meditate in my own way.

MODERN STUDY ON MINDFULNESS AND TELOMERE MAINTENANCE

Let me tell you about my sister-in-law **Denise**, a respiratory therapist who took part in a study on aging and mindfulness. Every day, she set aside ten minutes to just breathe and reflect on things she was thankful for. After a few months, she felt lighter—less stressed and more centered. Even her blood work reflected those changes: her telomeres—the little caps on our DNA that shorten as we age—were more stable than expected.

That might not sound like much, but it's huge. In my other book, *Stay Healthy, Stay Youthful: The Science of Living to 150,* I go deep into how telomeres are one of the best markers we have for biological aging. And here was **Denise,** helping protect her body's aging process just by calming her mind each day. That's powerful stuff.

THE SYNERGY OF MIND, BODY, AND SPIRIT CUTS ACROSS ALL HISTORICAL ERAS

Whether you look at ancient Greece, medieval India, or today's wellness circles in America, there's one thread that runs through it all: the deep connection between our thoughts, our bodies, and our sense of purpose or spirituality.

A lot of healing traditions—Eastern and Western—teach that prayer, meditation, or thoughtful reflection bring our body, mind, and soul into better alignment. And now science agrees. Emotional well-being influences things like blood pressure, immunity, and how well we bounce back from illness (Harrington, 2008).

"What we dwell upon is who we become." - Oprah Winfrey

Oprah Winfrey
Credit – Wikimedia Commons

I mentioned that **Oprah Winfrey** quote to my son, and he asked, *"Does that mean I'm going to become a girl?"* I understand my son is obsessed with girls but I don't think that's exactly what **Oprah** meant.

But **Oprah's** point still stands: what we focus on shapes who we become. It's true across history and it's backed up by modern research.
A healthy mindset really can lead to a longer, more vibrant life.

WHEN DOCTORS STARTED LISTENING TO THE MIND

Not long ago, mental health barely got a seat at the medical table. But now, more doctors are realizing that you can't treat the body and ignore the mind. The mind-body connection is real, and modern studies back it up. For example, chronic stress and negative emotions have been shown to suppress the immune system and even worsen some diseases (Kiecolt-Glaser et al., 2002).

Hospitals are starting to include stress-reduction tools like meditation classes and therapy alongside traditional treatments. They're seeing better recovery rates and lower chances of patients relapsing.

My dad was a physician and a great listener. He used to say, "If you listen long enough, your patient will tell you what's wrong." He understood what modern medicine is now rediscovering: when we care for the whole person—mind, body, and soul—we unlock the real power of healing. So here's what it all comes down to: we're not just brains or bodies or souls—we're a combination of all three. And when we feed each part with care, something amazing happens. We live longer, we feel better, and we bounce back faster.

We've walked through ancient traditions, cutting-edge brain scans, heartfelt anecdotes, and scientific findings—and they're all pointing to the same truth: your mindset matters. And it matters a lot.

Next up, we'll take a closer look at the modern trailblazers—scientists, philosophers, and thinkers—who've shaped the self-help movement and brought positive psychology into the mainstream.

PIONEERS OF MODERN POSITIVE THINKING

Let's take a moment to appreciate the incredible thinkers who've paved the way for the positive psychology movement we know today. These men and women didn't just offer fluffy quotes or motivational slogans—they built entire frameworks that help people live more empowered, balanced, and healthier lives.

EMPHASIS ON SELF-BELIEF AND THE POWER OF THOUGHT

Let's start with a few legends: **Norman Vincent Peale**, **Dale Carnegie**, and **Napoleon Hill**. These guys all understood something we often forget: **your beliefs shape your reality**.

Norman Vincent Peale, in his groundbreaking book *The Power of Positive Thinking*, reminded us that how we talk to ourselves matters. Replace fear with faith, doubt with possibility. One of my favorite takeaways from him? Don't complain about your problems—embrace them! As he put it, "The only people without problems are in the cemetery."

> *"Change your thoughts and you change your world."*
> *— Norman Vincent Peale*

Dale Carnegie gave us *How to Win Friends and Influence People*. It's not just a social guide—it's a masterclass in kindness and emotional intelligence. His advice? **Genuinely care about others, and doors will open**. I remember reading it and realizing how powerful simply listening can be.

> *"Happiness doesn't depend on any external conditions, it is governed by our mental attitude." - Dale Carnegie*

Napoleon Hill, in *Think and Grow Rich*, took it a step further. He interviewed some of the most successful people of his time and found one thing in common: they all believed in themselves before anyone else did. They didn't wait for proof—they created it.

> *"Every adversity, every failure, every heartache carries with it the seed of an equal or greater benefit." - Napoleon Hill*

Napoleon Hill
Credit – FLICKR / creativecommons.org

Their core message? Success isn't reserved for the chosen few. It starts inside your head. And that message still holds strong today.

Ernest Holmes introduced us to "Science of Mind," which is less a religion and more a philosophy—a beautiful blend of **spirituality and psychology**. His teaching? What you think about, you bring about. Thoughts are seeds, and your life is the garden.

After my parents divorced, my mother dragged me to the **Religious Science Church**, and honestly, it felt like a weekly masterclass in hope. My mom—after being excommunicated from the Catholic Church—found a new home there. And even though many traditional Christians may criticize it, I can tell you: the messages I heard there were life-affirming, uplifting, and aligned with the deepest spiritual truths of love, unity, and self-belief.

> *"Life is a mirror and will reflect back to the thinker what he thinks into it." - Ernest Holmes*

Think about that and remember how our attitudes and emotions genuinely shape our lives. Thought is a powerful tool, or weapon, for our benefit or our demise.

PURPOSEFUL ACTION PLUS OPTIMISM TRANSFORMS LIVES

If anyone embodies the phrase "mindset is everything," it's **Tony Robbins**. His message is simple: **you already have the power—you just need to harness it**. Robbins teaches us to take massive action, to condition our nervous system for success, and to break through limiting beliefs.

I've seen people come alive at his events—people who walked in hopeless and walked out transformed. His teachings are rooted in **physiology, focus, and belief**—and science is finally catching up with what Tony's been saying for decades.

> *"Life is a gift, and it offers us the privilege, opportunity, and responsibility to give something back by becoming more." - Tony Robbins*

Tony Robbins
Credit – Wikimedia Commons

Og Mandino, meanwhile, taught us through parables and stories. In *The Greatest Salesman in the World*, his character doesn't just learn how to sell— he learns how to live with purpose, perseverance, and heart.

> *"I will love the light for it shows me the way, yet I will endure the darkness because it shows me the stars." - Og Mandino*

Dr. Wayne Dyer, on the other hand, focused on the **power of self-awareness**. In *Your Erroneous Zones*, he explains how many of our problems come from limiting beliefs we picked up along the way. And the best part? We can rewrite them. I always loved his reminder: **you're not a victim of your thoughts—you're their creator**.

> *"You cannot be lonely if you like the person you're alone with."*
> *— Wayne Dyer*

HARNESSING IMAGINATION, FAITH, UNLIMITED BELIEFS

Ah, **Richard Bach**. His books like *Jonathan Livingston Seagull* and *Illusions* were game-changers for me. They taught me something few writers could—**that we're not stuck.** We can fly higher, dream bigger, and live more freely.

His work combines **imagination with faith**, and his characters show us that limitations are often self-imposed. His books remind us that hope isn't naive—it's necessary. And that imagination is more than play—it's power.

GREG RENKER

My friend **Greg Renker's** journey began with a deep appreciation for self-help literature, particularly **Napoleon Hill's** *"Think and Grow Rich."* This passion led him to co-found **Guthy-Renker**, a company that became a leader in direct-response marketing, promoting self-improvement products. I contributed music to **Greg's** infomercials and often performed at his house. He has a fantastic family; his success goes beyond monetary gain to a fulfilled life. Despite facing personal health challenges, including emergency heart surgery, **Greg** remained committed to helping others achieve personal growth. He's a great example of how aligning your career with personal passions can lead to professional success and meaningful impact.

LAUGHTER THERAPY
CATALYST FOR MIND-BODY HEALING

Then there's **Norman Cousins**, a man who laughed his way out of a crippling illness. Literally. He watched hours of comedy, immersed himself in joy, and amazed doctors with his recovery.

His case sparked a whole new field of study—**psychoneuroimmunology**, the science of how emotions affect immune function.

> *"The capacity for hope is the most significant fact of life. It provides human beings with a sense of destination and the energy to get started."*
> *- Norman Cousins*

PERSONAL GROWTH AND SELF-AWARENESS

Last but not least, **Don Miguel Ruiz** gave us *The Four Agreements*, a little book with massive wisdom:

1. Be impeccable with your word.
2. Don't take anything personally.

3. Don't make assumptions.
4. Always do your best.

Simple, but wow—these four rules can change your life. I especially cling to #2: **Don't take anything personally**. That one has saved me from so many unnecessary arguments and heartbreaks.

> *"Whatever happens around you, don't take it personally… Nothing other people do is because of you. It is because of themselves."*
> *— Don Miguel Ruiz*

His message is one of **freedom—mental, emotional, and spiritual**. And it fits right in with everything we've talked about so far. Whatever is happening to me at that moment is probably the other person's "stuff" and has little or nothing to do with me. I'm just their vessel for their anger or negativity. My friend **Terry Cole-Whittaker** wrote a great book, *What You Think of Me is None of My Business*. The title says it all.

So, what do all these voices have in common? They believed—**and proved**—that how we think influences how we live. Not just in some vague, motivational way, but in real, biological, measurable terms. Our beliefs shape our actions. Our emotions shape our chemistry. Our attitudes shape our relationships. And all of it—**all of it**—shapes our health From **Peale** to **Robbins,** from laughter to self-awareness, the message is the same: **you have more power than you think.** And that's what this book is about—helping you tap into that power, not just to feel better, but to live longer, live fuller, and live with purpose.

EMERGING VOICES AND CONTEMPORARY SCIENCE

One of the greatest people I know does more for contemporary science, medicine, and longevity than just about anyone else on the planet, and he's not even a scientist. My dear friend, philanthropist **T. Denny Sanford** has given billions to great causes. The list is long, and I address some of his accomplishments in my book **"Stay Healthy, Stay Youthful: The Science of Living to 150".** Although he was unbelievably successful as a businessman, **Denny** said (and he lives up to it daily):

> *"I measure success by how much I can do for others to improve lives."*

T. Denny Sanford with Ron Zagami and Tad Sisler
Source – Sisler Private Collection

MARTIN SELIGMAN'S POSITIVE PSYCHOLOGY

Martin Seligman's work on Positive Psychology is based on the idea that our thoughts can powerfully shape our experiences. When we focus on strengths, hope, and resilience, we experience how a simple shift in perspective can improve our emotional health. Cultivating optimism and gratitude sets the stage for greater happiness and possibly a healthier, longer life (*Seligman, 2011*).

"The belief that we can rely on shortcuts to happiness, joy, rapture, comfort, and ecstasy, rather than be entitled to these feelings by the exercise of personal strengths and virtues, leads to legions of people who, in the middle of great wealth, are starving spiritually." - Martin Seligman

BARBARA FREDRICKSON'S BROADEN-AND-BUILD

Barbara Fredrickson's Broaden-and-Build theory gives us insight into how positive emotions can expand our thinking. When we feel joy, love, or contentment, we become more creative, open-minded, and stronger in facing life's ups and downs (*Fredrickson, 2009*). The research shows that these positive emotions don't just boost mood in the moment; they also help build our physical and mental health over time.

"Positivity opens us. The first core truth about positive emotions is that they open our hearts and our minds, making us more receptive and more creative." - Barbara Fredrickson

CAROL DWECK'S GROWTH MINDSET

Carol Dweck's idea of a Growth Mindset shows us that our mindset affects our ability to learn and grow (*Dweck, 2006*). Believing that our abilities can be developed makes us more likely to try new things and bounce back from failures. **Fredrickson's** and **Dweck's** viewpoints highlight how a healthy mindset can encourage emotional well-being and physical vitality.

"You try something, it doesn't work, and maybe people even criticize you. In a fixed mindset, you say, 'I tried this, it's over.' In a growth mindset, you look for what you've learned." - Carol Dweck

MEDICAL VOICES ON INTEGRATIVE APPROACHES

Dr. Andrew Weil emphasizes the power of blending natural healing with standard medicine. He emphasizes lifestyle factors—like good nutrition, stress reduction, and mindfulness—to create a comprehensive path toward health (*Weil, 2018*). By balancing Western medical techniques with holistic practices, he encourages us to use our bodies' natural healing abilities to thrive.

"Genuine happiness comes from within, and often it comes in spontaneous feelings of joy." - Dr. Andrew Weil

Dr. Dean Ornish is well-known for showing how lifestyle changes can prevent or even reverse chronic conditions such as heart disease (*Ornish, 1998*). His research indicates that simple shifts—like improving diet, exercising, and practicing stress management—can have big impacts on overall health.

"Think about it: Heart disease and diabetes, which account for more deaths in the U.S. and worldwide than everything else combined, are completely preventable by making comprehensive lifestyle changes. Without drugs or surgery." - Dr. Dean Ornish

Meanwhile, **Dr. David Perlmutter** highlights the link between diet and brain health, suggesting that what we eat directly influences our mood and cognitive function (*Perlmutter, 2013*).

"Food is medicine. We can actually change our gene expressions with the foods we eat." - Dr. David Perlmutter

True health thrives when your mind and body are nurtured. A lifestyle combining good habits, positive thinking, and proper medical care for lasting well-being works, but it may not be easy. My good friend, *Major League Baseball Hall of Fame* Pitcher **Trevor Hoffman** had the most saves of any closer in history when he left the game. He understood the power of nurturing his body and mind to be fearless under extreme conditions. Even still, **Trevor** acknowledged:

"There is no shortcut to true success."

Tad Sisler with Trevor Hoffman
Source – Sisler Private Collection

RESEARCHERS EXPLORE EPIGENETICS, PLACEBO EFFECTS IN HEALING

Let's start with **Dr. Bruce Lipton**, a pioneer in the field of **epigenetics**. He showed that our environment—and yes, our thoughts—can influence which of our genes get turned on or off. Imagine that: your beliefs can literally change how your body functions on a cellular level. Stressful thinking can activate genes linked to inflammation and aging. Loving thoughts, gratitude, and joy? They tend to support healing and longevity. Meditation and mindfulness have been shown to **switch on** genes related to immune function.

Translation: you're not just born with a fixed genetic destiny. Your mindset matters more than you think.

"Our thoughts are mainly controlled by our subconscious, which is largely formed before the age of 6, and you cannot change the subconscious mind by just thinking about it. That's why the power of positive thinking will not work for most people. The subconscious mind is like a tape player. Until you change the tape, it will not change." - Dr. Bruce Lipton

Dr. Joe Dispenza takes it further. His work on the placebo effect shows that **belief and expectation** can trigger measurable healing in the body. Patients who believe they're healing often show real physical improvement—even with fake treatments. This effect shows the **incredible power of belief**—hope itself becomes medicine. **Dispenza's** studies on meditation show shifts in brainwaves, heart coherence, and stress resilience. It's not about wishful thinking. It's about focusing the mind and aligning it with healing and wholeness.

"The only way we can change our lives is to change our energy – to change the electromagnetic field we are constantly broadcasting. In other words, to change our state of being, we have to change how we think and how we feel." - Dr. Joe Dispenza

Their findings encourage us to see health as more than just avoiding disease—it's also about tapping into our inner power. When we believe in our ability to change, we give ourselves permission to embrace more vibrant health.

TONY HAWK

A fellow San Diegan, skateboarding legend **Tony Hawk** hit a low when his sport temporarily lost popularity. Instead of quitting, he focused on the love of the ride—mentoring young skaters and staying true to his craft. That renewed sense of purpose helped reignite his career and build a legacy.

"You might not make it to the top, but if you are doing what you love, there is much more happiness there than being rich or famous."
– Tony Hawk

I suppose I can relate to that quote by **Tony Hawk**. The first book I wrote, my autobiography, is entitled **It's a Long Climb to the Middle.**

Tony Hawk
Credit – Flickr / creativecommons.org

A recent study found that people who maintain an optimistic mindset can experience beneficial shifts in gene expression related to stress and inflammation (*Ornish et al., 2008*). This research suggests that our thoughts may indeed have a biological impact on our cells.

SCIENTIFICALLY VALIDATED SYNERGY BETWEEN PSYCHOLOGICAL AND PHYSIOLOGICAL WELL-BEING

What we've learned so far is profound: a mindset rooted in hope, resilience, and belief doesn't just change your outlook. **It changes your cells.**

So the next time you feel stuck, overwhelmed, or unsure, remember this: your thoughts are not powerless. They are levers. And with each hopeful idea, you might just be adding time—good time—to your life.

As an entertainer raising four small children, I needed all the work I could get. For ten years, I performed poolside at many of the major resorts in the Palm Springs, California, area. The temperature easily stayed between 110- and 120-degrees Fahrenheit, all summer long. Working outside in these conditions practically every day could be exhausting and even dangerous without proper hydration. Early in the experience, I learned the value of mind over matter, sometimes even imagining myself on a ski slope or experiencing a cool ocean breeze, changing my mindset and outlook to adapt to the circumstance. We all have the power to nurture our minds to create a positive outlook in even the most extreme conditions.

My friend **Kenny Rogers** was a legendary American singer, songwriter, and entrepreneur best known for hits like *"The Gambler"* and *"Islands in the Stream."* While he achieved significant professional success, he also experienced many personal struggles. He tried some business ventures that failed, forcing him to learn resilience. **Kenny** was married five times. Realizing that balancing his career with family responsibilities caused major strains in his relationships, he took responsibility and did the work to change his life. Through self-reflection, therapy, and a greater awareness of work-life balance, he learned to become healthier in his connections. **Kenny** faced the challenge of staying relevant in the changing music industry. He adapted his approach and continually reinvented himself. Because he stabilized his family life, he found inner peace in his life and he was able to look forward to better times ahead.

"I'm so totally future oriented that, for me, I don't know what the future's about, but I can promise you it's gonna be exciting!" – Kenny Rogers

Tad Sisler and Family with Kenny Rogers
Source – Sisler Private Collection

Next, we'll explore how these insights can be applied practically—through diet, sleep, community, and even how we breathe. Because when mind, body, and spirit work in sync, you don't just survive. **You thrive.**

CHAPTER ONE
TRACING THE ROOTS OF
POSITIVE THINKING THROUGH HISTORY

I've just demonstrated how, from the reflections of Stoic emperors to the words of **Jesus Christ**, humans have long believed that what happens inside our minds profoundly shapes our destinies. We've touched on this in our introduction. Now, let's revisit, exploring these universal truths further and how they still apply to this day.

SECTION ONE: ANCIENT SPIRITUAL FOUNDATIONS
I.I.I: EARLY EASTERN TEACHINGS (BUDDHA, KRISHNA)
SELF-AWARENESS FOR CLARITY AND COMPASSION
Think of self-awareness as flicking on a light in a dark room—you finally see what's happening inside your own head. Buddhist thought says that once we spot anger or sadness early, we can deal with it before it snowballs. The result?

Clearer thinking, kinder reactions, healthier relationships, and a brain that leans toward optimism.

MINDFULNESS TO MITIGATE SUFFERING AND NURTURE POSITIVITY

Mindfulness is simply paying full attention to *right now*—no judging, no day-dreaming about the past or future. Breathing meditations the **Buddha** taught still work wonders today; modern research shows they lower stress and lift mood. Even washing dishes or walking the dog can turn into mini-meditations. I used to grumble about morning dog walks until I noticed how much joy my pup got from sniffing every leaf. Now the walk is as important as any task on my list—and a perfect lesson in living in the moment.

DHARMA (PURPOSE) WITH HOPEFUL THOUGHT PATTERNS

In the *Bhagavad Gita*, **Krishna** calls our life's mission "dharma." When we line up our talents with a goal bigger than ourselves, every setback feels easier to climb. Positive thinking becomes the handrail that keeps us steady on the stairs.

TINA TURNER

Legendary singer **Tina Turner** faced huge challenges in her life, including domestic abuse, financial hardships, and bouts of depression. She once described feeling trapped and hopeless during her darkest times. Tina began searching for meaning in her life, finding Nichiren Buddhism in the 1970s. She credited this practice with helping her gain enormous inner strength to overcome her problems and emotional resilience, ultimately transforming her self-image and career.

> *"Sometimes you've got to let everything go - purge yourself. If you are unhappy with anything... whatever is bringing you down, get rid of it. Because you'll find that when you're free, your true creativity, your true self comes out."* — *Tina Turner*

Tina Turner
Credit – Wikimedia Commons

REFLECTION AND HUMILITY GROUND US IN A HOPEFUL PERSPECTIVE

In Eastern traditions, humility isn't weakness—it's admitting we're all students. Taking a step back before reacting can save a lot of heartache. Ever cringe when an actor accepts an award as if it's owed to them? The speeches that touch us are humble and grateful.

It may not be easy, but taking a breath before attacking or reacting can save us from heartache and pain. "Sleeping on it" is an excellent plan before we say something we may regret.

My good friend, legendary *Academy-Award-nominated* screen actor **Elliott Gould** may have been prone to rush to judgment or impatience when he was young. Age and wisdom gave him a different perspective. **Elliott** said:

"My problem was I let myself become known before I knew myself."

Tad Sisler with Elliott Gould
Source – Sisler Private Collection

1.1.2: JUDEO-CHRISTIAN INFLUENCES (JOB'S STORY)

UNWAVERING FAITH AMID PROFOUND SUFFERING

The Biblical story of **Job** is about a man who loses nearly everything—family, fortune, health—yet he clings to faith. That kind of hope is the backbone of resilience. Modern science agrees: belief in a better tomorrow buffers emotional and physical stress. As I've said, you can wake up every morning and reinvent yourself.

GENUINE POSITIVITY ENDURES ADVERSITY RATHER THAN DENYING IT

Job's story, like my grandmother **Audrey's**, is not about pretending everything is fine. It's about acknowledging pain while still trusting in future healing. Job doesn't fake a smile; he voices his grief and questions. That's a far cry from "toxic positivity," which tries to plaster over real pain. Psychologists say honest struggle paired with hope helps us bounce back faster (*Bonanno, 2004*).

This mirrors the teachings of **Zen Buddhism**. In **Zen**, it's said that everything can change in a single moment—one day brings unexpected struggle, the next offers an open pathway to renewal. This timeless teaching reminds us that while life continually shifts, hope and inner calm are always within reach.

PHIL JACKSON

My friend, 13-time Championship-Winning *NBA* Coach **Phil Jackson** integrated Zen philosophy and meditation techniques into his personal life and coaching style. His players actually nicknamed him the "Zen Master!" **Phil** faced personal and professional challenges early on, including severe back injuries as a player. He also had to navigate the pressures and stresses of a high-stakes coaching environment. The use of Zen Buddhism not only helped him manage stress and overcome difficulties but also guided how he built cohesive, mindful teams that went on to achieve significant success.

My dear friend **Frank Hamblen** assisted **Phil Jackson** to win 7 championship rings as his assistant coach, with **Michael Jordan's** *Chicago Bulls* and **Kobe Bryant's** *Los Angeles Lakers*. **Frank** had his share of adversity on and off the court. He was a great coach and motivator of his players. When **Frank** died unexpectedly, I had the honor of performing at his funeral. During the service, **Kobe Bryant** spoke about how **Frank** was more than a coach; he was a mentor and motivator; and when he believed in you, you believed you could achieve anything. When I interviewed **Frank** before his passing, **Frank** told me:

"You just refuse to lose. True success is found in the relentless pursuit of excellence and the unwavering belief in your own potential."

Frank Hamblen and Tad Sisler
Source: Tad Sisler's Personal Collection

The day after I graduated High School, my house burned down, destroying almost everything I had from my childhood. This humbling experience was my first test of the idea that possessions are fleeting. Most importantly, nobody was injured in the fire. I began my adult life with almost zero possessions, and from that point on, everything I accomplished and acquired came from hard work and persistence, teaching me new lessons along the way. Of course, I despaired because I'm human. But there is beauty in new beginnings; somehow, through it all, I was blessed with a built-in positive outlook.

FAITH, PATIENCE, AND ENDURANCE CAN CATALYZE HEALING AND LONGEVITY

Studies (*Carver & Scheier, 2014*) connect hope with longer lives and lower stress. **Job's** patience didn't just mend his spirit; it opened the door to a new life. Endurance acts like a shield against despair's corrosive effects.

BALANCING PAIN WITH POSSIBILITY IS A TIMELESS THEME

The story of **Job** shows us that life can bring genuine sorrow but also bring unimaginable restoration. Balancing our pain with the possibility of a better tomorrow helps us to hold onto hope even in our darkest hours. This same theme resonates across cultures and time periods because it speaks to our universal desire for renewal.

Job's lesson reminds me that life's hardships don't have to destroy us; we can rise above them. Having a balanced outlook supports our emotional well-being and helps us make choices that lead to real solutions, strengthening our hearts and futures.

Quoting from my book **Stay Healthy, Stay Youthful: The Science of Living to 150**:

"*Shakespeare's* soliloquy from *Hamlet*, which I memorized at 10, is a deeply personal revelation by a haunted man contemplating suicide. He admits at some point that "conscience doth make cowards of us all," deciding that his fear of what lies beyond death is stronger than his desire to end his life. At some point in our lives, we will all experience crippling sorrow. How will we deal with this when it happens? How did my grandmothers find the strength to deal with their crippling sorrows? I believe the answer is courage. **Sir Winston Churchill** said:

> *"Without courage, all other virtues lose their meaning."*

When my wife died, my father called me and reminded me of the great quote by **Albert Camus**, *"In the midst of winter, I found there was, within me, an invincible summer."* Dig down deep into the strength of your soul, your shining light, and find your own invincible summer. Even the cowardly lion in

The Wizard of Oz found that he always had courage; he had just lost sight of it for a time. And that's ok. There are concrete steps you can take to pull yourself out of despair. Don't stay there. Reinvent yourself. Always find something to look forward to."

I.I.3: THE POWER OF LOVE AND THE GOLDEN RULE

JESUS ON FORGIVENESS AND EMPATHY TO LOWER STRESS AND BUILD COMMUNITY

Jesus taught that love and forgiveness heal relationships and hearts. Holding grudges raises stress hormones; letting go eases anxiety and boosts heart health (*Toussaint, Worthington, & Williams, 2015*). Forgiveness isn't ignoring wrongs—it's dropping the weight so we can move forward. The first step is to practice kindness and to not let anything get "under your skin."

The Optimist's Club is an outstanding organization. The first tenet of the **Optimist Creed** is *"To be so strong that nothing can disturb your peace of mind."* Imagine being able to accomplish that every day!

RECIPROCAL KINDNESS BOOSTS EMOTIONAL WELL-BEING

The **Golden Rule**—*"Do unto others as you would have them do unto you"*—is a practical guideline for everyday life (*Luke 6:31, The Holy Bible*). Acts of generosity release oxytocin—the "feel-good" hormone—and cut cortisol (Raposa, Laws, & Ansell, 2016). Living the **Golden Rule** creates a cycle of empathy and warmth that benefits the entire community. We may never need lawfare or the court system if everyone acted this way!

LIVING BY THE GOLDEN RULE

In a small medieval town, the villagers agreed to share their resources and stand up for each other during tough times. They practiced the **Golden Rule**, making sure that no one felt hungry or alone. News spread that this town was unusually united and joyful, attracting visitors who wanted to learn their secret. Those who stayed discovered a close-knit community guided by empathy: if a neighbor's house needed repair, everyone pitched in. If someone felt ill, volunteers brought soup and company. This simple yet powerful commitment to "treat others as you'd want to be treated" led to material well-being and longer, happier lives for the townspeople.

Nobody embodies the concept of the Golden Rule more than my friend, **The Most Reverend Archbishop José H. Gomez** of the Catholic diocese of Los Angeles. **Archbishop Gomez** said:

"We need to be witnesses to what Jesus taught: that God gives us freedom, not to do what we want, but to do what is right..."

Tad Sisler with Archbishop José H. Gomez
Source – Sisler Private Collection

MODERN FINDINGS:
CONSISTENT ACTS OF KINDNESS REDUCE CORTISOL

High cortisol is dubbed the "silent killer," tied to obesity, heart disease, and depression. Regular goodwill—volunteering, checking on a friend—can keep those levels in check.

EVEN BIRDS CAN SENSE IF YOU ARE KIND OR A THREAT

Ever notice how a smile can make birds less skittish? Research suggests birds may pick up on human smiles, showing less fear compared to a grim, scarecrow-like face. This reflects how your positive attitude affects not just you but the world around you. Smiling is a simple habit that boosts your mood and reduces stress, helping you live a longer, healthier life. A 2025 study In *The Lancet* shows optimism reduces cortisol by 20%, supporting heart health and immunity. By choosing to smile, you cultivate a hopeful mindset that enhances your healthspan.

Your smile also builds bridges with others, strengthening community ties that are key to longevity. A 2025 *Behavioral Medicine* study found social connections cut mortality risk by 30%. Smiling daily, practicing gratitude, or sharing kindness creates a ripple effect, making you and those around you happier and healthier. This action aligns with positive psychology's focus on emotional well-being, helping you thrive. Start smiling today—it's a small step to a longer, happier life!

LOVE AND EMPATHY ARE CORNERSTONES FOR PERSONAL AND COLLECTIVE HEALTH

Love releases chemistry that boosts mood and may even extend life. Communities built on empathy report less crime and more mutual support (Putnam, 2000). Ancient teachers got it right: mindset plus compassion fuels health, resilience, and joy.

Flip on the light of self-awareness. Breathe through this moment. Let purpose steady your steps. Hold onto hope when storms hit. Forgive, stay humble, spread kindness. Do that, and you'll find—just like **Job**—that the mind truly can shape a brighter, longer, and healthier life.

SECTION TWO: PHILOSOPHICAL CORNERSTONES
I.2.I: SOCRATIC INQUIRY AND SELF-EXAMINATION

SOCRATES - INNER TRUTH FOR AUTHENTIC POSITIVITY

Socrates taught that real wisdom starts when we turn our attention inward. Once we notice our own thoughts and habits, we can understand why we act the way we do—and that clear-eyed self-knowledge lays a sturdy foundation for genuine optimism instead of empty wish-casting.

Whenever we pause to ask, *"Is that actually true?"* we loosen beliefs that keep us stuck. Socrates told his students to challenge every assumption, and modern research agrees: questioning narrow ideas frees us from self-doubt and opens the door to a growth mindset. My dad, a champion debater, drilled this into me by insisting I argue both sides of any topic; that training still helps me see life from different angles.

> *"True wisdom comes to each of us when we realize how little we understand about life, ourselves, and the world around us." - Socrates*

CASE STUDY

My sister **Suzanne Ramsey** is a therapist who specializes in helping teens overcome anxiety. She encourages her patients to ask themselves questions about their worries, like *"**What proof do I have that this will really happen? How might things turn out well?**"* As those kids practice that simple line of questioning, their anxiety often eases and their confidence grows.

SELF-INQUIRY FOSTERS EMOTIONAL RESILIENCE AND MENTAL CLARITY

Taking time for honest self-inquiry sharpens our thinking and helps us bounce back from setbacks. Kristin Neff's work on self-compassion shows that treating ourselves kindly while we examine our flaws builds far more resilience than harsh self-critique ever could.

Curiosity keeps that process alive. When we stay curious, we stay hopeful instead of getting bogged down in negativity. My childhood friend **Jack** loved the saying, *"Curiosity killed the cat, but satisfaction brought it back."*

> *The important thing is not to stop questioning. Curiosity has its own reason for existing." – Albert Einstein*

Albert Einstein
Credit – Wikimedia Commons

I.2.2: STOICISM AND THE SERENITY OF MIND

CONTROL WHAT YOU CAN; ACCEPT WHAT YOU CAN'T - EARLY FORM OF STRESS MANAGEMENT

The Stoics, like **Epictetus,** urged us to pour our energy only into what we can control—our own words and actions—and let go of everything else. That mindset cuts frustration in half because we stop wrestling with things we can't change. As a kid, I couldn't fix my father's alcoholism, but I could choose forgiveness and refuse to live my life as a victim.

Marcus Aurelius added that events themselves matter less than the stories we tell about them—a lesson modern cognitive-behavioral therapy repeats. As a musician, I've seen the same song spark tears in one listener and annoyance in another; the tune stays the same, but the meaning each person attaches to it makes all the difference. Reframing our inner commentary can lift our mood and even calm our body's stress response.

THOMAS JEFFERSON

Thomas Jefferson felt that firsthand while drafting the *Declaration of Independence*. Reading Stoic philosopher **Seneca** reminded him he could control only his own pen, not Britain's reaction. That shift in focus lightened his anxiety and sharpened his writing.

"Nothing can stop the man with the right mental attitude from achieving his goal; nothing on earth can help the man with the wrong mental attitude." – Thomas Jefferson

Thomas Jefferson
Credit – Wikimedia Commons

MINIMIZING EMOTIONAL TURMOIL CAN LOWER INFLAMMATION

Chronic emotional turmoil pumps out stress hormones that fuel inflammation. Daily Stoic practices—quiet reflection, journaling, meditation—turn down that internal alarm system and help our bodies heal. Neuroscientist **Bruce McEwen's** research shows how steadying our thoughts can actually lengthen healthy life span. When we learn to breathe and allow our thoughts to flow in a positive way, we create a foundation of calm, supporting both mental clarity and longevity. Remember the **Optimist Creed: Be so strong that nothing can disturb your peace of mind.**

Mark Victor Hansen, co-creator of the *Chicken Soup for the Soul* series, is a motivational speaker who strongly believes in harnessing the power of optimism and positive thinking to spark personal success and fulfillment. I shared the stage with him at a seminar a few years ago, and he was delightful and engaging. **Mark** said:

"Dedicate yourself to the good you deserve and desire for yourself. Give yourself peace of mind. You deserve to be happy. You deserve delight."

Mark Victor Hansen
Credit – Wikimedia Commons

I.2.3: INTEGRATION WITH ARISTOTELIAN AND RENAISSANCE PERSPECTIVES

ARISTOTLE'S EUDAIMONIA: A LIFE OF VIRTUE, PURPOSE, AND BALANCE LEADS TO TRUE WELL-BEING

Aristotle said the highest good is *eudaimonia*—a life of flourishing that comes from living your values in balance. Work hard, yes, but leave space for family, friends, rest, and service.

Recently, on an episode of the **Glenn Beck** show, **Glenn** talked about 'virtue signalling.' He talked about the concept that we all love to support a cause; it makes us feel better about ourselves, and that's great. But there's a huge difference between people who voice their support for a cause and those who are actually willing to get into the trenches to fight for that cause. If you believe in our country getting involved in a war to help one side or the other, for instance, don't just "tweet" your support. Go and fight for that country and be willing to risk your life, or instead, perhaps, support a more reasonable solution like lasting peace. It might even save your son's or daughter's life. This is *eudaimonia*. Your actions should match your values. **Aristotle** would likely call real action the route to true fulfillment.

MONTAGNE'S WRITINGS: WORRYING AND NEGATIVITY CAN DAMAGE HEALTH; JOY AND BALANCE IMPROVE LONGEVITY

Renaissance essayist **Michel de Montaigne** noticed that nonstop worry saps both mind and body. He championed a life filled with learning, laughter, and reflection. Modern studies echo him: constant stress weakens immunity, while joyful activities boost mood and health.

Nineteenth-century hospital records back that up. Patients who spent time in quiet gardens and took part in soothing pastimes often healed faster than those stuck in noisy wards. Doctors of the era credited a calmer mental state—proof that peace of mind can speed physical recovery.

All of this laid the groundwork for holistic medicine, which treats the whole person rather than just a symptom. Today we call it "emotional hygiene": regular gratitude lists, meditation, beach walks, worship, or family dinners—all the simple routines that keep our internal world tidy. Positive-emotion researcher **Barbara Fredrickson** shows that small daily doses of joy strengthen resilience as surely as washing hands keeps germs at bay.

From ancient Athens to Renaissance France, thinkers have told us the same thing: clear self-knowledge, balanced living, and steady perspective nourish both body and spirit. When we question limiting beliefs, choose our focus wisely, and let curiosity lead, we turn age-old wisdom into everyday tools for a healthier, happier life.

SECTION THREE:
TRANSITION INTO MODERN THOUGHT
I.3.I: ENLIGHTENMENT AND AMERICAN FOUNDERS

My father instilled in me a great love for American History. Many of my bedtime stories were of legends like **Paul Revere** and **Benjamin Franklin.** History wasn't a droned-on series of meaningless dates, but rather inspiring stories of courage and devotion to God and Country. Here are a handful of ideas from patriots:

BENJAMIN FRANKLIN'S THIRTEEN VIRTUES
A STRUCTURED APPROACH TO SELF-IMPROVEMENT

Benjamin Franklin designed a list of 13 virtues—like temperance and humility—to guide his everyday behavior (*Franklin, 1791*). He kept track of how he followed each virtue, aiming to improve a little bit every day. This personal system laid the groundwork for a more methodical way of growing our character and mindset. I particularly enjoyed his idea of focusing on each virtue until you've mastered it while holding yourself accountable.

> *"Be at war with your vices, at peace with your neighbors, and let every new year find you a better man." - Benjamin Franklin*

THOMAS JEFFERSON'S PURSUIT OF HAPPINESS AS A SOCIETAL IDEAL

Thomas Jefferson, along with using the wisdom of the Stoics, penned the famous phrase about the "pursuit of happiness" in the *Declaration of Independence* (*Jefferson et al., 1776*). I quote that simple idea in many places in my *Health and Longevity Mastery Series* of books. **Jefferson** believed everyone should have a fair chance to seek joy and fulfillment. This idea turned happiness into a public goal, influencing the way we all think today about well-being and personal rights.

> *"I believe that every human mind feels pleasure in doing good to another."*
> *- Thomas Jefferson*

CASE STUDY

Jacob is a college student who installs a habit-tracking app on his phone. Just like **Franklin** wrote down his progress each night, **Jacob** checks off daily tasks like "exercise" or "limit screen time." Over the semester, he notices that small improvements—tracked consistently—add up to big changes in his energy and outlook. Imagine the apps **Ben Franklin** could have designed for our daily use!

SHIFT FROM SURVIVAL TO THRIVING AS A CULTURAL GOAL

Back when America was just getting started, most folks were simply trying to stay alive—fending off brutal winters, poor harvests, and illness. But once Enlightenment thinkers like **John Locke** came along, the conversation shifted from *"How do we survive?"* to *"How do we actually live well?"* People began to believe that once food and shelter were covered, life should open up space for learning, creativity, and personal growth. Schools popped up, towns hosted lectures and debates, and self-improvement became a shared community value.

I felt that same tug-of-war as a young dad with four kids. For years I hustled two or three jobs at a time, terrified that one slip would leave the pantry empty. My children remember a happy, carefree childhood in safe neighborhoods; I remember racing the clock, counting every dollar, and wondering if I'd make rent. Oh, how I loved my family! But, looking back, I realize I was stuck in survival mode long after we were reasonably secure. If I'd embraced more of the "thriving" mindset—trusting that growth and joy were just as vital as a paycheck—my own memories might match the sunny ones my kids still talk about.

> *"Trust yourself. You know more than you think you do."*
> *– Benjamin Spock*

That shift toward thriving shows up in early personal-development ideas too. **Benjamin Franklin** drew up his famous list of virtues, and **Thomas Jefferson** baked *"the pursuit of happiness"* right into the *Declaration*. Those seeds sprouted into whole fields of goal-setting, positive thinking, and mastery of mind and habits. Fast-forward to today and you'll find shelves of self-help books, life-coaching podcasts, and seminars—all tracing their roots back to that simple Enlightenment notion: once survival is handled, we're meant to reach for something bigger, brighter, and deeply fulfilling.

1.3.2: ABRAHAM LINCOLN AND RESILIENCE

BATTLING DEPRESSION WHILE LEADING A DIVIDED NATION - REALISTIC OPTIMISM IN ACTION

Abraham Lincoln faced the tremendous burden of the Civil War while also struggling with bouts of depression (*Shenk, 2005*). We view **Lincoln** as a hero and martyr through the lens of history, but he was wildly unpopular through most of his Presidency while feeling the burden of thousands of war dead and the loss of his beloved young son, **Willie**. Through all of his challenges, he remained hopeful that the country could unite again. His realistic optimism shone through in speeches and policies aimed at healing the nation. He knew that without faith, all would be lost.

"With the fearful strain that is on me night and day, if I did not laugh, I should die." - Abraham Lincoln

Abraham Lincoln
Credit – PICRYL / creativecommons.org

LINCOLN DEMONSTRATES HOPE'S NECESSITY AMID EXTREME ADVERSITY

Lincoln's resolve to save the Union showed hope can guide us through even the darkest times. He refused to let fear or sadness stop him from doing what he believed was right. He somehow stayed positive while acknowledging real problems can drive us toward meaningful solutions.

LINCOLN'S LETTERS

Lincoln wrote to his close friends, usually late at night. He shared his worries about the war's toll but ended one letter by insisting that "right makes might." **Lincoln's** quiet yet firm belief lit a spark in him, reminding him that faith in a better future can carry us through overwhelming trials.

EMPATHY AND UNITY REDUCE COLLECTIVE STRESS

By valuing empathy, **Lincoln** worked to ease tensions between opposing sides. When leaders show concern for everyone, communities can heal faster and better (*Hatch, 2005*). When you show concern, empathy, and care for your soldiers, they will follow you to the ends of the earth. Fewer tensions mean less stress and a healthier mental and physical environment. Even when the war was ending, through all the pain, **Lincoln** insisted that soldiers and officers from the South be treated humanely, with whatever dignity they had left. If he had only lived to work for reconstruction, the path forward may have been somewhat easier.

POSITIVITY CAN COEXIST WITH PROFOUND STRUGGLE

Lincoln's story shows us that being positive doesn't mean we ignore hardships. Instead, positivity can stand strong alongside sadness, worry, or anger. When we accept pain while holding onto hope—this understanding can help us stay resilient, which is vital for both our emotional and physical well-being.

THEODORE ROOSEVELT

Theodore Roosevelt lived more than a hundred years after **Franklin** and **Jefferson**, but he also felt like he had the weight of the world on his shoulders. He served as President of the United States and dealt with tough decisions almost every day. To cope, he read *Meditations* by **Marcus Aurelius**. **Roosevelt** learned that he shouldn't waste time complaining about bad luck or other people's actions. Instead, he should pour his energy into the challenges right in front of him—like making fair laws and protecting the environment. By focusing on what he could control, **Roosevelt** became a successful and revered President.

> *"Nobody cares how much you know, until they know how much you care." – Theodore Roosevelt*

I.3.3: HUMANITARIANISM AND MORAL LEADERSHIP

GANDHI'S "SATYAGRAHA" (SOUL-FORCE) APPROACH: TRUTH AND COMPASSION AS INSTRUMENTS OF CHANGE

Mahatma Gandhi believed nonviolent resistance, guided by truth and compassion, could transform societies (*Gandhi, 1927*). This idea, known as *"Satyagraha,"* is about meeting hostility with patience and love. He focused on moral power instead of force. **Gandhi** inspired millions to see that a peaceful mindset can topple massive injustices. I love this concept.

> *"Power is of two kinds. One is obtained by the fear of punishment, and the other by acts of love. Power based on love is a thousand times more effective and permanent than the one derived from fear of punishment."*
> *- Mahatma Gandhi*

MARTIN LUTHER KING, JR. - ALIGNING LOVE WITH SOCIAL JUSTICE - OPTIMISM AS A COLLECTIVE FORCE

Dr. Martin Luther King, Jr. applied **Gandhi's** nonviolent methods in the American civil rights movement (*King, 1963*). He taught that love and courage could break down even the most challenging barriers of prejudice. His dream of racial equality proved that a strong, positive vision can rally entire communities to strive for a brighter future. His *"I Have A Dream"* speech motivated us to judge each other by the content of our character rather than the color of our skin.

> *"Darkness cannot drive out darkness; only light can do that. Hate cannot drive out hate; only love can do that." - Dr. Martin Luther King, Jr.*

Dr. Martin Luther King, Jr.
Credit – FLICKR / creativecommons.org

RALPH WALDO EMERSON: SELF-RELIANCE, COMMUNION WITH NATURE, INNER HARMONY CULTIVATE WELL-BEING

Ralph Waldo Emerson championed the power of the individual spirit and the healing energy of nature (*Emerson, 1841*). He urged people to think for themselves and connect with the natural world to find peace and purpose. Emerson's idea that we should strive for self-trust and simplicity helped me understand how a calm, hopeful mindset can nurture personal growth and overall health.

> *"Write it on your heart that every day is the best day in the year."*
> *- Ralph Waldo Emerson*

HELEN KELLER

Helen Keller was born unable to see or hear, which made everyday life incredibly challenging. As she grew older, she felt trapped and worried she'd never communicate with the outside world. But with help from her teacher, she learned to read using Braille. **Helen** discovered the writings of **Ralph Waldo Emerson**—especially his ideas about *Self Reliance* and believing in your own power. Encouraged by that message, she also noted how **Gandhi** achieved remarkable changes through peaceful persistence, and (towards the end of her life) **Dr. King** fought for equality without violence. **Helen** decided early that she wouldn't let her disabilities stop her from sharing her voice. Over time, she became a famous author and speaker, proving that anyone can shine a light through self-trust, kindness, and determination, even in the darkest circumstances.

> *"Optimism is the faith that leads to achievement. Nothing can be done without hope and confidence." – Helen Keller*

Helen Keller
Credit – Picryl / creativecommons.org

THESE LUMINARIES SHOWED POSITIVITY ISN'T PASSIVE; IT'S TRANSFORMATIVE ON SOCIETAL AND PERSONAL LEVELS

Gandhi, MLK, and **Emerson** all reveal how optimism can drive real change. They stood for compassion, unity, and respect for human potential—values uplifting individuals and entire nations. Their lives prove that positive thinking when we act on it can shape history and spark new possibilities for everyone. We've traced ancient roots and modern pillars of positivity. Next, we'll focus on how the 20th century and beyond ushered in the era of self-help, spirituality, and holistic well-being.

CHAPTER TWO
REVOLUTIONARY THINKERS WHO SHAPED MODERN POSITIVITY

C ould one idea—or one book—truly redefine how millions approach happiness, health, and success? We've already touched on some thinkers who proved it could. Here's a deeper dive:

SECTION ONE:
EARLY-TO-MID 20ᵗʰ CENTURY VISIONARIES

2.1.1: NAPOLEON HILL'S "THINK AND GROW RICH"
THE POWER OF FOCUSED THOUGHT AND DESIRE

Napoleon Hill liked to say that success begins in the mind. When we lock onto a specific goal, picture it in detail, and keep that desire burning, we kick powerful forces into gear (*Hill, 1937*). That crystal-clear vision fuels motivation, helps us brush aside setbacks, and keeps us moving until the dream becomes real. The idea was so strong that some World War II POWs later said **Hill's** principles helped them survive their darkest hours.

Years before anyone coined the phrase "law of attraction," **Hill** was already describing it. He believed vivid, repeated images of success shape our attitudes and nudge our behavior so we naturally head in the right direction. A positive mental picture, he argued, is the bridge between today's effort and tomorrow's results.

MARY KAY ASH

Mary Kay Ash proved him right. She had a tough time in the working world. As a woman in the mid-1900s, she was often ignored or not taken seriously. She felt frustrated because she knew she could do great things if only people would listen. One day, she read **Napoleon Hill's** book about staying positive, setting clear goals, and acting on them. That gave her the spark of an idea to start her own cosmetics company, *Mary Kay,* using a simple motto: **If you believe in yourself, you can accomplish incredible feats.** Even though people doubted her at first, she never lost faith. She reminded herself of **Hill's** words, stayed focused on her dream, and eventually built one of the largest beauty companies in the world.

"Everyone has an invisible sign hanging from their neck saying, 'Make me feel important.' Never forget this message when working with people." – Mary Kay Ash

Mary Kay Ash
Credit – Wikimedia Commons

NAPOLEON HILL SHOWED MENTAL ATTITUDE SHAPES DESTINY, BUT REQUIRES ETHICAL GROUNDING

Hill also warned that ambition without ethics is a dead end. He insisted that real prosperity demands honesty and compassion. I learned that the hard way: after twenty years growing a company, I took on an investor and tried to expand too fast. We lost everything. Keeping transparent books protected my reputation, and a **Hill**-style attitude—"wake up and reinvent yourself"—got me back on my feet.

His final message is simple: aim high, but weave service into those ambitions. When success lifts others too, it feels richer and lasts longer.

"Whatever the mind of man can conceive and believe, it can achieve." - *Napoleon Hill*

2.1.2: DALE CARNEGIE AND NORMAN VINCENT PEALE

DALE CARNEGIE'S FOCUS ON EMPATHY AND SOCIAL SKILLS NURTURES EMOTIONAL HEALTH

Dale Carnegie's classic *How to Win Friends and Influence People* argues that good manners and genuine interest in others are superpowers (*Carnegie, 1936*). Listen more than you speak, hand out honest praise, remember names—those small gestures lower stress for everyone and leave you feeling lighter too. I am not the first to gather ideas about positivity and success from great thinkers and compare them. **Dale Carnegie** said:

"The ideas I stand for are not mine. I borrowed them from Socrates. I swiped them from Chesterfield. I stole them from Jesus. And I put them in a book. If you don't like their rules, whose would you use?"

NORMAN VINCENT PEALE'S "THE POWER OF POSITIVE THINKING" INTEGRATES FAITH AND PSYCHOLOGY

Norman Vincent Peale took that interpersonal warmth and added faith. In *The Power of Positive Thinking* (*Peale, 1952*) he blends prayer, affirmations, and upbeat self-talk to help readers replace worry with confidence. I love hearing **Peale** read his own words on the old tapes—you can hear the conviction in his voice.

"Every problem has in it the seeds of its own solution. If you don't have any problems, you don't get any seeds." - *Norman Vincent Peale*

Norman Vincent Peale
Credit – Smithsonian National Portrait Gallery / Oscar White (b. 1921)

JOHNNY CARSON

You would never believe it, but if you're old enough to remember **Johnny Carson** hosting *The Tonight Show*, you remember him as a vibrant, outgoing, easygoing host. But when he was younger, he dreaded parties, family get-togethers, and public speaking. **Johnny** felt like he never knew what to say or how to act without feeling awkward. When he picked up **Dale Carnegie's** techniques, he realized that simply showing genuine interest in other people's stories made it easier to talk to them. Reading **Norman Vincent Peale** also inspired **Johnny** to replace negative *"What if I mess up?"* thoughts with positive ones, such as *"I have something fun to share."* Over time, he transformed from a shy teen to a smooth TV host, thanks to a mix of preparation and positive thinking.

"To be an entertainer, you gotta be a little gutsy, a little egotistical, so you have to pull back sometimes when people say, 'Well, he's stuck-up.' 'Stuck-up' is only another word for self-conscious." – Johnny Carson

Johnny Carson
Credit – PICRYL / creativecommons.org

POPULARIZED OPTIMISM AS A MAINSTREAM LIFESTYLE

Thanks to **Carnegie** and **Peale,** optimism moved from lecture halls into living rooms. They showed that simple habits—greeting people warmly, replaying your strengths—lift mood, tighten social bonds, and even improve physical health (*Pressman & Cohen, 2005*).

2.1.3: THE EMERGENCE OF PSYCHOSOMATIC MEDICINE

NORMAN COUSINS' USE OF LAUGHTER TO COMBAT LIFE-THREATENING ISSUES

Author-editor **Norman Cousins** shocked doctors in 1979 when he wrote that **Marx Brothers** marathons eased his debilitating illness. Laughter, he found, lowered pain and sped recovery. His takeaway: optimism works first on emotion, then on physiology.

"Optimism doesn't wait on facts. It deals with prospects. Pessimism is a waste of time." - Norman Cousins

PLACEBO EFFECT RESEARCH VALIDATED MIND-BODY CONNECTIONS

Around the same time, researchers confirmed the placebo effect. Give half a group sugar pills but tell them it's medicine, and many still improve (*Beecher, 1955*). A famous 1960s trial found placebo patients reported less pain and healed faster—proof that belief alone can set off real biochemical changes. Early skeptics called it wishful thinking; later studies (*Benson, 1975*) forced a rethink, showing that hope, joy, and confidence calm stress hormones and bolster immunity.

DEEPER RESEARCH INTO STRESS, EMOTION, AND PHYSICAL HEALTH CORRELATION

Neuroscientist **Bruce McEwen's** work (1998) tied chronic stress to disease, cementing the mind-body link. This new research underlined the fact that our mental state can boost or harm our health. With each new study, we see more proof that positive thinking isn't just wishful—it's truly powerful.

Nobody understands high-stress situations more than my friend **Mark Redman**, one of the great *Major League Baseball* pitchers of our time. **Mark** found himself pitching in the World Series. He learned how to cope with stress in big moments. **Mark** said:

"It came to the point where you try to do too much out there. You give up a couple of runs and in the back of your head, because of the way things have gone all year, I just tried to battle. It can be wearing on a person, but I've been there before."

Mark Redman and Tad Sisler
Source – Sisler Private Collection

These amazing thinkers laid the groundwork; then came others who added fresh dimensions of spirituality, psychology, and even flight metaphors.

SECTION TWO: LATE 20ᵗʰ CENTURY VISIONARIES
2.2.1 TONY ROBBINS, OG MANDINO, WAYNE DYER AND OTHERS

I'll be elaborating now on these thought giants I mentioned in my **Introduction**, while adding a handful more:

HIGH-ENERGY TRANSFORMATIONAL TECHNIQUES FOCUSING ON IMMEDIATE BEHAVIORAL SHIFTS

Tony Robbins is known for his dynamic seminars, where he uses intense activities—like firewalking or rapid goal-setting—to help people snap out of old habits (*Robbins, 1992*). These high-energy methods encourage swift action instead of merely talking about change. When we push past our comfort zones, we discover personal strengths they never knew we had.

Zig Ziglar was another charismatic motivational speaker who used humor, personal stories, and practical wisdom to inspire people to reach their full potential. His books and seminars influenced great thought leaders like **Tony Robbins.**

"Your attitude, not your aptitude, will determine your altitude."
- Zig Ziglar

Zig Ziglar
Credit – Wikimedia Commons

Yet another thought leader who employs similarly dynamic techniques is **Les Brown**, famous for his energetic stage presence and powerful personal story—urges his audience to "be hungry" for their goals, using fiery language and real-life examples to spark immediate shifts in mindset and action.

I met **Tony Robbins** in the 1990s at a church where I performed in Palm Desert, California. He is a giant, literally a very tall man, and his kindness matches his charisma. We spoke about my wife's recent passing, and in our conversation, he compassionately told me that I could use my grief and pain to my benefit for the sake of my children rather than allowing it to control me. His words of wisdom were precisely what I needed to hear.

> *"The secret of success is learning how to use pain and pleasure instead of having pain and pleasure use you. If you do that, you're in control of your life. If you don't, life controls you." - Tony Robbins*

Another **Tony Robbins** gem I love: He believes that you can kick any habit if you associate more pain than pleasure with that habit. When I was young, I smoked cigarettes, and I loved the nicotine rush and the light-headedness I felt when smoking. It wasn't until I started focusing on the stench of the cigarettes, and what it was doing to my lungs and my general health that I was able to quit smoking. I also wanted to be a singer and I believed that cigarettes would impede my ability to take deep breaths and project my voice. This is a great example of associating more pain than pleasure to let go of a bad habit.

CORE PREMISE:
CHANGE YOUR STORY TO CHANGE YOUR REALITY

Og Mandino's *The Greatest Salesman in the World* (1968) and **Wayne Dyer's** early work (1976) echo that theme: rewrite the story in your head, and your outer world follows. When we shift our mental story from self-doubt to self-belief, we pave the way for new possibilities to unfold.

> *"Conflict cannot survive without your participation." - Wayne Dyer*

KIRSTIE ALLEY

Kirstie Alley was an actress known for making people laugh—but privately, she felt embarrassed about her extra weight. Every time she tried a new diet she ended up feeling discouraged. Then, she came across **Tony Robbins's** concept of *raising your standards*, so she started expecting more from herself. She began visualizing the outcome she wanted, a technique **Wayne Dyer** recommended for creating a positive mindset. She also enjoyed reading **Og Mandino's** stories about *consistency and daily improvement.* **Kirstie** tried repeating an affirmation each morning: *"I am capable of the discipline and focus I need today."*

> *"You'll never be disappointed if you always keep an eye on uncharted territory, where you'll be challenged and growing and having fun."*
> *– Kirstie Alley*

Kirstie Alley
Credit – Wikimedia Commons (cropped)

Before long, **Kirstie** was cooking healthy meals, going for regular walks, and dancing for exercise. Her clothes fit better, and she felt a fresh wave of confidence on camera and off. Eventually, **Kirstie** became a spokesperson for *Jenny Craig* weight-loss programs.

POSITIVITY IS ACTION-ORIENTED, NOT PASSIVE

Robbins, Mandino, and **Dyer** agree that positivity means action. Dream big, yes—but tie those dreams to daily steps. At the same time, they warn against sprinting yourself into exhaustion. Real growth includes rest, renewal, and a little grace.

2.2.2: POSITIVE PSYCHOLOGY

MARTIN SELIGMAN'S "PERMA":

Psychologist Martin Seligman mapped flourishing with his **PERMA** model: Positive emotion, Engagement, Relationships, Meaning, and Achievement (*Seligman, 2011*). Happiness, he says, isn't just a mood; it's a life where these five pillars stay strong.

> *"Well-being cannot exist just in your own head. Well-being is a combination of feeling good as well as actually having meaning, good relationships, and accomplishment." - Martin Seligman*

Martin Seligman

BARBARA FREDRICKSON'S BROADEN-AND-BUILD: POSITIVE EMOTIONS EXPAND COGNITIVE CAPACITY

Barbara Fredrickson added the Broaden-and-Build theory. Joy, gratitude, and love don't just feel good; they widen our perception so we spot more options, learn faster, and build lasting resources (*Fredrickson, 2009*). She warns that positive thinking stuck only in your head won't move the needle—you need feelings that reach every cell.

"Positive thinking is just one small part of positive psychology. Plus, as an approach to well-being, positive thinking only helps you to the extent that it yields one or more positive emotions. The problem with positive thinking is that it sometimes just stays up "in the head" and fails to drip down to become a fully embodied experience." - Barbara Fredrickson

GRATITUDE STUDY

A 2012 study on daily gratitude and mindfulness (*Boehm & Kubzansky*) found moods brightened and blood pressure dropped within months, linking emotional warmth to heart health. Seligman and Fredrickson's data pushed "happiness research" into mainstream academia, turning optimism into a respected scientific field. So, we're seeing a pattern here of many different validities to the truth that a positive outlook really does breed greater health and longevity.

2.2.3: MODERN SPIRITUAL MOTIVATORS

EXPLORING FREEDOM FROM LIMITING BELIEFS

Richard Bach wrote stories that invite readers to imagine a life beyond constraints. *Jonathan Livingston* tells the parable of a seagull who dares to fly higher and farther than the rest (*Bach, 1970*). In *Illusions*, **Bach** challenges us to see that our perceived boundaries might be self-made illusions (*Bach, 1977*).

ENCOURAGES A SENSE OF WONDER, INTROSPECTION, AND FAITH IN ONE'S HIGHER POTENTIAL

Through dreamy narratives, **Bach** guides us to dream big and trust in our limitless nature. He blends mystical elements with personal growth themes, urging us to look within ourselves for answers. When we blend wonder and self-reflection, that action inspires us to step beyond the ordinary and follow our deepest calling.

NEIL DIAMOND

Neil Diamond came into a restaurant years ago, and I was performing in the other room. My voice sounded a lot like **Neil Diamond**, and he didn't realize I was singing. He asked the waitress if she could check to see what recording was playing of himself because he didn't remember ever recording that song. She told him it was actually me singing in the other room, and he was dumbfounded. We met and became friends, and later, he introduced me to his publisher.

Neil was an extremely talented singer-songwriter, and he confided in me that, for a while, he felt like he was going through the motions in the music business. His songs didn't thrill him anymore, and he wondered if people still cared about his work. Then he picked up a little book called *Jonathan Livingston Seagull* by **Richard Bach**, and he read about that determined seagull who wanted more out of life than just fighting for scraps of food. **Neil** connected with this story and with the idea of never giving up and aiming higher. Suddenly, he felt inspired to pour his heart into new music. Reading about the adventurous seagull convinced him that he, too, could fly beyond his old routines. This led him to write the soundtrack to the film *Jonathan Livingston Seagull.* What I loved about **Neil Diamond** was that he was constantly pushing his artistic boundaries and regaining his passion for music with every new album or project.

"I came back to performing with a different attitude about performing and myself. I wasn't expecting perfection anymore, just hoping for an occasional inspiration." – Neil Diamond

Neil Diamond
Credit – Wikimedia Commons

BROADER MOVEMENT OF SPIRITUAL SELF-DISCOVERY IN THE LATE 20th CENTURY

Often called the *"Queen of Affirmations,"* **Louise Hay's** message was that self-love and positive affirmations can dissolve negative beliefs. She suggested that changing your inner dialogue can transform your external reality. **Louise Hay** endured considerable hardship in her early years, including abuse and later a cancer diagnosis. In her late 40s, she discovered the power of self-forgiveness and kindness toward herself and others. She wrote *You Can Heal Your Life* at a time when many people might have been slowing down, but her renewed sense of hope and compassion ignited a second career as a best-selling author and founder of a major publishing house. She transformed her struggles into a worldwide message of healing and empowerment through affirmations, self-love, and service to others.

"I believe we create our own lives. And we create it by our thinking, feeling patterns in our belief system. I think we're all born with this huge canvas in front of us and the paintbrushes and the paint, and we choose what to put on this canvas...every thought we think is creating our future."
- Louise Hay

Best known for *The Power of Now,* **Eckhart Tolle** encourages us to become fully present and let go of limiting stories in the mind. In other words, true freedom arises when we detach from the "voice in our head." Whenever you see a young boy playing with his trucks in a sandbox, or a young girl playing with her dolls, they are immersed in their imaginations, yet fully in the moment. At what age do we start to lose the ability to be entirely focused on this very moment?

"It is through gratitude for the present moment that the spiritual dimension of life opens up." - Eckhart Tolle

Eckhart Tolle
Credit – Wikimedia Commons

While I was performing at this church in Palm Desert, California, there was a point in each service where we would do a "moment of meditation and giving thanks," and I would softly sing a meditative song entitled *"We Are One."* Over the years, scores of people came to me following services and told me that during that particular moment of the service, they felt actually present "in the moment" for the first time they could remember. Whatever it takes for you to get there (or here! Because here we are in this moment!), do it!

Deepak Chopra, the physician and best-selling author I mentioned in the **Introduction** of this book, blends Eastern wisdom with modern science, focusing on the mind-body connection for holistic well-being. He uses guided meditations, discussions on consciousness, and teachings about spiritual harmony to help people transcend limiting beliefs. Concentrating on our mindfulness and personal awareness encourages us to tap into deeper levels of healing, purpose, and self-realization.

> *"You can't make positive choices for the rest of your life without an environment that makes those choices easy, natural, and enjoyable."*
> *– Deepak Chopra*

As people searched for more than material success, motivators like **Bach, Hay, Tolle,** and **Chopra** paved the way for a wave of spiritual and self-help literature. Their works showed that personal growth might be better served by achieving goals and nurturing the soul. This era helped us to move towards deeper introspection and holistic well-being.

PERSONAL TRANSCENDENCE CAN COMPLEMENT EMOTIONAL AND PHYSICAL HEALTH

We can change our daily mindset by embracing these spiritual leaders' calls to push beyond our limiting beliefs, and when we do this we move towards lowering stress and sparking inspiration. Over time, feeling a greater sense of purpose may support better mental and physical health (*Koltko-Rivera, 2006*). We can try to see ourselves as more than our current circumstances, and in doing so we live with greater energy and hope.

Echoing **Seligman's** idea of the true meaning of engagements, community and relationships, my friend, legendary *multi-platinum* recording artist **Rod Stewart** whittled it all down when he said:

> *"You go through life wondering what is it all about but at the end of the day it's all about family."*

After years of touring and living the crazy rock-and-roll life, **Rod Stewart** came back around to the simple idea that love and family really holds the key.

Tad Sisler with Rod Stewart
Source – Sisler Private Collection

We've merged philosophy and spirituality with intellect, and we've looked at the ways our bodies physically react to a positive outlook. Now, the final piece is integrating mind, body, and community into a holistic view—as we enter the new world of science-backed wellness.

SECTION THREE:
INTEGRATIVE AND CONTEMPORARY THINKERS
2.3.1: HOLISTIC HEALTH PIONEERS

FUSING NUTRITIONAL SCIENCE, STRESS MANAGEMENT, AND EMOTIONAL WELL-BEING FOR DISEASE PREVENTION

You've probably heard that eating right and staying active are key to a healthy life, but did you know your mindset plays a huge role too? Experts like **Dr. Andrew Weil, Dr. Dean Ornish, Dr. Mark Hyman,** and **Dr. David Perlmutter** all agree that good health comes from a mix of smart eating, handling stress well, and keeping a positive outlook. Instead of just treating symptoms, they focus on the whole you—your diet, your stress levels, and how you feel emotionally. By making thoughtful choices in these areas, you can prevent a lot of chronic health problems.

NOTABLE SUCCESS IN REVERSING OR HALTING CHRONIC ILLNESS VIA LIFESTYLE CHANGES

Dr. Dean Ornish showed the world you can sometimes reverse heart disease with the right diet, regular exercise, and a supportive mindset. **Dr. Hyman** has helped people tackle issues like diabetes by connecting their struggles to food and stress. These examples remind us that lasting health comes from steady, everyday habits, not quick fixes. And honestly, we're only starting to understand how powerful our minds can be in all this. As **Dr. Ornish** once said:

"When we understand the connection between how we live and how long we live, it's easier to make different choices. Instead of viewing the time we spend with friends and family as luxuries, we can see that these relationships are among the most powerful determinants of our well-being and survival." - Dr. Dean Ornish

LARRY KING

My old friend, legendary CNN host **Larry King,** was famous for interviewing all sorts of people on television, but behind the scenes, he often felt stressed and hurried. His blood pressure numbers increased, and he knew something had to change.

After talking with **Dr. Ornish** on his show, **Larry** learned that simple shifts—like swapping processed snacks for veggies or lean proteins—could do wonders for the heart. **Dr. Hyman's** approach taught **Larry** to keep track of how certain foods made him feel and to slow down through daily meditation. **Larry** also kept a small journal of what he was thankful for, like his family and friends, and the chance to keep asking people curious questions on TV. That high blood pressure eased little by little, and he gained new energy for his work.

I'm grateful for my friendship with **Larry King** and for the Socratic wisdom he imparted to all of us with his pointed questions to just about every consequential person of his time. By remembering his roots of poverty and how far he had come, concentrating on the things that meant the most to him, and remembering what he was thankful for, **Larry** lowered his blood pressure and lived many years longer than his doctors told him he would.

"I never forgot being poor, and I never stopped thinking how fortunate I am."

Larry King and Tad Sisler
Source – Sisler Private Collection

RECOGNIZING POSITIVITY AS KEY TO PATIENT COMPLIANCE AND LONG-TERM SUCCESS

The doctors we're talking about all say a hopeful attitude helps people stick with healthy habits. When you believe things can get better, you're more likely to keep up with your meal plans, workouts, or stress-busting routines. People who stay optimistic also tend to recover faster from setbacks. It's not about being perfect—it's about making small, consistent choices, like eating more whole foods, taking a walk, or practicing mindfulness.

"The best advice is to avoid foods with health claims on the label, or better yet avoid foods with labels in the first place." - Dr. Mark Hyman

Dr. Mark Hyman
Credit – Wikimedia Commons

2.3.2: CUTTING-EDGE MIND-BODY RESEARCHERS

EXPLORING EPIGENETICS: BELIEFS POTENTIALLY INFLUENCING GENE EXPRESSION

Now, here's where things get really interesting: your thoughts might actually influence your genes. **Dr. Bruce Lipton** talks about epigenetics, which suggests our beliefs and emotions can affect how our genes work. It's like our DNA is a blueprint, and our mindset helps decide how it's built. A study even found that people who meditated and visualized positive things saw changes in genes tied to stress.

"Epigenetics doesn't change the genetic code, it changes how that's read. Perfectly normal genes can result in cancer or death. Vice-versa, in the right environment, mutant genes won't be expressed. Genes are equivalent to blueprints; epigenetics is the contractor. They change the assembly, the structure." - Dr. Bruce Lipton

Bruce Lipton
Credit – Wikimedia Commons

A PARADIGM SHIFT:
MIND AS AN ACTIVE PARTNER IN HEALING

Dr. Joe Dispenza takes this further, showing how meditation and focused intention can physically change your body, with brain scans and hormone tests to prove it. While some scientists want more research, these ideas are starting to gain traction, and many doctors now see the mind and body as partners in healing.

"Your personality is made up of how you think, act, and feel. It is your state of being. Therefore, your thoughts, actions, and feelings will enslave you to the same past personal reality. However, when you as a personality embrace new thoughts, actions, and feelings, you will inevitably create a new personal reality in your future." - Dr. Joe Dispenza

2.3.3: POPULAR SPIRITUAL LEADERS AND COACHES

MAINSTREAM PLATFORMS PROMOTING GRATITUDE, SELF-LOVE, AND MANIFESTATION

On the spiritual side, folks like **Oprah Winfrey, Gabrielle Bernstein**, and **Rhonda Byrne** have made positivity a household topic. Through TV shows, books, and social media, they've spread ideas like gratitude, self-love, and manifestation. Critics say these messages can oversimplify life's challenges, but for many, they're a game-changer.

"Remember, if you are criticizing, you are not being grateful. If you are blaming, you are not being grateful. If you are complaining, you are not being grateful." - Rhonda Byrne

SHANIA TWAIN

Shania Twain is a famous country singer whose life suddenly felt stuck after personal hardships and a difficult divorce. When she came on the **Oprah** show, she heard an uplifting message about gratitude: focusing on the good in her life rather than the things going wrong. She started writing down three things she was thankful for each morning—her son's laughter, supportive fans, and love of music. This daily practice helped **Shania** see that even when life seems dark, there is always a spark of hope. Thanks to that advice, she regained her passion for singing and later released new music, feeling more confident than ever.

"I don't take any day for granted anymore." – Shania Twain

Shania Twain
Credit – Wikimedia Commons

GLOBAL APPETITE FOR ACCESSIBLE POSITIVITY TOOLS

Oprah and her counterparts engage audiences worldwide through social media, podcasts, and events, making their teachings easy to follow. Their simple steps—like journaling or repeating affirmations—fit into anyone's busy schedules, encouraging consistent practice. This universal reach shows many people's hunger for straightforward methods to help us towards hope and resilience.

EVOLUTION FROM FRINGE SUBCULTURE TO WIDESPREAD PHENOMENON

These ideas—gratitude, affirmations, visualization—used to be considered out there, but now they're everywhere, from workplace wellness programs to casual chats. They're simple, fit into busy lives, and speak to a global hunger for hope and resilience. As **Ernest Holmes** wrote in *The Science of Mind*, when we affirm that what we want is already happening, we help make it real.

Remember what my dear friend, former championship-winning *NFL* Quarterback, **Congressman** and **Secretary of Housing and Urban Development Jack Kemp** said:

"There are no limits to our future if we don't put limits on our people."

Tad Sisler with Congressman Jack Kemp
Source – Sisler Private Collection

The science and stories all point to one truth: your mindset can add not just years to your life, but joy and quality too.

CHAPTER THREE
UNDERSTANDING THE MIND-BODY CONNECTION FOR LONGEVITY

W hat if your cells are eavesdropping on your thoughts? Evidence suggests they might be. From the work of **Dr. David Sinclair** at *Harvard* and other great researchers, we are now finding a direct connection between our thoughts and our health.

SECTION ONE:
CELLULAR AGING AND TELOMERE SCIENCE
3.1.1: TELOMERES 101

TELOMERES PROTECT CHROMOSOMES LIKE SHOELACE CAPS - SHORTER TELOMERES EQUAL FASTER AGING

You inherit telomeres from your parents, much like your DNA. These protective caps at the ends of chromosomes, similar to the plastic tips on shoelaces, prevent wear and tear. Keeping telomeres long and strong helps your cells function properly, reducing the risk of disease over time, as I discuss in my book **"Stay Healthy, Stay Youthful: The Science of Living to 150."**

CHRONIC STRESS ACCELERATES TELOMERE SHORTENING, INCREASING DISEASE RISK

If you're constantly stressed or overwhelmed, your body pumps out stress hormones that can harm telomeres, especially in kids exposed to chronic stress, which may cause lasting damage. Stress also triggers inflammation and oxidative stress, further shortening telomeres. Research shows this accelerates aging and increases disease risk. For instance, studies on stress-related aging—like *Epel et al., 2004*—reveal that chronic stress and poor coping mechanisms can shrink telomeres, leading to health issues such as depression and heart disease. Conversely, those who manage stress well tend to have longer telomeres and better health (*Epel et al., 2009*).

In the same way, **jealousy** or **resentment** triggers a mix of stress responses and negative thought patterns that can strain your body physically. Chronic stress often leads to unhealthy habits like overeating or sleep deprivation, which further harm telomeres and overall health (*Shalev et al., 2013*). These negative behaviors create a cycle: stress shortens telomeres, which worsens health, causing more stress. Like I've said before, all these **negative emotions act as acids that eat their own containers**; they eat you!

On the other hand, positive habits like mindfulness, exercise, and social support can protect telomeres and improve well-being, helping you cope with stress more effectively (*Schutte & Malouff, 2014*). You can slow cellular aging and literally create a longer, more vibrant life by actively working to replace lingering negativity with healthier coping strategies.

A handful of years ago, my brother-in-law called me, yelling about what a terrible brother I was to my sister and blaming me for things that had happened in his life years ago that were entirely out of my control. My initial reaction was shock and resentment. Nothing he said represented who I really am. He didn't even really know me! I didn't immediately react; it took me a few days to calm down from this personal attack. As I realized that this had nothing to do with me and it was all about his way of coping with his current situation, I sat down and wrote a long letter (which I never mailed) and got it "off my chest." I was able to let it go and move on from it. Hopefully, eventually, we may be able to repair the damage he caused, but I did not accelerate the situation with more anger; I let go of my resentment and realized it's always healthier for us to let go of toxic relationships that cause pain when we need to. Like my lovely daughter **Rachel** likes to say, *"Not my circus; not my monkeys."*

MEDITATION AND MINDFULNESS CAN SLOW OR REVERSE THIS PROCESS

Mindfulness and meditation can actually help slow down how fast you age. Studies show they work by keeping your telomeres—those protective caps on your chromosomes—nice and long (*Schutte & Malouff, 2014*). They help dial down stress hormones and boost your mood, which means better health overall (*Buric et al., 2017*). It's like a little shield against stress messing with your body!

THOUGHT PATTERNS CAN DIRECTLY IMPACT BIOLOGICAL AGING

Thoughts are things. Your thoughts can totally affect how fast you age on the inside. If you're always stressed, negative, or worrying about stuff, it can wear down your telomeres faster, speeding up aging and upping your risk for health issues (*Epel et al., 2017*). Think of it like this: if you're stuck feeling anxious or holding onto grudges, it's quietly aging you more than you'd like. But if you focus on positive vibes—like being grateful or just feeling content—it can slow that aging process down. It's not just about feeling good in the moment; it's about keeping yourself healthier for the long haul. So, let's not let those negative thoughts drag us down—time to let go and focus on the good stuff!

"Once you replace negative thoughts with positive ones, you'll start having positive results." – Willie Nelson

Willie Nelson

RESEARCH STUDY

A research team tracked a group of nurses working long, high-pressure shifts. They found that those with higher stress levels showed faster telomere shortening than their less-stressed colleagues. This striking discovery reinforced the link between chronic stress and accelerated cellular aging, emphasizing the need for us to all find positive coping methods. So, take a deep breath. Reframe your situation. Find the good in it. Let go and move on.

3.1.2: ROLE OF CORTISOL AND CHRONIC STRESS

PERSISTENT STRESS AND NEGATIVE EMOTIONS ELEVATE CORTISOL, LEADING TO INFLAMMATION AND CELLULAR DAMAGE

Stress isn't just a mental burden—it can really take a toll on your body. When you're stressed all the time, it ramps up inflammation and damages your cells, making it harder for your body to stay healthy. It's like a cycle that's tough to break: chronic stress messes with your immune system and even your sleep, which just adds more strain (*McEwen, 1998*). Over time, this can lead to bigger health problems and speed up aging.

OPTIMISTIC THINKING AND RELAXATION TECHNIQUES LOWER CORTISOL

There are some easy ways to help your body handle stress better. Things like deep breathing, gentle yoga, or just taking a moment to relax can really bring down your cortisol levels—that's the stress hormone that causes so much trouble (*West et al., 2017*). When you make these habits part of your routine, especially during tough times, they can help calm your body's stress response. It's all about giving yourself a chance to reset and support your natural healing systems.

JOHN GOODMAN

John Goodman is a popular actor who realized he was feeling tired and unhealthy almost always. He worried that people only knew him for being overweight rather than for his talent. When he came across **Tony Robbins's** idea that your mind can "fire you up" to take action, something clicked. He also read **Wayne Dyer's** advice to *focus on the good you can do right now* and **Og Mandino's** reminder that *every morning brings a new chance to change your life*. So, **John** started each day by saying an affirmation like:

"I am strong, determined, and ready to make healthier choices."

He then made a quick decision: he would exercise daily, no excuses. Over time, his routine—walking, light jogging, and later adding weight training—helped him shed pounds. His energy soared, and he felt proud that he hadn't let doubt keep him stuck. **John's** optimistic thinking lowered his cortisol levels, leading to better overall health.

John Goodman
Credit – Wikimedia Commons

CHRONIC STRESS IS A SILENT KILLER

Chronic stress builds gradually, so it can sneak up on you before you realize a problem; over time, this ongoing tension can harm your heart, raise your risk for diabetes, and even sap your energy and drive (*McEwen, 1998*). Managing stress is absolutely necessary for protecting your mental and physical health.

My good friend **Greg** had just turned 50. He had a ten-year-old daughter and had gone back to school to get his MBA. At 50, he finally got his dream job at a creative agency in Los Angeles. He called me and we signed a big deal to do creative on a huge new children's website project. Going through college late had added to his stress, and his desire to outperform everyone on the staff of his new job caused massive stress to build gradually. **Greg** had a massive heart attack and passed away. He left behind a beautiful wife and daughter, and we were all shocked at how quickly he left us and how seemingly healthy he looked before he died. There was no outside indication that he was unhealthy. So breathe, and let go of as much stress as possible. Nothing in a job or outside project is worth losing everything. It's like the saying I see everywhere now that nobody on their death bed wishes they had spent more time at the office...

BALANCED CORTISOL SUPPORTS METABOLIC HEALTH AND IMMUNITY

When cortisol levels stay in a healthy range—rising only when needed and lowering during rest—they help your body use energy wisely and keep immune cells functioning at their best (*Sapolsky, Romero, & Munck, 2000*). Find a good balance in your life through relaxation, positive thinking, and self-care to keep this critical hormone in check, supporting your long-term wellness.

My friend, former **Secretary of State, General Colin Powell** said:

"Perpetual optimism is a force multiplier."

Secretary of State, General Colin Powell and Tad Sisler
Source – Sisler Private Collection

3.1.3: NEUROPLASTICITY AND THE AGING BRAIN

YOUR BRAIN CAN REWIRE AT ANY AGE THROUGH NEW EXPERIENCES AND THOUGHT PATTERNS

Here's something cool—your brain never stops being able to change, no matter how old you are. It can keep growing and adapting through new experiences and the way you think (*Davidson & McEwen, 2012*). Scientists call this neuroplasticity, and it means you can shape your brain to support happier emotions and better thinking habits. It's like giving your brain a chance to refresh and grow stronger over time.

POSITIVE EMOTIONAL STATES ENHANCE NEUROGENESIS (CREATION OF NEW NEURONS)

When you're feeling good—think hopeful, engaged, or loved—it actually helps your brain make new neurons (*Kempermann & Gage, 1999*). This process, called neurogenesis, is super important for keeping your brain sharp. On the other hand, if you're stuck in negative emotions like anxiety or sadness, it can slow this down (*Duman, 2004*). So, focusing on positive feelings isn't just about being happy in the moment—it's also about keeping your brain healthy for the long run.

NEUROIMAGING STUDY

I read about this fascinating study where researchers looked at the brains of people who meditated a lot, like monks with thousands of hours of practice (*Lazar et al., 2005*). They found that these folks had thicker brain areas tied to focus and emotional balance. It's amazing to think that something like meditation can literally change the structure of your brain for the better—it's like proof that you can train your mind to be calmer and more resilient.

NEGATIVE RUMINATIONS CAN BECOME "HARDWIRED" BUT CAN BE UNDONE

Sometimes, if you keep dwelling on negative thoughts—like worrying or overthinking—it can become a habit that's hard to break (*Nolen-Hoeksema, 2000*). It's like your brain gets wired to keep going down that path. But here's the good news: you can change that! By practicing things like mindfulness or focusing on positive habits, you can rewire those patterns and create healthier ones. It takes some effort, but it's totally doable.

When I was 5, my father left on an assignment with the Navy for several months. I missed him greatly. Whenever I cried, my sister **Suzanne** would take me to the window and tell me to look for a red bird. She said it was a sign of hope that everything would be ok. I always found a red bird and immediately felt better. Redirecting your emotions will empower you.

HIGHLIGHTS HUMAN RESILIENCE ACROSS THE LIFESPAN

Here's the big picture—your ability to bounce back and grow stronger can keep improving your whole life. I heard about this Navy study where they taught sailors skills like mindfulness and optimism before tough missions (*Seligman, 2011*). It really helped them handle stress better. The idea is that by practicing these habits, you can build resilience at any age. It's never too late to learn, grow, and get better at handling life's challenges.

My dear friend, legendary *multi-platinum* recording artist **Glen Campbell** had his share of heartbreak, including overcoming addiction and being diagnosed with Alzheimer's Disease in the last years of his storied life. Through it all, he always came back around to a positive outlook. **Glen** said:

"I've laughed, and I've cried. Laughing has got it over crying."

Glen Campbell Performing with Tad Sisler
Source – Sisler Private Collection

Now that we've explained the basics of cellular and neural aging, let's investigate the biochemistry that ties our happiness to our health.

SECTION TWO: THE BIOCHEMISTRY OF EMOTIONS
3.2.1: DOPAMINE, SEROTONIN, OXYTOCIN – HAPPINESS CHEMISTRY

DOPAMINE DRIVES MOTIVATION AND REWARD-SEEKING - POSITIVE HABITS CAN NATURALLY ELEVATE IT

You know that feeling when you're super motivated to get something done? That's dopamine at work—it's like your brain's natural reward system kicking in. The cool thing is, you can naturally boost it with positive habits. Things like setting goals, learning new skills, or even doing something creative can give you that "feel-good" chemical surge (*Volkow et al., 2017*). It's all about finding healthy ways to keep your brain happy and engaged, like exercising or picking up a new hobby.

My loving sister has become overcome with Parkinson's disease. For years, she has struggled with this awful, debilitating illness, needing more and more drugs to increase the dopamine levels in her brain. This and so many other hormones and chemicals do their daily jobs for so many of us, and we have no clue about their necessity until something goes wrong and the need for this chemical to work correctly in our body becomes glaringly evident. When my sister started to get worse, I feared that I, too, might suffer from Parkinson's at some point in my life. I researched what I could do and was grateful that playing piano was high on the list of ways to help your brain produce dopamine. I've made my living as a pianist and musician for years.

Become involved in hobbies. Check out my MUSIC MASTERY SERIES of books on Amazon if you want to learn to sing, play piano, guitar, drums, or bass. Maybe that act alone will help extend a healthy life. If you're interested, use this QR code to access my music training books on Amazon:

SEROTONIN STABILIZES MOOD; GRATITUDE AND SOCIAL TIES HELP MAINTAIN HEALTHY LEVELS

Serotonin is like a mood stabilizer. It gives you a sense of calm and well-being (*Young, 2007*). Gratitude exercises—like writing down things you're thankful for—can raise your serotonin levels, partly because they shift your focus to life's bright spots. Strong social connections also nurture steady serotonin levels, reminding you you're loved and supported. Find reasons to be grateful each day. Try starting when you awaken; instead of being grouchy, smile and be thankful that you've been given another day on this beautiful planet to live, breathe, and achieve your purpose.

OXYTOCIN FOSTERS BONDING, REDUCING STRESS

You've probably heard of oxytocin—it's often called the "love hormone," and for good reason! It helps keep your mood steady, makes you feel grateful, and strengthens your connections with others. Things like writing down what you're thankful for, giving someone a hug, or just spending quality time with loved ones can boost your oxytocin levels (*Young, 2007*). And here's the best part: this also helps keep your dopamine levels balanced, so you feel more motivated and happy overall. It's like a little teamwork between these feel-good chemicals in your brain.

BALANCING "HAPPINESS HORMONES" STRONGLY CORRELATES WITH LONGEVITY

Here's something really interesting: keeping your happiness hormones—like dopamine, oxytocin, and serotonin—in balance can actually help you live a longer, healthier life. Research shows that people who have higher levels of these hormones tend to have less wear and tear on their bodies as they age (*Pressman & Cohen, 2005*). So, by nurturing your relationships, staying grateful, and finding joy in the little things, you're not just feeling good now—you're also setting yourself up for a better, longer life down the road.

SHAQUILLE O'NEAL

I was fortunate to meet and watch **Shaquille O'Neal** play basketball for the Los Angeles Lakers due to my friendship with coaches **Frank Hamblen** and **Phil Jackson**. **Shaq** was an unstoppable force on the basketball court. He put his heart and soul into the game. **Shaq** said:

"We want to win. We want to win big. We want to win the whole thing."

But after retiring, he found that his days felt long and quiet. He missed practicing with his teammates and traveling for big games. Determined not to sit around, **Shaq** reached out to charities that help kids and families in need. Whether delivering presents around the holidays or surprising students with school supplies, **Shaq** felt a wonderful sense of warmth spread through his chest every time he made someone smile. He also became a spokesperson for almost every product ever made, appearing in countless television commercials. Over time, he realized that by giving his time and energy, he was also giving himself a boost—his loneliness faded, replaced by the joyful feeling of making a positive impact—this was oxytocin in action, sparked by the simple act of compassionate connection.

Shaquille O'Neal

Credit – Wikimedia Commons / John Mathew Smith & www.celebrity-photos.com

My darling Pomeranian **Frankie** helps me release tons of oxytocin daily.

3.3.2: IMMUNE SYSTEM AND EMOTIONAL STATES
POSITIVE EMOTIONAL STATES BOLSTER IMMUNE RESPONSE

Feeling optimistic or joyful doesn't just lift your spirits—it can actually give your immune system a boost. When you're in a positive headspace, your body tends to fight off illness better, and it can even help you recover faster if you do get sick (*Cohen et al., 2006*). Studies have shown that happier people often have lower inflammation and stronger immune responses, which is a big win for your overall health. It's like your emotions are giving your body a little extra armor to stay well.

CHRONIC NEGATIVITY ELEVATES INFLAMMATION, LINKING TO CANCER AND OTHER DISEASES

On the flip side, being stuck in a negative mindset for a long time can really take a toll on your body. Constant stress, anger, or sadness can increase inflammation, which has been linked to serious conditions like cancer, heart disease, and diabetes (*Kiecolt-Glaser et al., 2002*). It's not just about feeling down—those emotions can create a chain reaction in your body, making it harder to stay healthy. The good news? By working on your mindset, you can help reduce that inflammation and lower your risk of these issues. Let go of those acids that eat their own container.

MEDICAL STUDY

I came across this interesting study about cancer patients that really stuck with me. Researchers looked at two groups of people with similar diagnoses—one group focused on staying positive, while the other struggled with more negative emotions (*Spiegel et al., 1989*). They found that the group with a more positive outlook often had slower cancer growth and better overall outcomes. It's not a cure, but it shows how much your emotional state can impact your body—it's pretty powerful to think about.

IMMUNE CELLS COMMUNICATE WITH NEUROTRANSMITTERS - MIND AND BODY ARE DEEPLY INTERTWINED

Your mind and body are more connected than you might realize. Immune cells actually "talk" to neurotransmitters—the chemicals in your brain that affect your mood—like serotonin and dopamine (*Ader et al., 1995*). That means your thoughts and feelings can directly influence how well your immune system works. When I learned about this, it really hit me how much our mental health matters for our physical health. It's a reminder that taking care of your emotions isn't just about feeling good—it's about keeping your whole body in balance.

I've had my own ups and downs with this, especially after losing someone close to me. The grief was heavy, and I could feel it in my body—I was tired all the time, and I even got sick more often. It wasn't until I started focusing on small things, like practicing gratitude or reconnecting with friends, that I began to feel better (*Fredrickson, 2001*). It made me realize how much our emotions can affect our health. Now, I try to live with more positivity—not because it's always easy, but because I know it helps me stay healthier and more resilient in the long run.

In other words, a calm and optimistic mind helps build a resilient body. My **Robin** and I both came out of extremely dysfunctional relationships, in situations where it always seemed our lives were in chaos, no matter how hard we tried. As soon as I was able to let go of my need to try to "fix" other women as I had tried to fix my mother, I was able to allow myself to find a healthy relationship. Living a life in an emotionally balanced relationship is far better than living in chaos. This reminds me of something my friend, legendary actress **Dyan Cannon**, said:

"Have you noticed when you start getting happy, you say, uh-uh, I'd better watch out. I feel too good. Something's going to happen."

Many of us are conditioned to expect the worst somewhere inside us. My friend, legendary trumpeter **Steve Madaio** lived with the idea that if you keep your hopes and expectations low, you can only be pleasantly surprised when good things happen. I believe in the power of prayer and affirmations. Believe in yourself, first and foremost, and always accept support and encouragement from others. You may soon find, like I did after living through my darkest of times, that a strong support system and emotionally balanced life will save you.

Dyan Cannon and Tad Sisler
Source: Tad Sisler's Personal Collection

3.2.3: THE PLACEBO EFFECT AND BRAIN RECEPTORS

BELIEF AND EXPECTATION CAN TRIGGER DOPAMINE RELEASE, FOR GENUINE PHYSIOLOGICAL IMPROVEMENTS

Here's something amazing—feeling hopeful or looking forward to something can actually spark a dopamine release in your brain, which makes you feel good all over. It's not just about big things; even small expectations, like looking forward to a good meal, can lift your mood and boost your well-being (*de la Fuente-Fernández et al., 2001*). It's like your brain rewards you for staying positive, and that can have a ripple effect on your overall health.

THE PLACEBO EFFECT EXEMPLIFIES THE MIND'S INFLUENCE OVER THE BODY - A TESTAMENT TO MENTAL POWER

You've probably heard of the placebo effect—it's such a great example of how powerful your mind can be. When you believe something will help you, like taking a pill, your body can sometimes respond as if it's real, even if it's just a sugar pill (*Benedetti et al., 2005*). Doctors have seen this in action for years, and it's pretty incredible to think about. It shows how much your thoughts and beliefs can actually shape what's going on in your body—it's like a little bit of mind magic. In *The Bible, Matthew 21:22*, it is written, **"If you believe, you will receive whatever you ask for in prayer."** Just as **Napoleon Hill** said, **"Whatever your mind can conceive and believe, it can achieve,"** we need to begin to realize we humans have way more power of mind than we may have believed up until now.

I read about this fascinating study with Parkinson's patients that really highlights the placebo effect. Researchers gave some patients a fake treatment, but told them it was a new drug to help with their symptoms (*Goetz et al., 2008*). Amazingly, a lot of them started feeling better—like their movement improved—just because they believed the treatment was real. It wasn't a cure, but it showed how much hope and expectation can influence the brain, especially when it comes to dopamine, which is so important for Parkinson's. My dear friend, legendary actress **Mary Tyler Moore** said:

"You truly have to make the very best of what you've got. We all do."

Tad Sisler with Mary Tyler Moore
Source- Sisler Private Collection

BRAIN RECEPTORS RESPOND TO OPTIMISM AND BELIEF

The placebo effect shows that when we anticipate a good outcome, our brains respond with chemical changes that ease pain, lower stress, and promote healing. This underscores a central theme of this book: positivity isn't just "in your head"—it has real, physical impacts. When you intentionally feed your mind hopeful messages, you can influence your body's natural ability to heal and thrive. It makes me feel better when I pray and give gratitude for the blessings around me. Like **Vince Flynn** said:

> *"No matter how bad you think you have it, there's always - always somebody who's got it way, way worse."*

Train yourself daily to find a million reasons to be hopeful and grateful!

We've explored how your emotions shape biology. Next, let's learn some practical ways to make these discoveries work for you to achieve a healthier, happier life.

SECTION THREE:
PRACTICAL INSIGHTS FOR PERSONAL HEALTH
3.3.1: EMOTIONAL AWARENESS AND MINDFULNESS
IDENTIFYING EMOTIONS EARLY PREVENTS TOXIC STRESS BUILDUP

When we notice our feelings—like anger, worry, or sadness—as soon as they appear, we need to prevent them from piling up and causing harm. Just like how a small leak is easier to fix than a flood, catching emotional waves early can help us process them in healthier ways. If you don't allow emotions like resentment to build up, you can prevent your stress from reaching toxic levels, which can weaken your body and mind over time.

By tuning in to our emotions, we give ourselves a chance to respond instead of just reacting. We can choose calming activities, talk things out with friends, or acknowledge our feelings before they grow stronger. Many mental health professionals have linked this simple habit to better stress management and overall well-being (*Kabat-Zinn, 1990*). As I did with my brother-in-law, just taking a breath, maybe letting it out in a way that is not harmful to others, like writing a letter you'll never send, you can find ways to get this pain off your chest.

BASIC MINDFULNESS PRACTICES (BREATHING, BODY SCANS) GROUND YOU

Mindfulness exercises—like taking slow, deep breaths or doing a quick body scan—keep us firmly rooted in the present moment. When we shift our focus to our breath, for instance, we help calm the racing thoughts that often spark anxiety. This simple act soothes both the mind and body.

When my generation was growing up, our fathers told us to "man up." Mindfulness was frowned upon as if we would show weakness. As I grew, I realized it's not about that. Being in tune with yourself will keep you strong for the long haul. It is actually a sign of strength not to act from primal anger or let worry or sadness get the best of you.

Body scans work by encouraging us to check each part of ourselves, from head to toe, relaxing areas of tension. When we do these practices regularly, we train our brains to stay centered, which can bring more peace into our daily lives. Studies show that these calming techniques help lower stress hormones and support better health over time (*Kabat-Zinn, 1990*).

KELLY CLARKSON

Kelly Clarkson was managing her singing career and a TV show while raising her children. She often felt as if she were running a race without a finish line. To deal with the stress, **Kelly** decided she needed some "quiet time" each day. So, she set aside ten minutes whenever she could—sometimes in the morning, sometimes before bed—to close her eyes and imagine standing by a peaceful lake with tall trees and a gentle breeze. At first, it felt silly, but each time she did it, her shoulders relaxed, and she felt more patient when her kids needed her. If she wasn't home with her children or dogs, she pictured these calming influences in her mind, and **Kelly** noticed she felt happier and more in control of her busy life. She found she could handle life's curveballs more easily simply because she paused to reset her mind. Mind-over-matter is a powerful thing.

"There is no greater feeling than hanging out with my dogs or just walking around the land with our horses. My rescue ranch is is where I feel the most at peace and where I'm reminded of the simple things in life and let the chaos of my crazy work life fade away." – Kelly Clarkson

Kelly Clarkson
Credit – Wikimedia Commons

EMOTIONAL AWARENESS LEADS TO IMPROVED DECISION-MAKING, CALMER PHYSIOLOGY

Being in tune with your emotions can really help you make better choices. When you're aware of how you're feeling—whether it's stress, excitement, or something else—you can step back and think more clearly about your decisions (*Damasio, 1994*). It's like having an inner compass that helps you weigh your options and go with what feels right, while also keeping your goals in sight. I've noticed that when I take a moment to check in with myself, I make decisions I feel better about in the long run.

RESILIENCE IS KEY - SMALL DAILY PRACTICES ADD UP

Building resilience is so important, and the good news is, it's something you can work on every day with small habits. Things like taking deep breaths when you're stressed, writing down three things you're grateful for, or even going for a quick walk can really add up over time (*Southwick & Charney, 2012*). These little practices help you bounce back from challenges and keep you grounded. I've found that even on tough days, doing one small thing for myself makes me feel stronger and more ready to tackle whatever comes next.

3.3.2: GOAL-SETTING WITH A HEALTH-DRIVEN MINDSET

ALIGN YOUR GOALS WITH DEEPER LIFE PURPOSES FOR STRONGER MOTIVATION

Here's a simple way to get started—focus on building a mindset that's all about your health and well-being. Set small, meaningful goals that feel good to you, like drinking more water, taking a moment to breathe deeply, or reaching out to a friend (*Lyubomirsky, 2008*). It's all about taking those first steps with intention. When you prioritize your health in these small ways, it creates a ripple effect, helping you feel more motivated and in control of your life.

CHRIS PRATT

Chris Pratt became famous, starring in big movies and juggling action scenes on set. On top of that, he had responsibilities at home: being a dad, planning family get-togethers, and trying to keep up with friends. One day, he realized he was feeling so wound up that he couldn't enjoy even the fun parts of his job. After talking with a friend, he learned about mindfulness—a simple practice of pausing to breathe deeply and focus on the present moment. **Chris** started to imagine a quiet beach, listening to the gentle waves in his mind. He also practiced paying attention to small details around him and celebrating things like the taste of his coffee or the feel of fresh air. Over time, these little breaks helped him stay calm and not get lost in a swirl of worries. His determination and celebrations kept him motivated. Each tiny triumph lifted his spirits and fueled his belief that he could let go by honoring each step on the way.

Eventually, Chris took his newfound knowledge to higher levels like developing unique bathing habits!

"My favorite way to blow off steam is to sing obnoxiously loud in the shower." – Chris Pratt

Chris Pratt
Credit – Flickr / creativecommons.org

USE MICRO-GOALS TO REINFORCE OPTIMISM

One thing I love to do is celebrate small wins—it keeps the positive vibes going! For example, try setting a tiny goal, like stretching for five minutes in the morning or finishing a task you've been putting off (*Amabile & Kramer, 2011*). Each time you do it, give yourself a little pat on the back. These small victories build momentum, making you feel good and encouraging you to keep going. It's a great way to stay motivated and make progress, one step at a time.

REFRAME OBSTACLES AS CHALLENGES TO OVERCOME, NOT DEAD ENDS

When you hit a roadblock, try to see it as a challenge to tackle rather than something that stops you completely. It's all about shifting your perspective—those obstacles can actually help you grow if you let them (*Dweck, 2006*). I've found that when I approach a problem with the mindset of "I can figure this out," it feels less overwhelming, and I often come up with solutions I wouldn't have thought of otherwise. It's like turning a hurdle into a stepping stone. **Dr. Norman Vincent Peale** said:

"Stand up to your obstacles and do something about them. You will find they haven't half the strength you think they have."

POSITIVITY BECOMES A SELF-SUSTAINING CYCLE

Here's the cool thing about positivity—the more you practice it, the more it becomes a natural part of your life. When you focus on the good stuff, like appreciating the little wins or staying hopeful, it starts to build on itself (*Fredrickson, 2001*). Over time, you'll notice that you're naturally more optimistic, and that positivity keeps fueling itself. I've seen this in my own life—once I started looking for the bright side, it got easier to keep that mindset going, even on tough days.

3.3.3: DESIGNING A POSITIVE ENVIRONMENT

SURROUND YOURSELF WITH UPLIFTING STIMULI LIKE MUSIC, NATURE, OR SUPPORTIVE PEOPLE

One of the best ways to keep that positive vibe going is to surround yourself with things that lift you up. Listening to your favorite music, spending time in nature, or hanging out with people who support you can make a huge difference (*Thoma et al., 2013*). I love taking a walk outside or putting on a good playlist when I need a boost—it's amazing how much those simple things can recharge you. They help create a space where you feel good, which makes it easier to stay positive.

It's also really helpful to clear out the chaos in your life, both mentally and physically. Things like decluttering your space, organizing your thoughts, or even cutting back on distractions can bring a sense of calm (*Saxbe & Repetti, 2010*). I've noticed that when my surroundings are tidy—like my desk or my room—it helps my mind feel less cluttered too. It's like giving yourself a fresh start, which makes it easier to focus on what really matters and keep that positive momentum going.

My darling stepsister **Kimberley** was brutally murdered when she was only 23. Her mother, **Sandra**, grieved so very heavily that she felt her life had ended. We were all in shock, and the grief for everyone was overwhelming. Without even realizing it, **Sandra** began to hoard things. I believe it was because she couldn't bear to let go of her daughter, which translated into being unable to let go of anything. In a way, this was comforting to her, but there came a point where nobody could make their way through their house anymore, and her sister had to intervene. Slowly, they worked together to start letting go of things. The pain never stopped, but clearing the surroundings was a way for her to move forward somehow to begin the slow healing process. God bless my little sister in Heaven, and God bless her mother for her courage through those dark times.

Sandra, Kimberley, and Tad Sisler
Source — Sisler Private Collection

RITUALS OF GRATITUDE LIKE STICKY NOTES OR VICTORY BOARDS FEED OPTIMISM

One great way to keep your spirits up is by focusing on things like optimism and gratitude. You can try writing down things you're thankful for, keeping a list of your small wins, or even putting sticky notes with positive reminders around your space (*Emmons & McCullough, 2003*). I love keeping a little "victory list" of things I've accomplished—it really helps me stay motivated. These habits remind you to focus on the good stuff, which can make a big difference in how you feel every day. Sometimes, I'll sneak a love note into **Robin's** lunch bag for work. It makes me smile as much as it does her.

ALIGN YOUR SURROUNDINGS WITH THE MINDSET YOU WANT TO CULTIVATE

Your environment plays a big role in shaping your mindset, so try to fill it with things that inspire the mood you want to have. Whether it's surrounding yourself with uplifting quotes, adding plants to your space, or playing calming music, these little touches can help you stay positive (*Kaplan, 1995*). I've found that keeping my space cozy and inspiring—like having a favorite candle or a photo that makes me smile—really helps me feel more optimistic and focused. For instance, when I went to paint my recording studio, I researched colors that boost productivity and calmness and found a nice green for the walls.

RIGHT SIDE BRAIN VS. LEFT SIDE BRAIN

It's also helpful to balance both sides of your brain to keep your mind sharp and creative. The right side of your brain is all about creativity and big-picture thinking, while the left side focuses on logic and details (*Sperry, 1968*). Doing things like painting or daydreaming can spark your right brain, while puzzles or planning can engage your left brain. I like mixing it up—maybe I'll do some journaling to get creative, then tackle a to-do list to stay organized. It keeps things fun and helps me feel more balanced.

My friend **Glen Myerscough** (the *Grammy-winning* Saxophonist with **Andraé Crouch and the Disciples** I mentioned in the Introduction) is a dear man. I've recorded **Glen** on about a thousand tracks in my recording studios, and I consider him to be one of my closest friends. **Glen** is a profoundly religious man and probably the finest saxophone/flute player I've ever worked with. For years, as we worked hundreds of corporate gigs together, **Glen** was putting himself through college, taking challenging courses like calculus and advanced science. He's the perfect example of someone who uses his left and right brain to the fullest, with kindness and compassion added in. I have nothing but admiration for him. Most of the saxophones or flutes you hear on my recordings on *Apple Music* and *Amazon Music* are **Glen's** mastery.

Tad Sisler with Glen Myerscough
Source – Sisler Private Collection

Before I continue, I have a personal request for you, my reader…
PLEASE MAKE A DIFFERENCE WITH YOUR BOOK REVIEW
Unlock the Power of Kindness

"Sharing our gifts helps others shine bright."

My father's example as an exemplary healer guided my perception of medicine and health. I was lucky to have great teachers and mentors who helped me grow and pushed me to learn more about enhancing the human condition. Now, I want to help others find their own way towards health and longevity, too.

Would you help someone just like you—excited about getting on the right track but not sure where to start learning how to master health and wellness?

My mission is to educate as many people as possible about new and upcoming age reversal discoveries leading us all towards longer, healthier lives.

But to reach more people, I need your help.

Most people choose books based on reviews. So, I'm asking you to help another by leaving a review.

It doesn't cost anything and takes less than a minute, but it could change someone's journey. Your review could help…

- …one more person find their way to healthy habits.
- …one more child know there's a possibility of loving grandparents longer.
- …one more person gain confidence to adopt a new lifestyle.
- …one more dream of a better life come true.

If you love helping others, you're my kind of person. Thank you from the bottom of my heart! **Tad Sisler**

Don't be afraid to keep challenging yourself—it's a great way to grow and stay engaged. Whether it's picking up a new hobby, trying a tricky puzzle, or setting a small goal, these challenges keep your brain active and boost your confidence (*Csikszentmihalyi, 1990*). I love trying something new every now and then, like learning a new recipe or taking on a project I've been curious about. It feels so rewarding to push myself a little, and it keeps life exciting.

Next, we'll focus on how gratitude, forgiveness, and even random acts of kindness serve as catalysts for a long, fulfilling life.

CHAPTER FOUR
EMOTIONAL WELL-BEING AS A CATALYST FOR HEALTHSPAN

C ould your emotional climate today predict how your body will age tomorrow? My mother was big on affirmations. She believed that positive thinking would help us to stay healthier. She told me that she knew negative people who died of cancer because their negative thoughts consumed them. Now, science is moving in the direction of proving she was close to the mark.

SECTION ONE:
GRATITUDE, FORGIVENESS, AND HEART HEALTH
4.1.1. POWER OF GRATITUDE ON INFLAMMATION

GRATITUDE PRACTICES LOWER INFLAMMATORY MARKERS (IL-6, CRP).

I've been showing you in different ways that practicing gratitude can actually help your body stay healthier. Studies show that when you take time to be thankful—like writing down three things you appreciate each day—it can lower inflammation markers in your body, like IL-6 and CRP (*Emmons & McCullough, 2003; Redwine et al., 2016*). It's amazing how something so simple can make a big difference. I've started keeping a gratitude journal, and it really helps me feel calmer and more grounded.

Not many people I've met have been more uplifting and positive than my friend, *multi-Platinum* artist **Sergio Mendes**, an icon of Latin popular music. He strongly believed that because of his joyful outlook, and because he had a deep belief in his ability to move people through his music, events unfolded for him by "happy chance", or serendipity.

There's a word in the English language that I like, "Serendipity"; it's the story of my life." – Sergio Mendes

Sergio Mendes and Tad Sisler
Source – Sisler Private Collection

REDUCED INFLAMMATION EQUALS REDUCED HEART DISEASE RISK

Lowering inflammation doesn't just make you feel better—it can also protect your heart. When inflammation levels go down, your risk of heart disease drops too, because there's less strain on your cardiovascular system (*Ridker et al., 2000*). I love knowing that by focusing on positive habits, like gratitude, I'm not only lifting my mood but also taking care of my heart. It's like a two-for-one deal for my health! I discuss the debilitating effects of inflammation extensively in my book, **"Stay Healthy, Stay Youthful: The Science of Living to 150."**

Combining gratitude with healthy habits—like balanced eating and regular exercise—gives our cardiovascular system the best chance to stay strong and resilient well into our later years.

GRATITUDE FOSTERS BOTH MENTAL AND PHYSICAL UPLIFT

Gratitude isn't just a "feel-good" emotion—it sparks fundamental, measurable changes in how we think and how our bodies function. People who make daily thankfulness a priority often report better sleep, brighter moods, and a more profound connection to life (*Wood et al., 2010*).

That improved emotional state translates into physiological benefits, too, from a calmer heart rate to healthier immune responses. In other words, gratitude works like a two-way street—what nourishes the mind also supports the body.

4.1.2: FORGIVENESS AND STRESS RELIEF

HOLDING A GRUDGE KEEPS YOUR STRESS RESPONSE HIGH, HARMING IMMUNITY

When we hold onto anger or resentment, our bodies stay in a constant state of tension. This tension can trigger higher levels of stress hormones—like cortisol—that weaken our immune system and make us more prone to illness (*Luskin, 2002*).

Over time, living with persistent grudges is like living next to a factory that never stops polluting—it wears down our physical and emotional defenses. Recognizing this cycle is the first step for us to break free and allow our bodies to heal.

FORGIVENESS IS SELF-HEALING RATHER THAN EXCUSING BAD BEHAVIOR

Many people think forgiveness lets someone "off the hook," but it's about freeing ourselves from the burden of anger. By letting go of resentment, we clear space for peace and emotional balance (*Worthington & Scherer, 2004*).

Forgiveness doesn't mean we approve of hurtful actions; it means we refuse to let those actions poison our hearts. Forgiving someone else (or even yourself) can lower stress levels, reduce anxiety, and even improve heart health.

> *"To forgive is to set a prisoner free and discover that the prisoner was you." - Lewis B. Smedes*

SUZANNE SOMERS

Suzanne Somers was my friend. We lived in the Palm Springs, California, area and worked many charity events together. **Suzanne** was known for her role on *"Three's Company,"* a popular sitcom, but she felt the weight of personal and professional problems piling up. She believed that this constant tension contributed to her developing breast cancer. Instead of letting worry take over, **Suzanne** chose to forgive people who had caused her pain and practiced healthier ways of dealing with stress, like gentle exercise and mindfulness.

Along with medical treatments, she explored alternative methods to support her recovery. **Suzanne** has since written several books, often reminding her readers that freeing yourself from grudges can bring emotional and physical healing. While forgiveness didn't erase the past, it helped **Suzanne** reclaim her future with a calmer, stronger mindset.

"Forgiveness is a gift you give yourself." — *Suzanne Somers*

Suzanne Somers
Credit – Picryl / creativecommons.org

EMOTIONAL RELEASE OFTEN TRIGGERS MEASURABLE HEALTH IMPROVEMENTS

Letting go of deep grudges can reduce blood pressure, heart rate, and overall stress markers (*Lawler et al., 2005*). Releasing heavy emotional baggage allows our natural healing processes to function more efficiently.

As a result, people often report better sleep, clearer thinking, and improved relationships once they let go of longstanding anger. Renewing our sense of well-being can support a healthy immune system and may even add years to our lives. Like **Elsa** in *Frozen, "Let it gooooo, let it go!"*

LETTERS, THERAPY, AND CONSCIOUS LETTING GO AS FORGIVENESS TOOLS

There are many pathways to forgiveness. Some people write letters they never send (like I did), to express and release hurt feelings. Others work with a therapist or join support groups where they learn to process unresolved pain. Find a safe way to confront and let go of past wounds. With regular practice, forgiveness will become a habit that steadily reduces stress, safeguards heart health, and helps you experience more joy in everyday life.

Some things may seem impossible to forgive. The five young men who raped and murdered my stepsister **Kimberley** were caught and sentenced to life in prison without the possibility of parole. Even though these men received a sentence that ended their lives as they had known it, that fact still didn't do the job of helping me forgive them for what they did. I didn't want revenge; I wanted retribution, but it took counselling, perspective, and a few years to begin forgiving them. Finally, one reached out to the family through a heartfelt letter asking for forgiveness, and I sobbed, asking God for direction. By not forgiving, I was keeping myself in a mental prison of sorts. As I said earlier in the book, forgiving does not mean forgetting. I forgave that man, but **Kimberley's** mother could never find it in her heart to forgive, and she died in her early 50s of a broken heart. Now **Kimberley** and her mother are joined again in Heaven, and there's nothing left to do but forgive.

"The lesson is that you can still make mistakes and be forgiven."
– Robert Downey, Jr.

Robert Downey, Jr.
Credit – FLICKR / creativecommons.org

4.1.3: HEARTFELT EMOTIONS AND CARDIOVASCULAR HEALTH

POSITIVE EMOTIONAL STATES CORRELATE WITH STABLE BLOOD PRESSURE AND HEART RATE VARIABILITY

Feeling positive can do wonders for your heart—literally! When you're in a good mood, like when you're happy or calm, it's linked to steadier blood pressure and better heart rate variability, which is a sign your heart is handling stress well (*Steptoe et al., 2005*). I've noticed that on days when I'm feeling upbeat, my body just feels more balanced—like I'm not as tense or on edge. It's pretty cool how our emotions can help keep our hearts healthy.

EMOTIONAL DISTRESS LINKED TO PLAQUE BUILDUP AND ARRHYTHMIAS

On the other hand, being stressed or upset all the time can really put your heart at risk. Chronic distress is tied to things like plaque buildup in your arteries and irregular heartbeats, which can lead to bigger problems down the road (*Kubzansky & Kawachi, 2000*). It's a reminder of how important it is to manage stress—not just for your peace of mind, but to protect your heart. I try to take it one day at a time and find ways to unwind so I'm not carrying that tension around.

FRAMINGHAM HEART STUDY

I came across this long-term study called the *Framingham Heart Study,* and it's really eye-opening. They followed thousands of people for years and found that those who stayed more optimistic and less stressed had a lower risk of heart disease (*Tindle et al., 2009*). It wasn't just about their lifestyle—their mindset played a big role too. It makes me think about how much our outlook can impact our health, and it's motivating to focus on staying positive.

ACTS OF KINDNESS AND EMPATHY RELEASE OXYTOCIN, REGULATING CARDIOVASCULAR FUNCTION

Doing something kind for someone—like helping a friend or even just listening—can actually help your heart by releasing oxytocin. This hormone helps regulate your heart rate and keeps your cardiovascular system in check (*Grewen et al., 2005*). I love how simple acts of kindness can make you feel good and do good for your body at the same time. It's like a little gift to yourself and others, all wrapped into one.

INVESTING IN HEARTFELT EMOTIONS IS AN INVESTMENT IN YOUR HEART'S LONGEVITY

At the end of the day, putting effort into feeling heartfelt emotions—like love, gratitude, or empathy—is like investing in your heart's health. When you nurture these feelings, you're not just making your days brighter; you're also supporting your heart for the long haul (*Rozanski et al., 1999*). I've found that taking time to connect with the people I care about or reflecting on what I'm thankful for really helps me feel grounded—and now I know it's helping my heart too.

> *"Empathy is about finding echoes of another person in yourself."*
> *- Mohsin Hamid*

Gratitude and forgiveness build an inner shield against disease, but…as my stepmother showed through her daily courage while outwardly experiencing her grief… resilience must also handle life's toughest hits without sugar-coating."

SECTION TWO:
DEVELOPING EMOTIONAL RESILIENCE

4.2.1: IDENTIFYING TRIGGERS AND BUILDING COPING STRATEGIES

RECOGNIZE PERSONAL TRIGGERS TO AVOID SPIRALING INTO NEGATIVITY

It's really helpful to figure out what sets off your negative emotions so you can avoid getting stuck in a downward spiral. Things like certain comments, challenging situations, or even memories can pull you into a tough spot, but once you recognize those triggers, you can start to manage them better (*Gross, 2002*). I've learned to pause and notice when something's starting to bother me—like if I'm overthinking a conversation—and that awareness helps me shift gears before I get too caught up in negativity.

We all know somebody who has a "low boiling point," and it just seems that whenever we are around them, we are on edge, just waiting for them to explode in rage for whatever reason they come up with next. You want to tell them to wake up and start recognizing their triggers! The sooner you catch those triggers, the more control you have over how you react. If you can spot the early signs—like feeling tense or starting to dwell on something—you can take a deep breath, step back, and choose a different response (*Linehan, 1993*). For me, it's been a game-changer to notice those moments early on. It feels empowering to know I can steer my emotions in a better direction, like taking a quick walk or focusing on something positive instead.

This may be too personal to share, but here I go...I was the youngest of five children with four older sisters, so I technically had five mothers. As we grew, there became a time when they all experienced menstrual cycles at once. One of my sisters recognized that her mood swings directly correlated with the time of the month, and she was able to exert self-control over her emotions when she became triggered. It was a free-for-all with the rest of them!

SIMPLE TACTICS LIKE JOURNALING OR SHORT WALKS CAN INTERRUPT STRESS LOOPS

There are some simple ways to break those stress cycles, and I've found them to be lifesavers. Things like journaling your thoughts or taking a short walk can stop that spiral in its tracks (*Pennebaker, 1997*). When I feel overwhelmed, I'll jot down what's on my mind or step outside for a few minutes—it helps me clear my head and feel more centered. These little habits can really shift your focus and bring a sense of calm when you need it most.

The best part is, you don't have to do everything at once—just take it one step at a time. Start with something small, like noticing your triggers or trying one calming tactic when you're feeling stressed (*Fogg, 2009*). I started by just paying attention to my mood in the mornings, and then I added in a quick journaling session when I felt off. It's all about building these habits gradually, so you can keep growing without feeling overwhelmed.

TYLER PERRY

Tyler Perry had achieved some success in writing plays and movies, but he still felt weighed down by painful memories from his childhood and wondered if he'd ever truly be happy. During his appearance on the talk show, the host's advice emphasized healing old wounds by being honest about them and allowing yourself to move forward. **Tyler** realized that part of feeling "stuck" was not facing the sadness he held inside. He began journaling, meditating, doing quick breathing exercises, and speaking openly about his fears. Little by little, he felt more hopeful and found fresh energy to create new shows and films—eventually building an entire movie studio where he could share meaningful stories with the world. **Tyler's** story shows us that shifting your focus through writing things down, meditating, or breathing can create a powerful pause, even amid turmoil. It reminds us that we don't need a private retreat or a vacation to find calm—we only need a few moments and our own breath (*Brown & Gerbarg, 2009*).

"Everyone can relate to love, hurt, pain, learning how to forgive, needing to get over, needing the power of God in their life." – Tyler Perry

Tyler Perry
Credit – Wikimedia Commons

CONSISTENCY TURNS THESE TACTICS INTO INGRAINED HABITS

While practicing a helpful skill once or twice is excellent, consistently practicing it can make it second nature. Think of it like learning to ride a bike—you keep trying, and your body knows what to do after a while. The same goes for healthy coping strategies like journaling, breathing exercises, or short walks. I always say, *"Once we learn how to ride a bike, we never forget how to fall off!"* Yes, we may keep falling off, but eventually, you're cruising every time.

When you repeat these actions every day or week, your brain starts to form new pathways. Over time, you won't have to think so hard about it. You'll catch yourself automatically stepping outside for a short walk when stress hits. That's how habits get locked in (*Clear, 2018*).

Stay consistent and you'll reinforce that you're in charge of your reactions. Soon enough, you may notice your mindset shifting. Negativity has a more challenging time taking root when you've built these resilience rituals into your life. Like I always say, take a deep breath and move on to the next fiasco!

RESILIENCE IS LEARNABLE, NOT FIXED AT BIRTH

Some people think you're either naturally tough or not, but that's only half the story. Resilience is like a muscle—it can be strengthened with the right exercises and practice. Researchers have found that with the right mindset and support, almost anyone can boost their capacity to bounce back from hardships (*Southwick & Charney, 2012*).

When you train your mind to meet setbacks with determination instead of defeat, you're actively growing that "resilience muscle." It doesn't mean you won't feel pain or sadness, but you'll have the inner tools to rise above those feelings. Knowing resilience is a skill that can be sharpened gives you the power to shape your future reactions.

When you learn and practice resilience, you tap into your ability to adapt and thrive. It's a personal decision that starts with noticing your triggers, creating healthy coping strategies, and staying consistent. From there, you'll grow more confident and calmer when life throws curveballs.

My darling sister **Kathleen** is a fantastic singer-songwriter. For years, I wanted to record her original music. When she finally was able to make the trip to my studio in California, she came into the studio, sat down with her guitar, and started sobbing. I didn't expect that! I asked her what was wrong, and she told me that she didn't know if she had the confidence to record her songs at the same level that she used to sing them. I reminded her that her incredibly strong soul had produced this incredible gift of music and talent, and the world needed to hear it. Her inner self was strong and resilient. She just needed to be reminded of this. **Kathleen** nailed it, and we ended up with three full albums of her material.

4.2.2: SELF-COMPASSION AND INNER-CHILD HEALING

SELF-COMPASSION FOSTERS A HEALTHY RESPONSE TO FAILURE, REDUCING CHRONIC STRESS

When you're as kind to yourself as you would be with a close friend, you create a cushion against life's ups and downs. Don't beat yourself up for mistakes. Gently explore what went wrong and how to do better next time. According to **Dr. Kristin Neff**, a pioneer in self-compassion research, this approach decreases stress and promotes emotional well-being (*Neff, 2011*).

Being self-compassionate doesn't mean ignoring what you've done wrong. Instead, you acknowledge it without over-judging yourself. That way, you can address the problem without drowning in negative self-talk. Over time, this healthier response to failure helps you protect your mind and body from the toxic effects of chronic stress.

The results are powerful: improved mood, stronger motivation, and a more balanced outlook on life. You become more resilient as you learn to show yourself grace during difficult times. With less time spent dwelling on mistakes, you have more energy to move forward.

During a sermon, my dear minister friend, **Dr. Tom Costa**, said, *"If I told you that you were a very valuable, worthwhile person, many of you would immediately think, 'he doesn't know me; he's talking about someone else,' but if I told you that you are a sinner and you're going to Hell, you might tell yourself, 'he knows me like a book.'"* Believe in yourself. Be kind to yourself. You are a very valuable, worthwhile person.

HEALING YOUR INNER CHILD: ACKNOWLEDGING PAST WOUNDS CAN FREE YOU FROM RECURRING NEGATIVE PATTERNS

Everyone carries some childhood memory that may still shape how they react to stress, rejection, or conflict today. Recognizing these wounds—like when you felt neglected or overly criticized—can explain why specific comments or situations still sting. Remember, from *The Four Agreements*: **"Don't take anything personally."**

When you work through these old emotions alone or with a professional, you can allow yourself to break free from patterns that no longer serve you. For instance, you might discover that your fear of speaking up in meetings traces back to being dismissed or shushed as a child. Once you see the link, you can begin to respond more healthily.

Healing your inner child involves patience and honesty. It probably will feel uncomfortable at first, but the long-term benefits can be life changing. Freeing yourself from those chains of the past will bring you a sense of emotional lightness and possibility.

"It sounds corny, but I've promised my inner child that never again will I ever abandon myself for anything or anyone else again." - Wynonna Judd

Wynonna Judd

Credit – Craig Oneal/Wynonna Judd-A Christmas Classic/creativecommons.org

RESEARCH STUDY

I came across this really interesting study from the Journal of Psychosomatic Research that I wanted to share. They worked with a group of adults who were dealing with chronic stress and split them into two groups—one practiced guided visualization, while the other focused on self-compassion exercises (*Smith et al., 2019*). After a few weeks, both groups showed lower stress levels, but the ones doing self-compassion had an even bigger drop in inflammation markers. It just goes to show how much taking care of your mind can help your body too—it's like a little reset for both.

> *"Caring for your inner child has a powerful and surprisingly quick result: Do it, and the child heals." - Martha Beck*

HEALTHIER BOUNDARIES, REALISTIC EXPECTATIONS, AND SELF-FORGIVENESS

After my parents divorced, I somehow felt responsible for my mother. I was the last child left at home with her, and as she grieved the loss of her marriage, I began to parent her for a time. A child should never be put into a position of parenting their parent. This had a long-lasting effect on me and bled into my relationships as I later worked to try to 'fix' my girlfriends as I had tried to fix my mother. Working with my inner child, I eventually let go of this subconscious need to make everything okay for someone else when that was their task to do for themselves.

Once you start being kinder to yourself and healing old emotional scars, you naturally set better boundaries. You become more aware of what you can handle emotionally and learn to say "no" when necessary. It's easy to just purse your lips together sometimes and say "no". Don't be afraid! It prevents burnout and keeps resentment at bay.

Doing this helps you have more realistic expectations. Instead of pushing yourself too hard or demanding perfection, you develop a balanced outlook on what you can achieve. With these healthy boundaries, you free yourself from old pressures and anxieties. We're all human. Because we're half god-like and half animal, we feel a constant tug between reason and instinct, between mental and physical pulls. We're not perfect, but we can be better tomorrow than we were today if we choose.

An added bonus is learning to forgive yourself for past mistakes, which can lighten your emotional load in profound ways. Self-forgiveness is like removing a constant, nagging weight from your shoulders. You stand taller, breathe easier, and show up for life more open-heartedly.

A STABLE INNER WORLD BOLSTERS LONG-TERM EMOTIONAL WELL-BEING

Having a steady sense of inner calm can really help you stay emotionally strong over the long haul. When you feel grounded and secure—like you've got a handle on your emotions—it makes it easier to bounce back from life's ups and downs (*Kabat-Zinn, 1990*). I've found that taking time to check in with myself, maybe through a few deep breaths or a quiet moment, helps me feel more centered and ready to face whatever comes my way. Remember again the *Optimist Creed*:

"To be so strong that nothing can disturb your peace of mind."

Staying optimistic isn't always easy, but it helps to be patient, kind, and confident in yourself. Optimism is like a muscle—you've got to keep practicing it, even when things get tough (*Seligman, 1991*). I've learned that being gentle with myself and others, and trusting that things will work out, keeps me in a more positive headspace. It's all about giving yourself the space to grow into that mindset over time.

4.2.3: HANDLING TRAGEDIES AND SETBACKS WITHOUT SUGAR-COATING

ACKNOWLEDGE PAIN HONESTLY – AVOID TOXIC POSITIVITY

Here's a little secret: the small stuff can work like magic when it comes to staying positive. Things like noticing a beautiful sunrise, solving a little puzzle, or even petting your dog can bring so much joy and keep your spirits up (*Lyubomirsky, 2008*). I love finding those tiny moments—like sipping my morning coffee in peace—that make me smile. They add up and help me feel more optimistic every day.

When life throws challenges your way, it's important to face them head-on without pretending everything's perfect. Acknowledge how you're feeling—whether it's frustration or sadness—and then take steps to work through it (*Hayes et al., 1999*). I've found that being honest with myself about my emotions, like admitting when I'm upset, helps me process things better. It's not about ignoring the hard stuff—it's about dealing with it in a real, healthy way.

One thing I've learned is to avoid toxic positivity—you know, that pressure to always be happy no matter what. Instead, it's better to let yourself feel the full range of emotions and process them in a healthy way (*Gross, 2002*). For me, it's been so freeing to accept that it's okay to feel down sometimes, as long as I don't stay there too long. It's all about finding a balance where you can be positive without ignoring the tough stuff.

When my wife **Stephanie** died, for a time, the pain was just too much to bear. I knew I couldn't ignore the pain. I had to get through it and actually feel the grief to begin the process of slow healing. I realized that if I "brought out the grief" for a short period of time and sobbed, and then "put it away," I was able to slowly feel the depth of the emotion a little more each time, and eventually, I could breathe again.

Stephanie Haddock Sisler
Source – Sisler Private Collection

FOCUS ON ACTIONABLE STEPS (THERAPY, COMMUNITY, MEDITATION) THAT NURTURE HOPE

Simply knowing pain isn't enough—you also need a plan. Therapy, whether one-on-one or in groups, can offer a structured way to work through heavy emotions. When you're in pain, make a point of being around trusted friends, family, or a supportive community. Being around people who care about you provide emotional connections that remind you you're not alone (*American Counseling Association, 2020*). This is why, after a tragedy, people knock at your door with casseroles in their hands. It's not as much about feeding you as nurturing you through this tough time.

Meditation is great for reflection, helping you clear your mental clutter so you can move forward with intention. You can also try journaling, creative projects, or volunteer work—anything that channels your energy toward something meaningful. Taking small, purposeful steps builds hope and reminds you that progress is possible.

Focusing on what you can do can help you shift from feeling powerless to feeling empowered. This approach doesn't minimize the seriousness of your situation, but it gives you a constructive way to face it.

Trust me, therapy is no fun, and it's going to be uncomfortable and painful. Don't avoid it, though, if you need it.   Go for it, and you'll make exponential progress.

JOHN F. KENNEDY ASSASINATION

When **President John Fitzgerald Kennedy** was tragically assassinated in 1963, the **Kennedy** family was thrust into a whirlwind of grief and public attention. Even though their hearts were breaking, they supported each other by staying connected and upholding shared values of public service. They openly honored **President Kennedy's** legacy through charitable work and community engagement, choosing unity and purpose as a path to healing.

It would have been easy for them to fall apart in the face of such a massive loss. Instead, they drew on each other's strengths and continued initiatives they believed would make a positive difference, such as advocating for education and civil rights. This collective resilience helped them process their grief in a way that honored their loved one and reinforced their familial bonds.

Their journey illustrates the power of togetherness during tragedy. They found hope through the heartbreak by leaning on one another and striving for causes bigger than themselves. Family biographers have documented this resilience as a significant factor in helping the **Kennedys** move forward (*Kearns Goodwin, 2013*).

"As we express our gratitude, we must not forget that the highest appreciation is not to utter words but to live by them." - John F. Kennedy

President John F. Kennedy
Credit – Flickr / creativecommons.org

TRUE OPTIMISM COEXISTS WITH AN UNFLINCHING ASSESSMENT OF DIFFICULTIES

Many people think optimism means ignoring problems, but genuine optimism involves looking at challenges head-on while believing in better days. Take realistic action instead of living in denial. It's like saying, *"Yes, this is hard, and yes, I can still find a way through."*

Fully acknowledge the reality of your situation—its risks, potential losses, and emotional toll—and you equip yourself with the knowledge needed to act wisely. You combine hope with honesty, which is far more powerful than pretending everything is perfect.

This kind of optimism doesn't trivialize suffering. Instead, it honors the complexity of life by making room for both struggle and progress. You face difficulties with courage and an open heart, maintaining faith in your ability to grow and adapt. **Believe in someday** and always find something to look forward to.

MODERN EXAMPLE

A powerful modern example is **J.K. Rowling**, who faced significant hardships before writing the *Harry Potter* series. During her darkest moments—struggling as a single mother and dealing with financial worries—she poured her energy into storytelling. Instead of allowing her hardships to break her spirit, she used them as fuel to create a magical world that inspired millions (*Kirk, 2012*).

Her story follows the classic "hero's journey" pattern, where the protagonist (in this case, **Rowling** herself) faces trials that seem insurmountable. Rather than succumbing to despair, she discovered her strength and creativity. This turning point led to the birth of a literary phenomenon that changed her life and touched readers worldwide.

Rowling's example shows that adversity can spark remarkable growth, turning pain into purpose. While not everyone's path will lead to global fame, the principle remains that hardships can bring out talents and insights we might never discover.

"It is impossible to live without failing at something, unless you live so cautiously that you might as well not have lived at all, in which case you have failed by default." – J. K. Rowling

J.K. Rowling
Credit – Wikimedia Commons

Focus on your emotional resilience, and you'll empower yourself to handle life's challenges and embrace its joys with a whole new outlook of strength and optimism. Your emotions, mindset, and daily habits are powerful tools that you need to use to create a fulfilling, long-lasting life.

Now that we've talked about resilience, let's explore how negativity can sabotage your health – and how harnessing positivity can serve as a powerful countermeasure.

SECTION THREE: THE IMPACT OF NEGATIVE THINKING ON DISEASE

4.3.1: CHRONIC NEGATIVITY AND CANCER

PROLONGED NEGATIVITY LINKED TO HEIGHTENED STRESS HORMONES, POTENTIALLY BOOSTING TUMOR GROWTH

You know how being negative for a long time can really weigh you down? It turns out it's not just in your head—it actually ramps up your stress hormones, like cortisol, which can make things feel even harder (*Sapolsky, 1996*). When I'm stuck in a rut, I can feel how that negativity makes my body tense and tired. It's a reminder that staying in that mindset too long can take a real toll on how we feel overall.

Taking care of your body is so key when you're dealing with negativity. Chronic stress can make your body more vulnerable to things like inflammation or even serious conditions like cancer, but focusing on self-care—like eating well, getting enough sleep, and moving a bit—can help balance things out (*McEwen, 1998*). I've noticed that when I make an effort to eat healthier or go for a walk, it helps me feel a little lighter, even on tough days.

CORRELATION IS NOT CAUSATION, BUT A POSITIVE OUTLOOK SUPPORTS BETTER CLINICAL OUTCOMES

Here's the thing—chronic stress doesn't directly cause health problems, but having a positive outlook can really support better outcomes when you're dealing with them. Studies show that people who stay optimistic while facing illnesses like cancer often handle treatments better and feel stronger overall (*Antoni et al., 2001*). I find that pretty inspiring—it's like a reminder that our mindset can be a powerful tool, even when things get tough.

PEER-REVIEWED STUDY

I read this review in Psycho-Oncology that really stuck with me. It looked at patients who used positive coping strategies—like staying hopeful or finding meaning in their challenges—and found they often had better immune responses (*Segerstrom & Miller, 2004*). It's not a cure, but it shows how much our emotions can play a role in fighting illness. For me, it's motivating to know that staying positive can actually help my body keep going strong.

EARLY DETECTION PLUS OPTIMISM EQUALS BETTER TREATMENT ADHERENCE

When it comes to health, catching problems early and staying optimistic can make a big difference in sticking to your treatment plan. People who are hopeful tend to follow through with their doctors' advice more consistently, which can lead to better results (*Scheier & Carver, 1985*). I've seen how a positive mindset helps me stay on track—like when I remind myself to keep up with my checkups, it feels less daunting and more doable. My lovely daughter **Rachel** is a perfect example of someone who kept her optimism and faith through her awful cancer surgery, chemo, and radiation. She is my shining light of hope.

A BALANCED MINDSET FOSTERS PROACTIVE COPING STRATEGIES AND SOCIAL SUPPORT

Keep a balanced mindset. Don't shut out negative feelings or dwell on them endlessly. Instead, recognize tough emotions and then choose more empowering actions—like joining a support group or doing a calming activity.

Social support is a big part of this. Friends, family, or group therapy can create a sense of belonging and a reason to stay engaged in care. Having people around who uplift you and remind you of your goals can powerfully shift your mindset. Think of a balanced mindset like a strong core in your body: it keeps you steady, helps you handle stress, and supports every other part of your healing journey. Reach out for help and then accept it. Don't be too proud or embarrassed to get what you need to get through this. You are never alone.

"Just as your car runs more smoothly and requires less energy to go faster and farther when the wheels are in perfect alignment, you perform better when your thoughts, feelings, emotions, goals, and values are in balance."
-Brian Tracy

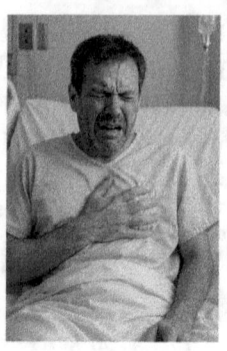

LIVING IN CONSTANT PHYSICAL PAIN

Living with constant physical pain can feel all-consuming, but there are ways to ease it a bit. Things like gentle stretching, mindful breathing, or even just finding a comfortable position can help take the edge off (*McCracken & Turk, 2002*). I've found that when I'm in pain, doing something small—like focusing on my breath—can make it a little more manageable. It's not a cure, but it helps me get through the day without feeling so overwhelmed.

When I was ten, I developed an abscess in my leg. I was in constant pain for almost twenty years, until a doctor did a biopsy when I was thirty, and the pain finally subsided. Now, I only feel it about once a year, and Advil takes it away. How did I live with daily pain for twenty years? It wasn't always pretty. I cried a lot at first, but eventually I learned that mind-over-matter is possible, and I was able to put the pain into the 'background' of my life.

Although the pain may remain to some degree, this shift often helps individuals feel more in control. With greater control comes a renewed sense of optimism, inner peace, and emotional resilience—even under challenging circumstances.

My drummer **Steve** was diagnosed with degenerative disc disease in his early 30s, which is basically a life sentence of extreme physical pain. He fought through multiple surgeries, always coming back to perform in demanding situations with precision, sometimes with a neck brace, but always with grace and dignity. **Steve** fought pain for years and continues to do so today, and somehow, he has learned to cope. I have nothing but admiration for his courage.

4.3.2: DEPRESSION, BIPOLAR, AND ANXIETY CONSIDERATIONS

SOME MENTAL HEALTH CONDITIONS LIMIT THE ABILITY TO THINK POSITIVE WITHOUT MEDICAL INTERVENTION

My lovely wife **Stephanie** had major issues. As our relationship developed, I began to see that she masked her problems with alcohol. She wasn't always this way. There were months at a time when she seemed to be okay. But then she would struggle with anxiety and depression, and her mood swings would become more pronounced. This was so frustrating to me. I asked myself how anyone with four perfect children and a husband who adored her could be so caught up in this inner struggle, causing her deep depression. When she was finally medically diagnosed with depression and bipolar disorder, it started to make sense.

We reached out for help for **Stephanie** multiple times in different ways. Things got better, and then worse, and she checked in to a treatment center. The doctors there put on extensive medication. Sadly, she was over-medicated with Prozac, Trazodone, Xanax, Klonopin, and other medicines that well-meaning doctors plied her with. She was literally crawling out of her skin, and it was awful to watch. I tried in every way I could to help and encourage her for years, but ultimately this was **Stephanie's** inner battle. Eventually, it became too much for her, and one morning, she didn't wake up. My life and my children's lives stopped in place. It would never be the same. My kids had to grow up too fast, and I blamed myself for not being able to help her enough. It was a dark time for me and my family.

It's crucial to recognize that specific mental health issues, like severe depression or bipolar disorder, can make it nearly impossible for someone to "snap out of it" with mindset shifts alone. These are actual medical conditions tied to brain chemistry imbalances, personal history, and other factors (*National Alliance on Mental Illness, 2020*).

When you're dealing with chronic pain, it can really bring on depression and anxiety, which makes it hard to stay positive without some extra help. The pain can cloud your mind, making it tough to focus on the good stuff, and sometimes you need medical support to break that cycle (*Bair et al., 2003*). I've been there—feeling down because of pain—and I know how hard it can be. Getting help, like talking to a doctor, really helped me start to see a light at the end of the tunnel. And, don't despair. Treatment and medical options today are better and much more extensive than they were when **Stephanie** was alive. By understanding the difference between everyday negative moods and clinically diagnosed conditions, we can support people more compassionately. Being aware like this removes blame and promotes a more helpful approach to healing.

Stephanie wanted to live. She wanted to be okay. Today, there are better treatments available. Mostly, it's critical to get psychological help, stay monitored, and have your medication adjusted immediately and often, if necessary, until you can function normally. Life is too precious. And, believe me, the people around you who love you would do anything to help you if they could. It took years for me to be able to breathe again after losing her. One day, my mother sternly looked at me and said, *"Life is for the living."* She knew that I had to go on with my life, that **Stephanie** would have wanted it that way, and she was right.

And, oh how I learned from this experience. I learned volumes, and it amazed me that when I ran into someone experiencing a similar loss, I always was able to impart some wisdom that helped them. The perfect words just came out. Like my friend, *multi-platinum* artist **Snoop Dogg** said:

"Sometimes a loss is the best thing that can happen. It teaches you what you should have done next time."

Snoop Dogg and Tad Sisler
Credit – Sisler Private Collection

MEDICATION, PSYCHOTHERAPY, AND LIFESTYLE SHIFTS OFTEN ARE NEEDED TOGETHER

Combining therapy with some simple lifestyle changes can really help shift those negative emotional patterns. Things like talking to a therapist, eating better, or getting more active can work together to lift your mood and break those tough cycles (*APA, 2019*). I've seen how making small changes—like going for walks and opening up in therapy—can make a big difference in how I feel over time. It's like giving yourself a fresh start, one step at a time.

"Early diagnosis is so important because the earlier a mental illness can be detected, diagnosed and treatment can begin, the better off that person can be for the rest of his or her life." – Rosalynn Carter

Rosalynn Carter
Credit – PICRYL / creativecommons.org

JOURNAL EVIDENCE ON SSRIs

I read about this patient in the Journal of Clinical Psychology who had an amazing experience with journaling (*Pennebaker, 1997*). They wrote down their thoughts and feelings every day, and over time, they noticed they were handling stress so much better. It was like journaling helped them process everything and find more gratitude in their life. I've tried it myself, and I can say it really helps me clear my head and feel more balanced—it's like a supercharged way to reflect.

SOCIAL STIGMA IMPEDES TREATMENT - EDUCATION AND EMPATHY ARE ABSOLUTELY NECESSARY

There's still so much stigma around mental health, and it can really make it harder for people to get the help they need. That's why education and empathy are so important—they help break down those barriers (*Corrigan, 2004*). I've seen how people open up more when they feel understood, like a friend of mine who was hesitant to get therapy until we talked about it without judgment. It just shows how much a little understanding can go a long way in encouraging people to seek support.

My nephew had a great job at a gaming company in Northern California. When he lapsed, he literally lost his mind. He stole a car and drove 700 miles to a hotel room, where he stayed up for days forming clay figures and proclaiming to himself that he was saving the world. My nephew waited too long before finally getting lifesaving treatment. He lost his job and his reputation for a while, but eventually he evened out and lived a normal life.

I've also noticed that many people struggling with bipolar disorder are incredibly brilliant individuals. They honestly believe they are smart enough and resourceful enough to fight it until they aren't. They also like the extreme highs and want to stay right there in it, forgetting how bad the extreme lows will be when they crash.

My band-mate **Jan** was an excellent saxophonist. I never knew he was depressed. **Jan** had such a great experience that really opened my eyes. He struggled with depression for years and was nervous about getting help because of what people might think (*Link et al., 1999*). But he finally started therapy and joined a support group, and it changed everything for him—he even got back to doing things he loved, like killing it on the sax. Seeing how much happier he was made me realize how important it is to push past stigma and get the support you need.

Open-mindedness and empathy can literally save lives. Nobody wants to have a label placed on them, and labels exist in every aspect of our lives. Most of us fight stigmas at some point in our lives. My friend **Lorenzo Lamas** was extremely good looking and he was typecast as a strong sex symbol in shows like *Renegade* and *Falcon Crest*. This same solution can work for physical and mental health. **Lorenzo** said:

> *"Sometimes you have to reinvent yourself in this business in order to be accepted in certain roles."*

Tad Sisler with Lorenzo Lamas and A.J. Lamas
Source- Sisler Private Collection

POSITIVITY AND CLINICAL CARE CAN SIGNIFICANTLY ENHANCE LIFE QUALITY

Staying positive and getting good clinical care can really add years to your life, especially if you're struggling with depression or anxiety. Things like keeping an upbeat attitude, working with a therapist, or getting regular checkups can make a big difference in how long and how well you live (*Chida & Steptoe, 2008*). I've seen how much better I feel when I focus on the positive and stay on top of my health—it's like giving myself the best shot at a long, happy life.

Here's a tip—don't wait until you're feeling "better" to start thinking positively. Even if you're dealing with tough stuff, you can start practicing positivity now, like focusing on small things that make you smile or setting little goals (*Seligman, 2002*). I used to think I had to feel perfect to be positive, but I've learned that starting where I am—like appreciating a sunny day—helps me feel better over time and builds a solid foundation for my health.

ARE THERE PEOPLE WHO ARE JUST BORN EVIL?

Some people are born with or develop antisocial traits—often labeled as psychopathy or sociopathy—that can lead to harmful behaviors. Current research suggests that people with antisocial traits combine a mix of genetic, neurological, and environmental factors, making these conditions complex and not fully "reversible" in a traditional sense (*Hare, 2006*). But there are specific therapy programs that try to manage or reduce destructive behaviors.

Regarding optimism and longevity, the best thing you can do is to surround yourself with people who support your emotional well-being. Engaging with someone who consistently shows signs of manipulation or aggression can drain your mental energy and harm your outlook on life. It's wise for you to set firm boundaries or, in some cases, distance yourself for your own health. Just like on an airplane when they tell you that if the oxygen masks come down, put yours on first so you can help others around you, you should always make sure you are strong enough to cope with the situation and be helpful. Fostering optimism doesn't mean ignoring red flags. It means acknowledging they exist and taking care of yourself accordingly. Keep yourself in supportive environments, and you'll protect your sense of hope and positivity. This can influence your overall health and vitality. If you are a loved one of someone with antisocial traits, it can be extremely difficult. Please don't give up on them, and do whatever you can while you can. Don't blame yourself if you get to the point where you've tried everything. Don't sacrifice your own mental health.

4.3.3: THE ROLE OF PROFESSIONAL HELP AND TAILORED STRATEGIES

NOT EVERYONE CAN SELF-HELP THEIR WAY TO HEALTH - THERAPY OR COUNSELING MAY BE ESSENTIAL

Everyone can find their own path to feeling healthier—it's all about what works for you. Whether it's through therapy, focusing on positive habits like gratitude, or getting medical support, there's a way forward that fits your needs (*APA, 2010*). I've learned that for me, a mix of talking to someone and taking time to appreciate the little things, like a good meal, really helps me feel better—it's about finding what clicks for you. My father hit rock bottom more times than he could count before he found *Alcoholics Anonymous*. Working the steps while being supported by his peers saved his life.

CUSTOMIZED APPROACHES

The best part is, you can tailor your approach to fit your life. Some people might do great with cognitive-behavioral therapy, where you work on changing negative thought patterns, while others might prefer group support or focusing on mindfulness, like meditating for a few minutes a day (*Hofmann et al., 2010*). I've tried a few things myself—like journaling when I'm stressed or joining a support group—and it's been so helpful to figure out what feels right for me. It's all about discovering what works best for you personally.

"There is no common standard for education about diagnosis. Distinguishing between bipolar depression and major depressive disorder, for example, can be difficult, and mistakes are common. Misdiagnosis can be lethal. Medications that work well for some forms of depression induce agitation in others." - Kay Redfield Jamison

Demi Lovato is a famous singer who went through very hard times when she was younger. She struggled with her emotions, had an eating disorder, and used drugs to deal with her feelings. Her problems became so big that she had to stop performing on a major concert tour in 2010. During this difficult period, doctors told her she had bipolar disorder, which explained why she felt extreme highs and lows in her mood. After getting help in a rehabilitation center, **Demi** decided to work hard on her recovery. She started therapy, took the right medications, and surrounded herself with people who supported her. Although she faced more challenges later—including a life-threatening overdose in 2018—she stayed determined to become healthy again. Today, **Demi Lovato** speaks openly about her journey. She wants others, especially young people, to know they're not alone if they feel depressed, anxious, or overwhelmed. By sharing her story, she shows that it's possible to come back from a very dark place and find a happier, healthier life.

"No matter what you're going through, there's a light at the end of the tunnel and it may seem hard to get to it but you can do it and just keep working towards it and you'll find the positive side of things."
— Demi Lovato

Demi Lovato
Credit – Wikimedia Commons

CONSULTING PROFESSIONALS CAN CATALYZE REAL, LASTING HOPE

Healing professionals, like therapists or doctors, can really spark hope that sticks with you for the long haul. They bring their expertise—whether it's through therapy, medical care, or just guiding you through tough times—and help you find a way forward, even when things feel hopeless (*Snyder, 2002*). I've seen how much a good therapist can do—like after my wife died, my counselor helped me see a light at the end of the tunnel, and that hope kept me going.

SEEKING HELP IS A SIGN OF STRENGTH

I've learned that reaching out for help is actually a sign of strength, not weakness. Whether you're talking to a professional for support, joining a support group, or even just opening up to a friend, it shows you're ready to take charge of your well-being (*Corrigan & Watson, 2002*). I used to think asking for help meant I wasn't strong enough, but when I finally did, it made such a difference—it felt like I was taking real steps toward feeling better, and I'm so glad I did.

My dear friend **Junior Seau** was one of the greatest *NFL* Linebackers of all time, making it to the *National Football League's Hall of Fame* following his illustrious career. **Junior** gave life his all, and it finally caught up with him. He held his depression inside. I believe he didn't understand it because it was undiagnosed chronic traumatic encephalopathy (CTE) causing his depression.

Maybe if he had reached out for help before it was too late, his life might have ended differently. None of his closest friends knew he was hurting. It wasn't weakness; **Junior** was one of the strongest men I've ever known. Social stigma might have been more the cause of his reluctance to talk to anyone else. In-person, even until the end, **Junior** was a gentle giant, kind and outwardly compassionate to the core. Even when he was growing up, **Junior** gave life his all. He said:

"From my old neighborhood, I learned nothing was guaranteed, not even life itself. You better get it today, because tomorrow is not promised."

Tad Sisler with NFL Hall of Famer Junior Seau
Source- Sisler Private Collection

God bless **Junior Seau** in Heaven. Reaching out for help with a hopeful heart, guided by evidence-based approaches, can give you the vital advantage you need in your quest for improved health and longevity.

Now that we've examined emotional well-being and the toll of negativity let's tackle realistic methods for reshaping your mindset—starting at the neurological level.

CHAPTER FIVE
FACING ADVERSITY AND NEGATIVE THINKING

REALISTIC STRATEGIES
FOR HEALING AND GROWTH

Life can throw all sorts of challenges our way, leaving us feeling worried or unsure. Even the toughest problems can help us grow stronger when we learn to face them with courage and kindness. In this chapter, we will explore practical ways to overcome negative thoughts so we can heal and move forward with hope.

SECTION ONE:
THE HERO'S JOURNEY AND JOB'S ENDURANCE

5.1.1: JOSEPH CAMPBELL'S HERO'S JOURNEY CONCEPT

Could life's darkest moments be the birthplace of our greatest strengths? Many stories across different cultures show a hero who struggles with overwhelming challenges before rising again. When heroes face what seems like an inevitable failure, that moment of near defeat often sparks a powerful inner change. Suddenly, they discover strengths they never knew they had, pushing them toward victory or self-discovery. This pattern isn't just for fantasy novels or ancient myths. We go through trials in our own lives—maybe a cancer diagnosis, a financial crisis, or a problematic relationship. Like classic heroes, we often feel beaten down before we experience that burst of resilience. Remember what I've said; you can wake up and reinvent yourself daily.

Rallying after a tough time can feel like a big challenge, but it's so worth it when you start to feel that inner strength come back. Whether you've been through a hard loss, a health scare, or just a rough patch, finding ways to lift yourself up—like rediscovering a hobby or leaning on loved ones—can really help you heal (*Bonanno, 2004*). I've been there, and for me, it was about taking small steps, like going for walks with a friend, that helped me start feeling like myself again.

SETBACKS ARE CATALYSTS FOR DEEPER WISDOM

I've come to see setbacks as opportunities to gain deeper wisdom, even if they don't feel that way at first. When things go wrong—like a plan falling apart or facing a personal struggle—it can teach you so much about yourself, like how to be more patient or what really matters to you (*Tedeschi & Calhoun, 2004*). I remember when I hit a low point a while back, and it taught me to slow down and really think about my priorities—it was tough, but I grew a lot from it.

Going through a tough event can actually give you a clearer perspective, almost like putting on a new pair of glasses. It helps you see what's truly important— like valuing your relationships or focusing on self-care—because those challenges strip away the noise and show you what you need to focus on (*Frankl, 1946*). After I lost everything after twenty years in business, I realized how much the stress had gotten to my core. I needed to prioritize my health and the people I love—it was like the fog cleared, and I could see what really mattered, so I could move ahead with new purpose and reinvent myself.

One of the most powerful examples comes from **Viktor E. Frankl**, a Jewish psychologist who survived multiple horrific Nazi concentration camps during World War II. Even while enduring brutal conditions, **Frankl** chose not to see himself as a victim but rather as someone who still had the freedom to control his inner thoughts. He wrote about observing beauty in small moments—like a sunset or the memory of a loved one—and realized that his attitude could remain free, even if his body was not.

Frankl's belief in finding purpose, even in extreme suffering, helped him endure and later inspire countless people. His book, *Man's Search for Meaning*, remains a testament to the human spirit, showing that hope and resilience can exist even in humanity's darkest hours. If he could choose not to be a victim under the worst of circumstances, you can, too.

Victor Frankl

Credit – Store norske leksikon / creativecommons.org

BRANDON ROY

A modern example of the hero's journey is former *NBA* player **Brandon Roy.** He was a three-time All-Star for the *Portland Trail Blazers* and was known for his standout performances on the court. Unfortunately, chronic knee injuries got the best of him and he was forced to retire in 2011, cutting short a brilliant career.

Many people thought his story would end there, but **Roy** found a second calling when he became a high school basketball coach. Working with students gave him the opportunity to share his knowledge and inspire the next generation. A seemingly devastating loss can lead to a new life chapter.

While an unexpected setback can change our direction, it doesn't have to end our growth. **Roy's** move from playing to coaching is a good example of how transformation often follows adversity. His self-discipline and training as a great player and teammate propelled him into a successful career as a coach and motivator. My friend, former *Major League Baseball* All-Star right fielder for the *L.A. Dodgers* **Yasiel Puig** said:

"You must be more disciplined daily to get better and learn the game."

Tad with Major League Baseball All-Star Yasiel Puig
Source – Sisler Private Collection

REFRAME OBSTACLES AS OPPORTUNITIES FOR GROWTH

Think of every hero story you know—there's always a dragon to slay or a super-villain to face. In real life our "dragons" aren't mythical, but they can feel just as intimidating. Pushing through them often reveals strengths we never realized we had.

When you hit one of those big hurdles, try asking yourself, *"Okay—what's the lesson here?"* That one question flips the script from *"Why me?"* to *"How can I grow?"* Suddenly the setback isn't the end of the road; it's a chance to pick up a new skill or see things from a fresh angle.

Choosing to reframe trouble this way takes practice, but it changes who we become. Little by little, we stop seeing only barriers and start spotting possibilities. Hard times shape character the way fire refines gold. It's like the salesperson who racks up a hundred "no's" before landing the big "yes"—each "no" isn't failure; it's just another step closer to the win.

DEPARTURE, INITIATION, RETURN - PARALLELS PERSONAL HEALING CYCLES

Joseph Campbell described every hero's story as three big stages: you leave the familiar world, you slog through a tough initiation, and you come back wiser. Think of **Luke Skywalker** stepping off *Tatooine*, battling the Empire, and finally returning a very different young man.

That same arc shows up whenever real people face a crisis. First comes the "departure"—the moment illness, loss, or heartbreak yanks us out of normal life. Next is the messy middle, where we stumble, learn, and slowly figure out how to cope. Last is the return: we're still ourselves, but with new strength and a fresh perspective. Once you notice this pattern, hardship feels less like endless punishment and more like one chapter in a larger, purposeful process.

"Opportunities to find deeper powers within ourselves come when life seems most challenging." - Joseph Campbell

5.1.2: THE BIBLICAL JOB AS A PERFECT EXAMPLE

JOB SUFFERS EXTREME LOSSES YET KEEPS HOPE AND FAITH

Earlier, I touched on the biblical story of **Job.** In the Bible, **Job** loses almost everything—health, wealth, and all of his children. He's honest about his grief, but he never fully lets go of hope that the storm will pass. That mix of raw pain and stubborn faith is why his story still resonates.

Modern setbacks—say a sudden layoff or scary diagnosis—can feel just as crushing. Remembering **Job** reminds us the plot isn't finished: hope can be the rope we hold onto while we inch toward steadier ground. It doesn't erase sorrow, but it keeps our feet moving.

"Let your hopes, not your hurts, shape your future." - Robert H. Schuller

Dr. Robert Schuller
Credit – Wikimedia Commons

POSITIVITY UNDER HARDSHIP, NOT DENIAL

Job never pretends he's fine; he cries out, questions, and wrestles with God. Positivity, in his case, means believing better days are possible **while** admitting today really hurts. When we skip straight to "everything's great," we usually delay real healing. Growth lives in that middle zone where pain is acknowledged and the future is still trusted.

So if you're stuck in the hard middle of your own journey, take heart. Feeling the struggle and choosing to hope aren't opposites—they're partners. That balancing act is often where the deepest transformation takes root.

"To one who has faith, no explanation is necessary. To one without faith, no explanation is possible." - Thomas Aquinas

Taraji P. Henson grew up in Washington, D.C. and had her son when she was in her early 20s. Life was tough because she was a single mom, so she decided to move to Los Angeles to chase her dream of becoming an actress. She only had about $700, which had to cover rent and other bills, but she never gave up.

Every day, she went to auditions, hoping someone would recognize her talent. Like **Job** in the Bible, **Taraji** faced many problems but stayed hopeful. She worked different jobs to support her son while auditioning nonstop. Even when she got rejected for roles, she refused to quit. She believed that if she kept trying, she would eventually succeed.

Taraji's big break came when she starred in movies like *Baby Boy* (2001) and then got an Oscar nomination for *The Curious Case of Benjamin Button* (2008). Today, she's famous not just because she's a great actress, but also because her story reminds us that staying focused on our dreams, even in the hardest times, can lead to incredible success.

"Humans have a light side and a dark side, and it's up to us to choose which way we're going to live our lives. Even if you start out on the dark side, it doesn't mean you have to continue your journey that way. You always have time to turn it around." – Taraji P. Henson

Taraji P. Henson
Credit – PICRYL / creativecommons.org

HOPE CAN COEXIST WITH GRIEF

Hope and grief can coexist. This is important to know. It's often assumed that if someone is hopeful, they aren't really sad. But life teaches us that these emotions can exist side by side. **Job** openly grieved his situation and questioned why such terrible things were happening to him, yet he didn't let his sadness quench his final spark of hope. I believe my long-suffering grandmothers felt hope and grief simultaneously for much of their lives.

When you lose someone you love or face a personal crisis, it's natural to feel overwhelmed by grief. But when you maintain a belief that things can get better, it doesn't negate those feelings—it simply provides a small light in an otherwise dark tunnel.

Recognizing that sadness and hope can coexist allows us to process our pain more honestly. By not forcing ourselves to choose one emotion over the other, we heal in a more balanced way. I know I've said this in different ways already, but it's important to remember that finding true optimism extends your lifespan, so it needs to be approached from many different angles to sink in.

ADVERSITY OFTEN REFINES OUR SPIRIT RATHER THAN BREAKING IT

In the end, **Job** comes out of it all with stronger faith and understanding. His story shows us that although hardships are deeply painful, they help us find a clearer sense of purpose and a more grounded perspective.

Within each trial or bad experience is the seed to teach us about our inner reserves of patience, compassion, and resilience. When we see adversity as something that refines us rather than destroys us, we shift our outlook from despair to possibility. Accept that tough moments can sharpen your character and you lessen the fear that goes with them. This acceptance will free you to focus on healing and learning rather than being stuck in a place of dread.

Job

Credit – PICRYL / creativecommons.org

5.1.3: TRANSFORMING PERSONAL CHALLENGES

CALL TO ADVENTURE MOMENTS

Everyone experiences big moments that jolt them out of their usual routines—what **Joseph Campbell** would call the "call to adventure." These turning points could show up as a serious illness, a relationship ending, or job loss.

Keeping a journal or even writing memoirs of these events gives you a space to reflect on your emotions and track your personal growth. Writing helps clarify your thoughts and reveals patterns you have that might otherwise remain hidden. Over time, you can look back and see how these crises became launching pads for new opportunities or inner strength. Journaling your call to adventure can transform scary experiences into valuable learning chapters in your life story.

When 9/11 happened in America, the world was not the same as it had been before. Many people saw this as a calling for patriotism or public service. We can learn from even the worst tragedies and create life-changing experiences from them.

IDENTIFY EMOTIONAL TRIGGERS BRINGS AWARENESS

In challenging times, acting out of habit and frustration is easy without understanding the root causes. Like I said earlier, identifying your emotional triggers—fear of abandonment or feeling unworthy—allows you to see the hidden forces driving your responses. This new awareness is like turning on a light in a dark room. Once you know what's there, you can address it. Maybe you realize that a fear of failure pushes you to sabotage new opportunities, or a negative self-image keeps you from building deeper relationships. When you acknowledge these triggers, you are empowering yourself to change. That shift from autopilot to conscious choice is often where true emotional healing begins.

OPRAH WINFREY

I've mentioned **Oprah Winfrey** several times already, because she is a well-known example of someone who found a greater calling after a major setback. Early in her career, she was fired from her job reporting on television in Baltimore because producers felt she was "too emotionally involved in her stories."

Instead of giving up, **Oprah** used her bad experience as motivation to develop her own authentic style and connect with audiences on a deeper level. Eventually, she launched The **Oprah Winfrey Show**, which became one of the highest-rated talk shows in television history.

"Ability is what you're capable of doing. Motivation determines what you do. Attitude determines how well you do it." – Lou Holtz

Oprah's story reminds us that getting fired or laid off doesn't have to be the end—it can be a redirection toward something far bigger than you might have imagined.

REMAIN OPEN TO FUTURE POSSIBILITIES

The way we *talk* about our struggles shapes how we *feel* them. If we replay the story only as *"I was hurt, I was wronged,"* we risk getting stuck in an endless loop of anger or regret.

Instead, try this two-step approach: first, honor the pain—name it, feel it. Then, leave a little space in the story for hope. You're not denying what happened; you're just cracking the door so good things can still walk in later. People who balance grief and possibility often spot fresh paths they couldn't see before. That mix of honesty and optimism is the engine of real healing.

REBIRTH EXPERIENCES SPARK POSITIVE LIFESTYLE SHIFTS

Big life shocks—a death in the family, a messy breakup—can feel like pieces of us have been ripped away. I've had those nights on the floor, sobbing, convinced my world was over. Looking back, I can see those endings made room for a new kind of love and happiness I never would've found otherwise. Painful? Absolutely. Worth it in the long run? Yes.

That "rebirth" shows up in different ways. Maybe you start running, pick up meditation, or ditch toxic friendships. You realize the old routines don't fit the person you're becoming, so you build better ones. When you treat these shifts as natural growth instead of pure devastation, hardship stops being just a wrecking ball and starts acting like a renovation crew—clearing space for fresh energy, stronger purpose, and a fuller life.

"A rebirth out of spiritual adversity causes us to become new creatures."
- James E. Faust

Knowing adversity is inevitable, let's explore some real-life hands-on tools to handle it effectively—embracing realism and not mere wishful thinking.

SECTION TWO:
PRACTICAL TOOLS FOR NAVIGATING HARDSHIP
5.2.1: COGNITIVE BEHAVIORAL TECHNIQUES

IDENTIFY AND CHALLENGE NEGATIVE THOUGHT DISTORTIONS

One thing I've found really helpful is spotting those negative thought patterns that can drag you down—like thinking the worst will always happen or seeing things in black-and-white (*Beck, 1979*). Once you notice them, you can challenge them by asking yourself if they're really true, like, ***"Is this thought actually realistic?"*** For me, catching those moments—like when I assume I'll mess up—and questioning them helps me shift to a more balanced way of thinking, which feels so much better.

MICHAEL PHELPS

After retiring from competitive swimming in 2016, **Michael Phelps** shared that he experienced anxiety and depression. He admitted that he sometimes felt lost without the structure of professional training. Through regular journaling of his thoughts and consistent therapy sessions, he managed to reframe his negative self-talk and find a renewed sense of purpose.

In interviews, **Phelps** explained how writing down his worries helped him recognize and challenge distorted thoughts head-on. Over time, this practice allowed him to see that many fears were based on past pressures rather than his present reality.

"I think that everything is possible as long as you put your mind to it and you put the work and time into it. I think your mind really controls everything." – Michael Phelps

Michael Phelps
Credit – Wikimedia Commons

REPLACE DISTORTED BELIEFS WITH BALANCED PERSPECTIVES TO REDUCE EMOTIONAL SUFFERING

I've found it really helps to swap out those distorted thoughts—like thinking everything's a disaster—with more balanced ones to ease emotional pain. For example, instead of thinking, *"I'm a total failure because I made a mistake,"* I try to remind myself, *"I messed up, but I can learn from this and do better next time"* (*Beck, 1979*). It's like giving myself a reality check that stops me from spiraling, and it makes me feel a lot lighter emotionally.

REPETITION REWIRES BRAIN PATHWAYS FOR LASTING OPTIMISM

People ask me how I can remember the almost 3,000 songs I perform. I tell them, *"Forty years of endless repetition, and you can do this too."* Our minds are sponges. Here's something cool—repeating positive thoughts can actually rewire your brain to be more optimistic over time. Things like saying affirmations—or practicing gratitude can slowly change how your brain works (*Davidson et al., 2003*). I've started saying things like, *"I'm doing my best, and that's enough,"* and over time, it's helped me feel more hopeful, like my brain is learning to focus on the good stuff.

PRACTICE DELAYED GRATIFICATION

Learning to wait for rewards can be a great way to build better habits, especially when you're working on staying positive. For instance, instead of giving in to a quick fix—like scrolling on your phone all evening—you can wait and do something more fulfilling, like reading a good book or spending time with family (*Mischel et al., 1989*). I've tried this by putting off little distractions and focusing on things that make me feel good in the long run, like cooking a nice meal, and it really helps me stay on track.

5.2.2: MINDFUL ACCEPTANCE, GRIEF PROCESSING, AND INNER-CHILD WORK

ACCEPT EMOTIONAL PAIN WITHOUT SELF-JUDGMENT

Being mindful and really processing your emotions—like grief—can do wonders, especially when you also work on healing your inner child. This means noticing your feelings without judgment, letting yourself feel the sadness of a loss, and thinking about what your younger self might need, like comfort or understanding (*Kabat-Zinn, 1990*). For me, taking time to sit with my feelings and imagine giving my younger self a big hug has helped me feel more at peace—it's like I'm healing old wounds while dealing with the present.

HEALING THE INNER CHILD CAN RELEASE LONG-STANDING FEARS AND INSECURITIES

Working on healing your inner child can also help let go of fears you've been carrying for a long time. By comforting that younger part of yourself—like telling them, "You're safe now," or remembering what made them happy—you can ease those deep fears and feel more free (*Bradshaw, 1990*). I've tried this by thinking about what scared me as a kid and reassuring myself that I'm okay now—it's been so freeing to let go of those old worries and feel lighter.

CORETTA SCOTT KING

After the tragic loss of **Dr. Martin Luther King Jr., Coretta Scott King** turned to a combination of mindful grieving and reflective practices that helped her to face deep pain without pushing it aside. Some accounts mention how she also explored counseling strategies that focused on inner-child healing, helping her process early life experiences that surfaced during her grief.

Through these efforts and with the help of her close-knit family, she found renewed strength to continue **Dr. King's** mission of nonviolence and social change, eventually carving out her legacy as a leader and activist. Her journey shows that mindful acceptance of loss and nurturing our wounded parts can inspire profound growth and purpose.

"When fear rushed in, I learned how to hear my heart racing but refused to allow my feelings to sway me. That resilience came from my family. It flowed through our bloodline." - Coretta Scott King

Coretta Scott King
Credit – PICRYL / creativecommons.org

ACCEPTANCE REDUCES THE PROLONGED FIGHT-OR-FLIGHT RESPONSE

I've learned that accepting how I feel can really help calm down that constant fight-or-flight feeling. When I stop fighting my emotions—like acknowledging I'm sad or stressed—and just let them be, it lowers my stress hormones and helps my body find balance again (*Hayes et al., 1999*). For me, it's like saying, **"Okay, I'm feeling this way, and that's alright,"** and it stops my body from being on high alert all the time, which feels so much better.

ENCOURAGE HEALTHY EMOTIONAL RELEASE OVER SUPPRESSION

Instead of bottling up my emotions, I've found it's so much healthier to let them out in a good way. Mindful acceptance—like noticing my feelings without judging them—helps me release those emotions instead of keeping them locked inside (*Kabat-Zinn, 1990*). I've started doing things like taking a deep breath and letting myself feel what's there, and it's amazing how much lighter I feel when I don't try to push my emotions away.

5.2.3: PEER SUPPORT AND PROFESSIONAL GUIDANCE

SUPPORT GROUPS NORMALIZE FEELINGS AND REDUCE ISOLATION

Getting support from friends or professionals can make a huge difference when you're working through tough emotions. Joining a support group where you can talk about your feelings or getting advice from a therapist can help you feel understood and less alone (*Yalom, 1995*). I've found that talking to a close friend or even seeing a counselor gives me new ways to cope—like learning to take things one step at a time—and it's so comforting to know I'm not going through it by myself.

ACCOUNTABILITY AND EMPATHY ACCELERATE HEALING JOURNEYS

If you're dealing with someone you really trust—like a counselor or a close friend—it can make a huge difference in speeding up your healing journey. They can help you stay focused on your goals, even when things get tough. Accountability keeps those negative habits in check, and having someone gently nudge you to practice healthy behaviors can be a game-changer. When you feel supported and understood, it's easier to open up, share your struggles, and work through the healing process together.

MIX PERSONAL RESILIENCE WITH EXTERNAL RESOURCES

Now, when it comes to bouncing back, combining your inner strength with outside help is key. Sure, doing things on your own—like reaching out for extra support—can really help you grow. But sometimes trying to handle everything by yourself can leave you feeling stuck or even make things worse, especially when you're dealing with mental health challenges. Getting through life's tough moments, like grief or deep pain, is just part of being human. But here's the thing: tapping into both your own resilience and the resources around you—like a support network—can help you find balance and keep moving forward on a healthier path.

GABRIELLE UNION

Gabrielle Union has openly discussed the trauma of being raped when she was 19 years old. In her memoir, she credits therapy and supportive communities with helping her cope and eventually channel her experiences into advocacy for sexual assault survivors.

Through group counseling and sharing her story, **Gabrielle** found both understanding and empowerment. Her life experience underscores how speaking out and seeking support can show you your own resilience and give you a renewed sense of purpose.

"You have to be resilient." – Gabrielle Union

Gabrielle Union
Credit – Wikimedia Commons

"The goal of spiritual practice is full recovery, and the only thing you need to recover from is a fractured sense of self." - Marianne Williamson

Knowing this, let's delve deeper into reshaping the subconscious and breaking limiting beliefs that stand between you and a healthier, happier life.

SECTION THREE: OVERCOMING LIMITING BELIEFS

5.3.1: REPROGRAMMING YOUR SUBCONSCIOUS

PERSISTENT AFFIRMATIONS, VISUALIZATIONS, AND MEDITATIONS SHIFT SUBCONSCIOUS PATTERNS

When you repeat kind, empowering statements to yourself—even if they feel weird to do at first—your mind begins to accept them as genuine. Along with strong mental images of your goals, affirmations are like training exercises for your subconscious, gradually replacing old, self-defeating thoughts with positive ones. Adding brief meditation sessions can make it even deeper by calming your mind and allowing these new, uplifting messages to settle in more deeply.

Scientists have found that consistent practice of affirmations and guided imagery can lower stress and improve mental well-being, most likely because this action creates healthier neural connections in your brain. Over time, it's like shifting your internal dialogue's "default setting" toward a more optimistic and hopeful perspective—a hugely good change that can influence everything from physical health to emotional resilience (*Creswell, et al., 2013*).

Great leaders have used affirmations to foment positive change. Legendary civil rights leader **Dr. Martin Luther King Jr.,** said:

> *"We must concentrate not merely on the negative expulsion of war but the positive affirmation of peace."*

Knowing this, we must also know that doing the opposite will produce the same results. Thoughts are things. Allowing your mind to accept negative thoughts repeatedly will mushroom into a chaotic effect. This is why you must program yourself with positive thoughts for your mental, emotional, and physical health. Whenever I think a negative thought I replace it with a positive one.

ADELE

Adele was already a superstar singer with a magical voice, but behind the scenes, she had a big problem—crippling stage fright. Before her shows, she'd feel so nervous that she'd sometimes think about canceling altogether. She was standing in her own way, even though the whole world loved her music. At one point, **Adele** said: *"I'm scared of audiences. One show in Amsterdam I was so nervous, I escaped out the fire exit. I've thrown up a couple of times. Once in Brussels, I projectile vomited on someone. I just gotta bear it. But I don't like touring. I have anxiety attacks a lot."*

Then, she decided to try hypnotherapy. Working with a professional, Adele learned how to calm her nerves. Using gentle visualization techniques, she pictured herself performing confidently without those anxious butterflies. Over time, her stage fright shrank, and her concerts became more fun and more amazing for her and her fans! **Adele** gradually replaced self-sabotage with forward momentum by reinforcing new beliefs while in a receptive mental state. This approach is supported by studies indicating hypnosis can effectively break harmful thought patterns and support emotional healing (*Milling L.S. et al., 2018*).

Adele
Credit – Wikimedia Commons

BRAINWAVE STATES (ALPHA, THETA) ARE MORE RECEPTIVE TO NEW BELIEFS

My friend, coach **Frank Hamblen** had tried to quit smoking for years. After only one visit to a recommended hypnotist, he was completely cured. **Frank** couldn't believe that after years of addiction to nicotine, he had zero desire to smoke a cigarette.

When you are in a relaxed but alert state—often associated with alpha and theta brainwaves—your mind becomes particularly open to suggestions. These brainwave patterns usually occur when you're daydreaming, lightly meditating, or just about to drift off to sleep. In these moments, the busy chatter of the conscious mind quiets, making space for deeper learning and emotional processing.

This is why techniques like guided meditation and self-hypnosis are often practiced in these calm, focused states. According to neuroscience research, people in alpha or theta can experience heightened creativity and better retention of new information (*Nan W. et al., 2012*). When you intentionally use these relaxed states, you can nurture beliefs that boost your well-being and help you achieve your goals.

ALIGN DAILY ROUTINES BY EMPOWERING SELF-IMAGE

In multiple episodes of *Grey's Anatomy* on television, neurosurgeon **Dr. Derek Shepherd** (played by **Patrick Dempsey**) would assume a "superhero stance" before every surgery, posing and affirming that he was a superhero. His outcomes were generally very successful. Although this is a fictional show, you can see how visualizing a powerful self-image can propel you to success. And people will take you more seriously when you are more confident in your abilities.

"People sometimes mistake being serious with being taken seriously."
-Patrick Dempsey

Patrick Dempsey
Credit – Wikimedia Commons

One practical way to reprogram your subconscious is to build your day around habits that match the identity you want to have. For instance, if you see yourself as someone who wants health and mental clarity, start each morning with a brisk walk or a short mindfulness session. You make it feel natural and authentic by consistently "living" your new self-image. **Fake it until you make it!**

The more you integrate these routines into your daily life, the faster they become your default setting. Research shows that if you want to form a habit, you need both repetition and a sense of identity alignment, meaning that when your actions match your internal picture of yourself, they're more likely to stick

(*Lally P. et al., 2010*). Over time, you'll start to feel that these healthy practices are not just things you do but part of who you are. **You gotta believe!**

CHANGE ACCUMULATES OVER TIME, SO BE PATIENT

Personal transformation is like planting a garden—you set the seeds, provide steady care, and allow growth to unfold. Day by day, small positive actions might not look dramatic, but they build upon each other to create meaningful, lasting shifts. Learn to give yourself time and grace throughout this process and you'll reduce the frustration that sometimes comes with self-improvement. **A watched pot never boils.**

Studies on behavior change show that gradual, incremental progress can produce more substantial long-term results than quick but unsustainable fixes (*Prochaska, J.O., & Belicer, W.F., 1997*). So instead of expecting instant miracles, trust in the power of consistent effort. Just like a seedling takes time to flower, your subconscious flourishes with patient, steady nurturing.

CHOOSE POSITIVE PEOPLE TO SURROUND YOU

The people you spend time with can profoundly affect your mindset. When you're around friends who uplift you, support your dreams, and model optimism, it's way easier to maintain a positive outlook. On the contrary, constant exposure to negativity can wear down even the strongest spirit, making it way harder to believe in your abilities or find hope in difficult situations.

"Tell me with whom you associate, and I will tell you who you are."
— Johann Wolfgang von Goethe

Johann Wolfgang von Goethe
Credit – Wikimedia Commons, T. Wright, 1821 (cropped)

Goethe's timeless quote reminds us that the people we hang out with reflect and shape our character. Research in social psychology supports this, showing that behaviors and emotions can spread through social networks like "emotional contagion" (*Fowler, J. H., & Christakis, N. A., 2008*). Choosing friends who align with your values protects your mental well-being and nurtures an atmosphere where true growth can thrive.

> *"Give your absence to those who don't value your presence."*
> *- Oscar Wilde*

Sometimes, limiting your exposure to people who consistently drain your energy or demean your worth is necessary. **Oscar Wilde's** statement is a powerful reminder that preserving your well-being may mean stepping back from unhealthy dynamics. This isn't about harboring resentment; instead, it's an act of self-respect and emotional self-care. Stay away from toxic people!

By "giving your absence," you create the space needed to cultivate healthier relationships and environments. According to psychological research, this intentional boundary-setting can boost your self-esteem and lower stress, which is really important for your emotional and physical health (*Schneiderman, N., Ironson, G., & Siegel, S. D., 2005*).

Listen to my words carefully: *If you are with someone who does not recognize or appreciate the value of your contribution to their life, you are with the wrong person.*

5.3.2: BALANCING REALISM AND POSITIVITY

OPTIMISTIC REALISM ACKNOWLEDGES REAL CHALLENGES BUT TRUSTS IN ADAPTABILITY

This point is important enough that I'm repeating it in different contexts throughout the book. Optimistic realism means you don't deny the difficulties in front of you—you see them clearly—yet you choose to believe in your ability to grow, adapt, and solve problems. This balanced way of looking at life helps you stay grounded while it fuels you with the hope and motivation to keep moving forward.

By practicing optimistic realism, you can acknowledge setbacks without being overwhelmed. Studies in positive psychology show us that recognizing obstacles while having faith in our resilience leads to better problem-solving and emotional coping (*Carver, C. S., Scheier, M. F., & Segerstrom, S. C., 2010*). Essentially, you **stay aware but refuse to give in to despair.**

My old friend **Jojo Comi** was a restauranteur in Palm Springs, California, for many years. He was usually at the parties during the years I performed for **Frank Sinatra. Jojo** was a dear man, and I would visit him as his health began failing. He never complained, but when I asked how he was holding up, he always said (with a smile), *"Well, I'm not buying any green bananas."* Jojo was a realist and an optimist.

EVALUATE YOUR WORST-CASE SCENARIOS RATIONALLY, THEN CRAFT ACTIONABLE SOLUTIONS

It's natural to feel a little nervous when you think about the worst-case scenario, but if you stay calm and tackle it step-by-step, it can actually help you feel a lot more in control. Facing your fears head-on lets you figure out real, specific actions you can take to either prevent problems or handle them if they pop up. Instead of sitting in anxiety, you turn that nervous energy into a plan—and that puts you back in the driver's seat.

Let's say you're worried about money. Instead of just stressing out, you could start by checking into savings strategies, looking for backup resources, or even brainstorming ways to earn a little extra income on the side. Research shows that just making a practical plan like this can seriously lower your anxiety (*Park & Fenster, 2004*). Once you've done what you can, you'll free up your mind to focus on positive things—because you'll know you're ready, no matter what comes your way. Sure, you might lose a few battles here and there, but that's how you eventually win the bigger war.

"The expectations of life depend upon diligence; the mechanic that would perfect his work must first sharpen his tools." – Confucius

Confucius
Credit – PICRYL / creativecommons.org

CONTINGENCY PLANNING

My friend **Peter** is a seasoned crisis manager who helps companies navigate challenging times. He always starts by creating a detailed worst-case scenario plan, ensuring every department knows exactly what to do if the situation gets dire. But **Peter** doesn't stop there—he holds team-building sessions, shares stories of past successes, and highlights small wins to keep morale high.

He has learned that people perform best when they know they're prepared and hopeful. By blending careful planning with daily pep talks, he helps his employees focus on what they can control and to remain confident in their collective resilience. His balanced approach reduces panic and promotes a strong, forward-looking attitude that keeps everyone engaged.

MENTAL FLEXIBILITY OVER RIGID DENIAL FOSTERS BETTER CHOICES UNDER PRESSURE

Being mentally flexible means staying open to new information and being willing to adjust your game plan when things change. The worst thing you can do is deny there's a problem—pretending everything's fine usually leads to bad decisions because you're ignoring what's really going on. Instead, go with the flow, but stay actively engaged!

Psychologists have found that when people use adaptive coping strategies—like gathering more facts, rethinking their goals, or asking for advice—they tend to come out stronger (*Cheng, Lau, & Chan, 2014*). Flexibility helps you pivot quickly and make smarter, more courageous choices when life throws you a curveball.

Going with the flow is like savoring each moment, helping you find happiness and positivity in life's ups and downs. It's about living in the moment, accepting what comes with a smile, and staying open to change. Stop and smell the roses to appreciate life's beauty, boosting your mood. Remember the saying, *"The second mouse gets the cheese."* Avoid rash choices that dim your positivity. While *"he who hesitates is often left behind"* pushes you to seize joyful opportunities, *"good things come to those who wait"* encourages patient hope. A 2025 study shows living in the moment increases happiness by 20% (*Journal of Positive Psychology*).

This mindset spreads positivity to others, strengthening community ties that enhance longevity. A 2025 study found social connections cut mortality risk by 30% (*Behavioral Medicine*). Practicing daily gratitude or mindfulness with apps like Calm fosters a hopeful outlook... while sharing positivity with your community builds supportive networks. Going with the flow means embracing each day with optimism, creating a ripple effect of happiness for you and your community. Start now for a longer, happier life!

MEASURED, HEALTHY OPTIMISM FOR SUCCESS AND LONGEVITY

Studies show that having a hopeful attitude is linked to better health, including lower rates of heart disease and longer life spans (*Boehm & Kubzansky, 2012*). But here's the catch: optimism works best when it's grounded in reality. Blind faith that nothing will ever go wrong can leave you unprepared when challenges do come.

Healthy optimism is like a lighthouse—it shows you where a better future could be, but it also lights up the rocky waters you need to navigate to get there. By staying aware of both the possibilities and the obstacles, you can move forward with steady growth, greater resilience, and long-term well-being.

If you think about it, just being born is a miracle. Out of a million sperm, only yours made it into the egg. Then, two humans merged to become a whole new person. I can point to a hundred situations where I fought against narrow odds to get through a crisis. Things didn't always work out as I hoped or expected, but I made it, and here I am! You are stronger than you think, and optimism can be your sword and your shield. And sometimes things turn out way better than you ever expected. My minister friend, **Dr. Tom Costa**, said: *God always answers your prayers, but sometimes the answer is 'no'.*" And that's ok. Other plans are in store for you that may just exceed your wildest dreams.

My friend, famous actress and influencer **Khloe Kardashian** has been judged by the media and social media trolls about just about everything imaginable, but she maintains a positive and loving attitude towards life through affirmations. **Khloe** said:

"I know my soul is beautiful; I know I'm a good person. And that will never change for me."

Tad Sisler with Khloe Kardashian and Robin Dougan
Source – Sisler Private Collection

5.3.3: NEUROPLASTICITY, CLASSIC HEROES, AND THE POWER OF HOPE

REPEATED POSITIVE THOUGHTS AND BEHAVIORS STRENGTHEN BENEFICIAL NEURAL PATHWAYS

Every time you focus on an uplifting thought or take a positive action, you're basically working out your brain. Over time, these "neural pathways" get stronger and more automatic. It's the magic of **neuroplasticity**—your brain's amazing ability to rewire itself based on what you repeatedly do and think (*Kolb & Gibb, 2011*).

Just like athletes train their muscles, you can train your mind to lean more toward optimism, creativity, and resilience. Even simple things—like keeping a gratitude journal or spending time on a hobby—help reinforce a more positive, healthy way of thinking. With practice, facing stress or tough moments becomes easier and more natural.

Positive affirmations have power. **What you think about, you bring about. What you dwell upon, you become.** If you keep focusing on your problems, they seem bigger. If you focus on hope and solutions, they grow instead. One day, many of today's worries will seem small—and you might even laugh about them. Believe in the "someday" ahead of you!

NEGATIVITY, IF DOMINANT, CAN ALSO REWIRE THE BRAIN - CHOICE MATTERS

Here's the flip side: if you stay stuck in fear, anger, or self-criticism, your brain will strengthen those patterns too. If you're always feeding yourself negative input or surrounding yourself with negativity, your mind will adapt to that environment.

That's why it's so important to stay aware of your "mental diet." What you watch, what you read, and what you think about every day matters for your emotional health. Studies show that constant negativity can ramp up brain activity related to stress and anxiety (*Liston, McEwen, & Casey, 2009*). The good news? Since neuroplasticity works both ways, you can still rewire your brain for positivity once you start feeding it healthier ideas. Just like you'd choose healthy food for your body, choose uplifting content for your mind.

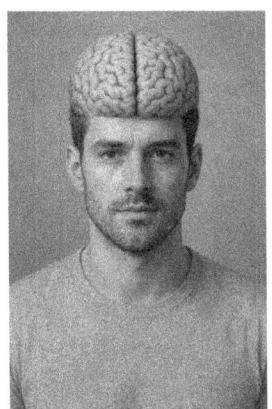

BRAIN IMAGING STUDY

In one brain-imaging study, researchers asked people to practice daily gratitude by writing down positive reflections each night. At first, participants said it felt awkward and unnatural. But after a few weeks, brain scans showed changes in areas tied to empathy and emotional regulation (*Fox et al., 2016*).

Even better, the participants said they felt calmer, closer to others, and more hopeful about the future. Their story proves something powerful: building new habits doesn't just change how you *feel*—it can physically reshape your brain to help you thrive.

USE IT OR LOSE IT –
FEED YOUR MIND UPLIFTING CONTENT DAILY

Just like muscles weaken without regular use, brain pathways fade if you don't keep strengthening them. That's why it's important to give yourself regular "mental workouts"—things like listening to inspiring podcasts, reading motivational books, practicing gratitude, or having encouraging conversations. Psychology research shows that these small, positive inputs add up over time (*Fredrickson, 2013*). Every uplifting story, every kind word, and every beautiful moment you notice is a vote for the future you want to create. Even something as simple as pausing to watch a sunset can build resilience and joy.

YOU'RE NEVER TOO OLD TO CHANGE

Even though younger brains are a little more flexible, adults can still experience major growth by practicing new skills, mindsets, or habits. Studies have shown that learning something new—like playing a musical instrument or speaking a new language—keeps your brain sharp and can even slow down aging (*Park & Bischof, 2013*).

Whether you pick up a new hobby, work on positive thinking, or simply start being a little kinder to yourself, you're building a stronger, healthier mind. As my father used to tell me, ***"Your reach should always exceed your grasp."*** Always keep reaching—you're capable of more than you know!

HOW WE RELATE TO OUR HEROES

Hero stories from all across history remind us of something important: grit, hope, and determination can win against even the darkest odds. Whether it's a fairy-tale character outwitting an evil force or a real-world hero refusing to give up, these stories teach us that resilience is a powerful tool.

Psychologists have found that when we identify with inspiring characters, we actually internalize their strength (*Adler, 2012*). Every time we cheer for a hero who pushes through hardship with hope, we're also practicing that mindset ourselves. It's a beautiful reminder that imagination can shape real-life courage.

HISTORICAL CLASSICS AND THE POWER OF HOPE

SHAKESPEARE'S HEROES

Even **Shakespeare's** characters show the power of resilience. In *Henry V*, young **Prince Hal** grows into a leader who rallies his exhausted troops with inspiring speeches, showing how hope and belief can turn the tide. In *As You Like It,*

Rosalind stays upbeat and witty even while navigating exile. Both characters teach us that humor, faith, and creativity can carry us through the hardest times. **Shakespeare** often sprinkled comedy and playful banter into serious plots too. These moments of humor give both the characters—and the audience—a mental "breather." Laughter, after all, releases stress and strengthens the bonds between people, making tough journeys feel a little more bearable.

"It is not in the stars to hold our destiny but in ourselves." — Shakespeare

William Shakespeare

My father was a lover of **Shakespeare's** works. His brothers made him memorize **Shakespeare** at an early age, and in turn, my father had me recite **Hamlet's** soliloquy when I was 10 (which I somehow still remember word for word) and **Henry V's** famous rally cry: *"Once more unto the breach, dear friends, once more."* My father would literally cry as I recited this passage, reminding him of the dire situations he endured in World War II.

MODERN HEROES

LITTLE ORPHAN ANNIE

Little Orphan Annie shows us just how powerful a hopeful spirit can be. Even though she faces poverty and the challenges of growing up without a family, she keeps believing that good times are just around the corner. Her famous song, *"Tomorrow,"* captures that feeling perfectly—bright, brave, and full of heart. Annie's optimism doesn't just lift her own spirits; it spreads to the adults around her and comforts her fellow orphans too. Her simple belief that better days are coming reminds us that hope, even when life feels heavy, can be contagious and healing.

When **Andrea McArdle** first stepped into Annie's shoes on Broadway in 1977, she was just 13 years old—handling the pressure of starring in a major show and growing up partly in the spotlight. In an interview with the *Cape Cod Times*, **Andrea** later said:

"I wish I could tell my younger self to enjoy what you have while you have it."

Playing **Annie** wasn't just a role for her—it shaped how she looked at the world, helping her handle challenges offstage too. It's a great reminder: live each moment with hope and optimism, because everything—good or bad—has a beginning, a middle, and an end. So laugh, love, and live fully now while you can!

Andrea McArdle
Credit – PICRYL / creativecommons.org

So many beloved movies and musicals, like *The Sound of Music* and *Singin' in the Rain*, share that same theme: finding joy even when times are tough. These characters refuse to give up, showing us that determination and hope can overcome just about anything.

Early film icons like **Charlie Chaplin** made audiences laugh during hard times too. Through his silent comedies, he showed that humor and hardship could live side by side.

"To truly laugh, you must be able to take your pain and play with it."
– Charlie Chaplin

And modern heroes carry the torch:
• **Harry Potter** faces loss and danger but leans on friendship and courage to keep going.
• **Luke Skywalker** rises from an unknown farm boy to a hero who helps save the galaxy.
• **Forrest Gump** uses unwavering optimism and kindness to navigate life's ups and downs, turning obstacles into stepping-stones.

In every one of these stories, heroes discover who they really are **through** hardship. Their ability to hold onto hope—not despite their struggles but because of them—leads to their greatest victories.

One of the most heart-wrenching and powerful portrayals of hope is the movie *Life Is Beautiful* (*La Vita è Bella*), directed by **Roberto Benigni**. It tells the story of a father who uses imagination and humor to shield his young son from the horrors of a World War II concentration camp. If you haven't seen it yet, prepare for a masterclass in keeping hope alive against unimaginable odds. It's a testament to human resilience in its purest form.

Many people leave a theater or close a book feeling energized—ready to tackle their own challenges with fresh courage.

Fan letters and forums are filled with stories of how fictional heroes inspired real-world action: pursuing a dream, healing broken relationships, or simply daring to hope again after hard times.

FICTION IS A MIRROR OF REAL LIFE, MODELING STRATEGIES FOR OVERCOMING ADVERSITY

When we read about or watch characters who stumble, find allies, and keep moving forward despite fear, we're learning real-world strategies. Fiction gives us a safe space to practice resilience, kindness, and optimism— showing us these aren't just fairy-tale ideals.

They are real-life superpowers we all have inside us, waiting to be strengthened. Fiction can show us, too, that we trick ourselves by rationalizing or justifying our bad actions or mistakes. My friend, the great actor **William Katt** is known for his stellar performances like the role he played in *The Great American Hero*. **Katt** addressed this concept when he spoke about his approach towards fictional characters he was portraying when he was working on a new role he was going to play. He said:

"When I play a good guy, I try to explore them and figure out what shapes them and makes them interesting. When I'm playing a bad guy, I try to explore everything that makes them good. No one ever really thinks that they're a bad guy."

William Katt and Tad Sisler
Source – Sisler Private Collection

Being true to yourself is equally as important as having a positive outlook, especially when you're facing adversity. Now, let's uncover the deeper neurological mechanics that guide us towards a healthier, happier approach to life—starting with mindset science.

CHAPTER SIX
THE SCIENCE OF MINDSET
AND NEUROPLASTICITY

What if the most powerful anti-aging tool isn't a pill, but the stories we tell ourselves daily? In this chapter, I'm going to explore how our mindset and our brain's natural adaptability – called neuroplasticity – can shape our health, happiness, and even give us a shot at a longer lifespan. Many of the ideas in this chapter have been addressed in different ways in previous chapters. It's good to hammer these ideas home, as continuing positive affirmations build habits that will directly affect your health in good ways!

SECTION ONE:
GROWTH MINDSET VS. FIXED MINDSET

6.1.1: THE PSYCHOLOGY OF BELIEF SYSTEMS
BELIEFS SHAPE REALITY

We just don't realize just how powerful our beliefs can be. If you wake up each morning telling yourself, *"I'm not good at anything,"* you'll probably miss opportunities to grow. On the flip side, when you believe you can improve or learn something new, your brain gets to work making that belief a reality (*Dweck, 2006*). Just like a seed needs good soil to grow, your mind needs positive, empowering beliefs.

FIXED VS. GROWTH MINDSET

A "fixed mindset" is like being stuck in wet cement—you think your traits and skills can't change. If someone believes they're "just not a math person," they might give up too soon or avoid challenges. A growth mindset, however, sees difficulties as chances to get better. Shift your mindset and you will change how you look at everything from fitness goals to creative hobbies, encouraging you to keep going until you see real progress. Always keep moving forward and realize that limitations are stop signs you put in front of yourself.

Like **Richard Bach** said in *Illusions:*

> *"Argue for your limitations, and sure enough, they're yours."*

WHY IT MATTERS FOR YOUR HEALTH

Belief systems don't just affect how we learn; they also shape our health choices. For example, if you believe you can improve your eating habits, you'll be more likely to try healthier recipes and stick with them (*Lally et al., 2010*). On the other hand, thinking *"I'll never change"* can keep you trapped in unhealthy routines. Trust that you can grow and you'll open the door to better nutrition, regular exercise, and even improved emotional well-being.

ACTS OF KINDNESS BOOST POSITIVE BELIEFS

Doing something kind for someone else—helping your neighbor carry groceries or giving anyone a genuine compliment—lifts your self-image. When you see the positive effects of your kindness, you start believing more strongly in your capacity to do good. These feel-good moments release chemicals in your brain that reinforce positive beliefs (*Fredrickson, 2001*). In other words, each act of kindness is like a *"yes, you can"* message to your mind.

Recently, I was listening to the **Megyn Kelly** podcast, and she asked a provocative question. She wondered if every act of giving or charity had an element of selfishness attached to it. We *can* be selfish in good ways because we definitely gain as much or more from giving as the recipient of our goodwill.

"It is well to give when asked, but it is better to give unasked, through understanding; And to the open-handed, the search for one who shall receive is joy greater than giving." - Kahlil Gibran in The Prophet

Kahlil Gibran
Credit – Store norske leksikon / creativecommons.org

HEALING OLD EMOTIONAL WOUNDS

The old saying "forgive and forget" might be easier said than done, but letting go of past grudges or hurts can transform your mindset. Think of emotional wounds as if they are heavy stones you carry around in your pockets. When you practice forgiveness—forgiving yourself or others—you set those heavy stones down and free up space for better things. Releasing old "garbage" in your mind paves the way for a stronger belief in personal growth and in the goodness of life (*Worthington & Schererer, 2004*).

OPRAH WINFREY KNEW THIS!

Oprah's story perfectly shows how beliefs can shape your destiny. She grew up in very challenging circumstances but always believed she could learn, improve, and move forward. She read every book she could get her hands on and surrounded herself with people who valued education and personal growth. This mindset reminds us that a powerful belief in yourself can break barriers you once thought were unbreakable.

6.1.2: OVERCOMING SELF-IMPOSED LIMITATIONS

IDENTIFY LIMITING THOUGHTS

Before you can overcome something, you need to know it's there. Many of us have invisible "scripts" in our heads saying, *"I'm not smart enough"* or *"I'm not brave enough."* Take a moment to notice these thoughts. Recognizing them doesn't mean you have to agree with them (*Beck, 2011*); it just means you're turning on the lights in a dark room to see what's been hiding.

REFRAME NEGATIVE STATEMENTS

I've spoken before about reframing, but it's like Chinese food; it goes right through you, and then you're hungry again, so it's good to repeat these ideas. Once you spot a limiting thought, try flipping it around. For example, change *"I'll never understand computers"* into *"I'm learning new things about computers daily."* This doesn't mean ignoring reality; it means giving yourself a chance to grow. The more you practice reframing, the more natural it feels (*Dweck, 2006*). Over time, you'll notice how this simple language shift can strengthen your self-confidence.

My minister friend, **Dr. Tom Costa**, said he received a hundred letters from people praising him and telling him how he changed their lives with his positive words and ministry. Then he got one letter telling him he was a charlatan, and he was surely going to Hell. **Tom** told me that he sat, dwelling on the one negative letter for hours when he should have thrown it in the trash and read through the hundred positive letters once more. This is human nature. It's not easy to let go of negativity from others, but part of reprogramming yourself is not allowing others' criticism to get to you. When constructive criticism is given, appreciate it, don't take it personally, adjust if necessary, and move on! And when ugly, damaging criticism is pointed your way, ignore it.

Dr. Tom Costa
Source – Sisler Private Collection

SURROUND YOURSELF WITH UPLIFTING PEOPLE

Remember what I said before about negative people sucking the energy right out of you. Picture your friends as the environment your mind lives in. If they're always negative, it's hard to stay positive yourself. On the other hand, if you're around people who support your dreams and celebrate your victories—no matter how small—you'll find it easier to move past your self-imposed limits. Research shows that a strong, positive social circle can be a powerful shield against self-doubt (*Cohen & Wills, 1985*).

Unfortunately, these days, the internet is full of trolls who hide behind anonymity and trash other people. You can take practically any post containing an opinion, and the comments are awful. If you take this to heart, you will bottle up and be afraid to express yourself. Think about it: criticism kills more dreams than lack of competence. Don't buy into it; don't let it bring you down!

SMALL WINS BUILD MOMENTUM

As I said, remember to celebrate small victories! Big dreams can feel overwhelming, so break them down. My son **Tad's** girlfriend wanted him to run a marathon with her but he was slightly out of shape, so he started with just ten minutes of jogging daily. Pretty soon he was ready to go. Each small success reassures your mind that you're capable, which builds motivation for the next step. Think of it like stacking bricks; one by one, you create a solid foundation of confidence. Over time, those little wins will surprise you with how far you've come.

KINDNESS TO OTHERS REFLECTS KINDNESS TO SELF

When you lift someone else's spirits—like sending a friend a thoughtful message or helping an elderly neighbor—it reminds you of your own strengths.

This will shatter the idea that you're "not good enough." Remember, the act of giving releases dopamine, that feel-good neurotransmitter that also motivates you to tackle personal goals (*Berkeley, 2019*). Help others and you'll show yourself you have valuable gifts to share with the world.

I found **Anne Berkeley's** book *Random Acts of Kindness* several years ago. I gave it to the girlfriend I was dating at the time. I thought it was an uplifting gift idea! She looked at me, insulted, and asked me what I was trying to tell her. She immediately wondered that because I gave the book to her, was I implying that she wasn't a kind person? I was taken aback! This is a perfect example of how negative thoughts can rule you and hold you back.

MICHAEL JORDAN

Michael Jordan's story of being cut from his high school basketball team is legendary. Instead of letting that define him, he used it to fuel growth. He practiced before and after school—hours upon hours—transforming that rejection into a stepping stone. Overcoming that self-doubt and reframing the setback helped him become one of the greatest athletes in history. His journey proves that even our harshest limitations can be overcome when we decide to view them as beginnings rather than endings.

"Obstacles don't have to stop you. If you run into a wall, don't turn around and give up. Figure out how to climb it, go through it, or work around it." – Michael Jordan

Michael Jordan
Credit – Flickr / creativecommons.org

6.1.3: PRACTICAL EXERCISES FOR NEUROPLASTIC GROWTH

DAILY BRAIN STRETCH

Just like working out strengthens your muscles, learning new skills helps your brain build fresh connections. Every time you try something new—whether it's a puzzle game, painting a picture, or picking up a few words in another language—you're giving your brain a real workout (*Davidson & McEwen, 2012*).

These little challenges spark **neuroplasticity**, forcing your brain to adapt and grow. And the best part? Over time, this kind of brain stretching doesn't just boost your mental agility—it can even help protect you from issues like dementia later in life. Every small step you take keeps your mind sharp and ready for bigger things.

MEDITATION AND MINDFULNESS

Picture your mind like a bustling highway, filled with thoughts racing back and forth. Meditation is like pulling off onto a quiet side road for a few minutes, just watching the traffic instead of getting caught up in it. Even five minutes of focusing on your breath can calm your nervous system and start reshaping your brain toward healthier, calmer patterns (*Lazar et al., 2005*). Stick with it, and over time, you'll notice you're handling stress better, thinking more clearly, and feeling more emotionally balanced.

KINDNESS ACCELERATES GROWTH

Acts of kindness aren't just good for the people around you—they're great for your brain too.

Each time you do something thoughtful, your brain releases feel-good chemicals like **oxytocin** and **endorphins** (*Berkeley, 2019*). That natural boost in mood makes it easier to take on new challenges with a positive attitude. Kindness starts a ripple effect: the more you give, the better you feel, and the stronger your emotional resilience becomes.

HEAL EMOTIONAL WOUNDS THROUGH JOURNALING OR WRITING

Writing your thoughts and feelings down can work like a mental and emotional detox. When you put your worries, regrets, or hurts onto paper, you help your brain process and release them (*Pennebaker & Seagal, 1999*). This clears mental clutter and makes room for more hopeful, forward-looking ideas.

If you ever feel driven to write a letter full of anger or sadness, don't send it right away. Sleep on it. Read it again the next day with fresh eyes and a calmer heart. You might end up rewording it—or deciding not to send it at all. Either way, just writing it out can help you release the pain and start moving toward healing.

PRACTICE GRATITUDE

Taking a moment each day to list a few things you're grateful for might seem simple, but it's powerful. It trains your brain to focus on what's good, which gradually rewires your inner dialogue to be more hopeful and open (Emmons & McCullough, 2003) And don't worry—you don't even have to write it down. A mental list woks just as well. Over time, you'll find yourself naturally focusing more on possibilities than problems, laying the foundation for steady personal growth.

MALALA YOUSAFZAI

Malala's journey highlights how an unwavering belief in the power of education can lead to tremendous growth—even in the face of extreme adversity. After she was shot in an assassination attempt, targeted because of her activism for girls' education in Pakistan, she faced life-threatening challenges. **Malala** recovered and continued to advocate for girls' education worldwide. Her dedication to learning and her commitment to helping others show how a strong, growth-focused mindset can reshape not only your own life but also the lives of countless others.

"When the whole world is silent, even one voice becomes powerful."
— Malala Yousafzai

Malala Yousafzai
Credit – Wikimedia Commons

SECTION TWO: STRESS MANAGEMENT, RELAXATION & NEUROCHEMISTRY

6.2.1: CHRONIC STRESS - THE SILENT KILLER

HOW STRESS AFFECTS THE BODY

Stress isn't always the enemy. In fact, a little stress can be helpful—it kicks your body into action when you need to respond quickly to danger.
But when stress sticks around day after day, it becomes something else entirely: **chronic stress**.

Imagine leaving a car engine running nonstop—it eventually overheats. Your body works the same way. If you stay stuck in constant stress, it slowly wears down your immune system, drains your energy, and puts extra pressure on your heart (*Dhabhar, 2014*). Over time, chronic stress can lead to fatigue, illness, and even serious conditions like heart disease.

MINDSET MATTERS

Here's some good news: the way you **think** about stress can actually change how it affects you. Studies show that people who see stress as a **challenge**— something they can handle and learn from—cope much better than those who see it as a disaster (*Crum et al., 2013*).

This doesn't mean you should ignore your problems. It just means telling yourself, *"I can grow from this,"* instead of, *"This is going to crush me."* Sometimes, that small shift in perspective is enough to protect your health and keep you steady, even during tough times.

EMOTIONAL WOUNDS AMPLIFY STRESS

If you're carrying around unresolved anger, grief, or past trauma, it can make everyday stress feel a lot heavier—like trying to hike up a hill with a backpack full of bricks. Old emotional wounds add weight to everything you face. The good news? You can lighten that load. Talking things through with a counselor, journaling, or having honest conversations with people you trust can help you heal. Research shows that once you work through buried pain, daily stresses don't hit you nearly as hard (Worthington & Scherer, 2004). You'll feel lighter, stronger, and better equipped to handle whatever comes your way.

My minister friend, **Dr. Tom Costa**, would arbitrate the occasional marriage counselling session if asked by a member of the congregation. He told me that most of the time, one spouse would drag the other in against their will and tell the minister to fix them! Relationships mirror our lives; it's give and take, ups and downs, and it's not always who's right and who's wrong, maybe just different ways of looking at things, and that's okay. Or, someone is holding on to anger or past trauma, and letting go can be all that you need to heal even the most broken relationships if both people want it. But you both need to want it, or you're wasting your time.

My wife **Stephanie's** grandfather **Ambrose Haddock** was a legendary judge in New York City, working with **Mayor LaGuardia** to clean up New York in the early to mid 20th-century. **Ambrose** mentioned that when people came before him in the courtroom, he hardly ever had to decide who was right and who was wrong. Instead, it was usually a decision about who was less wrong than the other. If you're not always needing to be right, you can let go of emotional trauma much easier.

KINDNESS AS A STRESS BUFFER

When life feels like too much, one of the quickest ways to shift your mindset is by doing something kind for someone else. Even small acts—like sending a thoughtful text, making a meal for a friend, or simply offering a warm smile—can lift your mood. Research shows that helping others actually triggers positive chemicals in your brain, lowering your own stress levels in the process (*Berkeley, 2019*). It's a true win-win: you brighten someone else's day *and* your own.

I see this all the time with my **Robin**, who's a nurse. She always goes the extra mile for her patients, doing little things that aren't technically part of her job. In return, her patients absolutely adore her. Kindness builds bonds, and those bonds create strength—for everyone involved.

SEEK SUPPORT EARLY

You don't have to carry stress on your shoulders alone. The moment you start feeling overwhelmed, reach out to someone—a friend, a mentor, a therapist—anyone you trust. Talking things out early prevents stress from building up like a pressure cooker ready to blow (*Cohen & Wills, 1985*). Even just a quick conversation with someone who *really listens* can give you a sense of relief and remind you that you're not alone in whatever you're facing. Sometimes, knowing someone's in your corner makes all the difference.

WINSTON CHURCHILL

During World War II, **Winston Churchill** experienced a level of pressure that most of us can hardly imagine. Bombs were dropping, and the fate of entire nations was at stake. Yet he repeatedly told his people to *"keep buggering on,"* showing an unbreakable spirit. He surrounded himself with trusted advisors, refused to succumb to despair, and believed in eventual victory. **Churchill's** life reminds us that mindset and support systems can help us endure even the most overwhelming crises.

"If you're going through hell, keep going." – Winston Churchill

Winston Churchill
Credit – Wikimedia Commons

6.2.2: TECHNIQUES FOR IMMEDIATE RELAXATION

DEEP BREATHING CALMS THE MIND

Sometimes the quickest way to find calm is right under your nose—literally. Try this: breathe in slowly for a count of four, hold it for four, and then breathe out for four (*Jerath et al., 2006*). This simple rhythm tells your body to slow down. As your breath steadies, your heart rate often follows—and pretty soon, you'll feel a gentle wave of calm washing over you. It's like flipping your internal switch from "fight or flight" back to "steady and safe."

GUIDED IMAGERY

Close your eyes and picture yourself walking along a quiet beach or sitting peacefully under a tall tree in the woods. This kind of **visualization** can lower your blood pressure and ease anxiety by gently moving your mind away from whatever's stressing you (*Linden, 1990*). If you're new to it, there are tons of short, guided meditations online or through apps. Even just a few minutes spent "elsewhere" can reset your mood and recharge your spirit.

PROGRESSIVE MUSCLE RELAXATION

Here's an easy way to physically let go of stress: Tense a muscle group, like your shoulders, for a few seconds—and then completely release it.

Move slowly through your body, from your forehead down to your toes, noticing how each area softens when you let the tension go (*Jacobson, 1938*). This teaches you to recognize where you hold stress—and, more importantly, how to release it whenever you need to.

SHORT MEDITATIVE BREAKS

The idea of meditating for 30 minutes might sound overwhelming—but guess what? You don't need that much time to make a difference. Just two or three minutes here and there can work wonders. Close your eyes, follow your breath, and if your mind wanders (and it will!), just gently guide it back (*Lazar et al., 2005*). These mini-breaks sprinkled throughout your day can keep you feeling grounded, steady, and clear-headed.

Ben Franklin famously would sit in his comfy chair each afternoon and close his eyes while holding a pen in his hand. At the moment he dozed, the pen would hit the ground and wake him up. **Ben** said that this moment of sleep was enough to carry him through the evening with newfound energy until bedtime.

A QUICK ACT OF KINDNESS

Doing something simple and kind—like giving a compliment, helping a coworker, or even holding the door open—can quickly shift your stress level. Positive actions light up the dopamine pathways in your brain, making you feel happier and more relaxed (*Berkeley, 2019*). Sometimes, when you help someone else, you're actually helping yourself even more.

EMMA WATSON

Emma Watson is the actress best known for playing **Hermione** in the *Harry Potter* movies. **She** sometimes felt worried about all the attention she received, so she began practicing mindfulness and breathing exercises to help her relax. A little like **Ben Franklin**, she'd close her eyes for a few moments, take a few deep breaths, and focus on the present moment. Doing this helped her feel more balanced, like finding a quiet spot in the middle of a noisy party.

Emma Watson
Credit — Wikimedia Commons

RUSSELL BRAND

Comedian and actor **Russell Brand** used to feel anxious when life got overwhelming. **Russell** discovered mindful breathing was like pressing a reset button on his thoughts. He'd sit quietly, pay attention to his breath going in and out, and let stressful feelings float away. This simple practice helped him keep calm when performing on stage or dealing with busy schedules.

"No-one really feels self-confident deep down because it's an artificial idea. Really, people aren't that worried about what you're doing or what you're saying, so you can drift around the world relatively anonymously: you must not feel persecuted and examined. Liberate yourself from that idea that people are watching you." – Russell Brand

6.2.3: HORMESIS.
USING SHORT-TERM STRESS FOR LONGEVITY

GOOD STRESS VS. BAD STRESS

Believe it or not, not all stress is harmful. Short bursts of stress—like taking a quick cold shower or sprinting for a few seconds—can actually teach your body how to bounce back stronger (*Mattson, 2014*). It's the same principle behind lifting weights: you briefly stress the muscles, then let them recover, and they come back even stronger. This healthy, short-term type of stress is called **hormesis**—and when used wisely, it can make you more resilient over time.

FASTING FOR FOCUS

When done safely and responsibly, **intermittent fasting** can sharpen your mind and help your body better regulate blood sugar (*Longo & Mattson, 2014*). It introduces a mild stress to your cells, encouraging them to adapt and become more efficient. A lot of people say they feel more clear-headed and energized during a fast—something that might sound strange at first, but actually makes a lot of sense once your body adjusts.

Of course, fasting isn't for everyone. Always listen to your body, and definitely talk to a healthcare professional before making any big changes. Health is personal, and what works beautifully for one person might not be the right fit for another.

COLD EXPOSURE PACKS

Ever jumped into a chilly pool and felt completely awake in an instant? That's your body's natural stress response kicking in—releasing adrenaline, increasing blood flow, and even sparking a boost of dopamine, the feel-good chemical (*Shevchuk, 2008*). Cold showers, brief dips in icy water, or cold exposure packs can be a surprisingly invigorating way to train your body to handle challenges better. It's a bit uncomfortable at first, but it teaches your system that it can survive and adapt—which is exactly the kind of mental and physical resilience we want to build.

In my book **Stay Healthy, Stay Youthful - The Science of Living to 150: Cutting-Edge Longevity Science for Reversing Aging and Living a Healthier, Longer Life,** I delve much deeper into intermittent fasting and cold exposure.

KINDNESS AND DOPAMINE

The same dopamine surge that can come from cold exposure also appears when you do a random act of kindness (*Berkeley, 2019*). Positive social actions are another form of "good stress" that energizes you and uplifts your spirit. Combining short, healthy stressors like fasting or cold exposure with acts of kindness creates a strong, optimistic mindset supporting longevity. Two for one!

HEAL THROUGH CHALLENGE

Facing minor discomfort on purpose—such as skipping a meal or taking a cold shower—can build mental toughness. When you learn to adapt to small stresses, you're better prepared for bigger life hurdles. Staying resilient can help you move past old emotional wounds and see yourself as strong, adaptable, and ready for new beginnings (*Davidson & McEwen, 2012*). Tell yourself, "I've got this."

TONY ROBBINS

Tony Robbins famously takes daily cold plunges. He starts his day by jumping into cold water, shocking his system awake. **Robbins** says it's a physical jolt and a mental reminder that he can handle discomfort. This practice sets a high-energy tone for his day, helping him stay sharp and motivated—an excellent example of hormesis in action.

SECTION THREE: LAUGHTER, JOY AND COGNITIVE FLEXIBILITY

6.3.1: THE PHYSIOLOGY OF LAUGHTER

LAUGHTER AS MEDICINE

As I mentioned earlier when talking about **Norman Cousins** and his groundbreaking book, laughter really is a form of medicine. When you laugh, your body releases endorphins—those natural "feel-good" chemicals that can lift your mood and even reduce pain (*Dunbar et al., 2012*). It's like giving your nervous system a mini-vacation. Plus, a good laugh slows your heart rate, helps you breathe more deeply, and pulls extra oxygen into your system, giving your cells a refreshing boost of energy.

LAUGHTER EASES MUSCLE TENSION

If you've ever felt your shoulders drop or your mind clear after a good laugh, you're not imagining it. Laughter physically relaxes your muscles because it reduces stress hormones while increasing those feel-good brain chemicals (*Martin, 2001*). It's almost like a quick, invisible massage for your mind and body—a reset button you can press anytime you find something funny. Sure, it's not quite as luxurious as an actual massage, but it's a great start, and you can do it anytime you need a lift.

LAUGHTER BOOSTS IMMUNE FUNCTION

Believe it or not, laughing can even strengthen your immune system. Studies show that laughter increases infection-fighting antibodies in your bloodstream (*Bennett & Lengacher, 2008*). That might explain why a good sense of humor feels so comforting when you're under the weather. It's not just in your head—your body is actually supporting its own defenses while you're laughing.

SOCIAL BONDING

Sharing a laugh with someone does more than just lighten the mood—it helps build real trust and closeness. When you laugh with friends, family, or even coworkers, you naturally feel more relaxed and open with each other (*Fredrickson, 2001*). Those moments of shared joy strengthen bonds and create relationships that lift you up, helping you grow in positive ways over the long haul.

LAUGHTER IS EASY TO PRACTICE!

You don't need a professional comedian in your back pocket to get more laughter into your day. It can be as simple as watching a funny video, reading a silly story, or reminiscing about a hilarious memory with a friend. Even just recalling one of those deep, unstoppable belly laughs—the ones that leave you practically gasping for air—can bring back that incredible rush of relaxation and release. Laughter is one of the simplest, most powerful tools you have to fight negativity and lighten even the heaviest moments.

LUCILLE BALL

Lucille Ball, the famous star of *"I Love Lucy,"* was known for her comedic genius. Fans still watch her shows decades later because her laughter and slapstick moments are timeless. She often noted how humor helped her cope with the stresses of show business and personal trials, illustrating that laughter can be a dependable lifeline when life gets tense.

"One of the things I learned the hard way was that it doesn't pay to get discouraged. Keeping busy and making optimism a way of life can restore your faith in yourself." – Lucille Ball

Lucille Ball

Credit – Picryl / creativecommons.org

6.3.2: JOYFUL HABITS FOR DAILY LIFE

MORNING GRATITUDE

Each morning when I wake up, I take my dog, **Frankie**, outside to do his duty and take a deep breath of the cool morning air. It is in these moments that I find it most perfect to thank God for the opportunity to be alive yet another day and for all of my blessings, one by one.

Start your day by listing three things you're thankful for—maybe a good night's sleep, a roof over your head, or a friendly conversation you had yesterday (*Emmons & McCullough, 2003*). This simple exercise can steer your mind toward positivity, setting the stage for a better day.

LIGHT-HEARTED EXERCISE

How many people do you see frowning while grunting and groaning at the gym? It's good to put in strenuous exercise, but it doesn't have to be grim or punishing. Turn on your favorite upbeat music and dance like nobody's watching or go for a fun walk with a friend. When you enjoy your physical activity, you're more likely to keep doing it. Plus, it boosts your mood and strengthens your body all at once. At the gym, I usually have a ridiculous smile on my face. They must think I'm crazy!

MICRO-KINDNESS MOMENTS

Remember those small, everyday acts of kindness—like smiling at a stranger or holding the door open—and you'll inject bright spots into your routine. These micro-moments of positivity can build up over time, helping you feel connected to others (*Berkeley, 2019*). A single act of goodwill can ripple out, inspiring more kindness and smiles.

LAUGHTER BREAKS

Schedule short "comedy breaks." Check out a funny clip on your phone or recall a ridiculous inside joke with a friend. These tiny bursts of humor can reboot your mindset, especially when stress starts to creep in (*Martin, 2001*). Laughter breaks don't take long, but they can keep negative emotions from piling up. My children chide me and groan for telling my "dad jokes," but they always laugh (at least inside, I know they're laughing!).

HEAL THROUGH JOY

When you actively bring joy into your daily routine, handling tough conversations or past emotional pain becomes easier. Feeling upbeat often softens defenses, making it less scary to face your hurts (*Fredrickson, 2001*). Joy isn't just about being happy; it can also be a pathway to deeper healing and self-discovery.

FRED ROGERS

I can't think of a kinder persona than **Mr. Rogers**. When **Fred** was a kid, he was sometimes bullied because he was quiet and liked to play alone. He felt sad and lonely. But **Fred** decided he wanted to help other children feel better about themselves. He created a TV show where he spoke gently, sang cheerful songs, and taught important lessons about friendship, kindness, and being proud of who you are. Grown-ups loved him too, because he reminded them that everyone deserves respect and compassion. *Mr. Rogers Neighborhood* gently taught generations of children to love and respect one another and to honor their elders.

"I think everybody longs to be loved and longs to know that he or she is lovable. And, consequently, the greatest thing that we can do is to help somebody know that they're loved and capable of loving." – Fred Rogers

Fred Rogers
Credit – PICRYL / creativecommons.org

6.3.3: BUILDING COGNITIVE FLEXIBILITY THROUGH PLAY AND NOVELTY

TRY NEW THINGS

Your brain loves novelty. You spark fresh neural pathways when you pick up a new hobby—like cooking food you've never made or learning basic guitar chords—(*Park & Bischof, 2013*). This can help you stay sharp mentally while adding fun and excitement to your life. Routine is good; it supports self-discipline. But when you change things up, it keeps life fresh. **Variety is the spice of life!**

PLAYFUL FREEDOM

As I just quoted earlier in this chapter, author **Richard Bach** often wrote about how we put limits on ourselves that aren't really there. Approaching everyday things we do playfully can peel away those imaginary barriers (*Bach, 1977*). Try treating problems like puzzles you get to solve instead of chores you have to do.

Keeping a playful mindset can unlock creative solutions you might miss otherwise.

EMBRACE CURIOSITY AND NEVER COMPARE

Curiosity is the engine of mental growth. If something fascinates you, follow that spark—read articles, watch videos, and ask questions. Each new piece of knowledge or experience opens up another branch in your mental "roadmap," making you more adaptable (*Kashdan & Steger, 2007*). Keep your wonder alive, and you'll stay flexible.

Remember also, **comparison is the first step to unhappiness.** One person might look at you with envy as if you have everything, and another person may look down their nose at you as if you are a peasant. Bugs look at you as if you are a giant, and whales might think you are a bug. Always come from kindness and don't covet anything anyone else has. It's not worth it. Whether you're comparing yourself to someone else or it's being done to you, it makes you either envious or the subject of someone else's envy. Celebrate other people's successes, especially your friends, be happy for them, and surely it will come back to you tenfold.

USE NOVELTY TO HEAL

Sometimes, a new experience can help you reframe an old hurt. Travel to a new place, learn a new dance or try a sport you've never attempted. Focusing on what's fresh and exciting gives your brain a chance to step away from negative thought loops. This can soften painful memories and give you a fresh sense of possibility.

SMALL ACTS OF KINDNESS SPARK CREATIVITY

Doing something thoughtful for another person can jump-start your creative thinking. When you feel good about helping others, you're more willing to explore new solutions and take healthy risks (*Berkeley, 2019*). In a way, generosity cracks open your mind, making embracing new ideas easier and adapting to life's twists and turns.

ALBERT EINSTEIN

Einstein once said, *"I have no special talents. I am only passionately curious."* He followed his curiosity wherever it led, leading to groundbreaking physics theories. By keeping a playful, open mind, **Einstein** came up with ideas that changed how we see the universe. His story shows how cognitive flexibility and a willingness to explore the unknown can spark remarkable breakthroughs. Embrace a growth mindset, learn how to manage stress, and welcome laughter and play into your life. These acts will activate the natural power of your brain to adapt and grow. Remember: every act of kindness, every new skill you try, and every time you laugh can literally help rewire your mind for better health and a brighter future. Small, consistent steps add up to major transformations. I hope this chapter inspires you to take those steps with optimism and excitement for what lies ahead.

Strengthening our mindset and neural pathways sets the stage for daily routines that enhance both our physical and emotional well-being.

"Creativity is just connecting things. When you ask creative people how they did something, they feel a little guilty because they didn't really do it, they just saw something. It seemed obvious to them after a while. That's because they were able to connect experiences they've had and synthesize new things." — Steve Jobs

CHAPTER SEVEN
DAILY HABITS, ROUTINES, AND NUTRITION THAT FUEL POSITIVE LIVING

If you're waking up each day feeling tired and grouchy, you're not doing yourself any favors. Here, we'll explore how daily habits—like morning rituals, exercise routines, and accountability practices—can lift your mood, strengthen your body, and even help heal old emotional wounds.

SECTION ONE:
MORNING RITUALS AND SLEEP HYGIENE

7.1.1: GENTLE WAKE-UPS TO HEAL YOUR INNER CHILD

EMBRACE A PEACEFUL START

Growing up with an abusive, alcoholic parent made my childhood rough. For a long time, until I worked on healing my inner child, emotional roadblocks kept popping up in my relationships. One of the most healing changes I made was learning to start my mornings in a calm, nurturing way. Instead of grabbing my phone the second I woke up, I gave myself a few minutes to stretch gently, breathe deeply, or put on some soft music. Research shows that easing into your day like this can lower stress hormones and help stabilize your mood (*Morgan, 2003*). Treating yourself with kindness first thing in the morning sets a gentle, steady tone that often lasts all day.

MORNING GRATITUDE CHECK

One of the simplest but most powerful habits you can build is a morning gratitude check. As soon as you wake up, think of—or even better, jot down—three things you're grateful for. This tiny practice shifts your focus onto the good things in life and helps create a healthier emotional foundation (*Emmons & McCullough, 2003*). Even if you know you're about to face challenges that day, starting off with gratitude reminds you that there are bright spots everywhere, if you're willing to look.

LIGHT HYDRATION AND A HEALTHY BREAKFAST

After a night's sleep, your body is thirsty for water and energy. Drinking a glass of water right when you wake up can jump-start your metabolism and clear out mental fog. Pair that with a balanced breakfast—something like oatmeal with berries—and you'll help stabilize your blood sugar and feed your brain for better focus and energy (*Gómez-Pinilla, 2008*). Think of breakfast not just as food, but as essential fuel to launch you into a sharper, more energized day.

7.1.2: CALM TRANSITIONS FOR BETTER SLEEP

A good morning actually starts the night before. Giving yourself a peaceful wind-down routine—maybe with calming music, a warm bath, or turning off bright screens—helps you fall asleep faster and wake up feeling rested (*Morgan, 2003*). If you struggle with sleep, it's better to avoid relying on pills, alcohol, or drugs. A small, gentle dose of melatonin might be a safer option to support your body's natural rhythms. Building this gentle cycle of restful nights and peaceful mornings is one of the best gifts you can give yourself.

Of course, it's not always that easy. When I was a young parent, I worked nights as a musician, getting home late and still trying to be up early to help my kids get ready for school. Sometimes I had to sleep in shifts. It wasn't perfect, but because I loved my work and loved my children, I found a way to make it feel joyful instead of exhausting.

We all chase money because we think it will buy us happiness. And for a lot of us, especially at certain times in life, we have to do jobs we don't love just to survive. But if you find yourself stuck and miserable, it might be time to rethink your path. Life is too short to spend most of it doing something that drains you. When I was younger, I asked myself: **What does success really mean to me?** And my answer was simple: When I reach a point where I spend more of my life doing what I **want** to do—and less time just doing what I **have** to do to survive—that's when I've truly made it.

Getting good sleep, winding down peacefully at night, and waking up gently the next morning—it all stacks up. Each small choice leads you a little closer to a calmer, happier, and more fulfilled life.

DOLLY PARTON

Dolly Parton said that she wakes up early to spend quiet time thinking, reading, and even songwriting. Known for her warm, optimistic personality, Dolly has often shared how she values peaceful mornings, gratitude, and self-reflection before a busy day of performing or running her businesses. Her experience shows that starting with calm, loving self-care can set a positive tone that carries you long after sunrise.

"You can be rich in spirit, kindness, love, and all those things that you can't put a dollar sign on." - Dolly Parton

Dolly Parton
Credit – Wikimedia Commons

7.1.3: RANDOM ACTS OF KINDNESS IN THE MORNING

Even though I was tired, I loved waking up with my kids and nurturing them with breakfast and love, sending them to school with smiles. Including a small act of kindness as part of your morning routine can have a ripple effect on your day. Maybe you send a positive text to someone who needs it or quickly volunteer to take out a neighbor's trash. These small gestures release "feel-good" chemicals in your brain (*Berkeley, 2019*), helping you feel more cheerful and connected before you even leave the house.

SECTION TWO:
MOVEMENT AND EXERCISE FOR BRAIN HEALTH

7.2.1: START WITH SIMPLE MOVEMENTS

STROLL BEFORE SCROLL

Instead of reaching for your phone the second you wake up, try stepping outside—or even just pacing your hallway—for a quick stroll. A few minutes of gentle movement gets your blood flowing and clears out those early-morning mental cobwebs (*Hillman, Erickson, & Kramer, 2008*). It's like a natural wake-up call for your entire body, no caffeine needed. Personally, I love my morning walks. They feel almost meditative—giving me a chance to breathe in the fresh air, clear my mind, and set a positive tone for the day ahead.

MINDFUL STRETCHING

After your stroll, add a few easy stretches—nothing fancy, just rolling your shoulders, reaching for the sky, or stretching your arms wide. Simple, mindful movement like this can help loosen up tight muscles and lift your mood (*Field,*

2011). It's also a quiet reminder to reconnect with your body instead of diving headfirst into the chaos of the day. Stretching out first thing is like giving yourself a small gift: a calm, centered start that helps shake off any leftover tension from sleep. I notice that my dog stretches his entire body first thing every morning! It's instinctive for him and it should be for us too.

7.2.2: HEALING THROUGH PLAY

Remember how much fun it was to play tag or jump rope when you were a kid? You can tap into that same playful spirit now, and it's good for you! Adding activities like dancing around the kitchen, tossing a frisbee, or even hula-hooping can turn exercise into pure joy (*Fredrickson, 2001*). When you keep things lighthearted, you naturally lower your stress hormones and remind yourself that moving your body doesn't have to feel like a chore. It can feel like recess all over again.

BRAIN-BOOSTING BENEFITS

Exercise doesn't just strengthen your muscles—it sharpens your brain, too. Physical activity has been linked to better memory, sharper focus, and even the growth of new brain cells (*Hillman, Erickson, & Kramer, 2008*). Every time you move your body, you're giving a beautiful gift to your future self—boosting both your mental sharpness and emotional health. It's a small investment today that can pay off in clearer thinking and better resilience down the road.

INCLUDE ACTS OF KINDNESS IN YOUR ROUTINE

Here's a simple bonus tip: If you're heading to the gym or taking a fitness class, bring a friend who could use a lift—or offer a kind word to someone who looks like they're struggling. Studies show that acts of kindness can boost dopamine for both you and the person you help (*Berkeley, 2019*). When you weave encouragement and support into your exercise routine, you're not just building a stronger body—you're also building a stronger, more positive community around you. And that's the kind of strength that truly lasts.

DWAYNE "THE ROCK" JOHNSON

Dwayne "The Rock" Johnson is famous for his early-morning workout routine, which often starts before most people wake up. In spite of his busy schedule, **Johnson** never misses his exercise sessions. He credits this discipline for keeping his mind focused and his spirit strong. Because he pairs dedication with a friendly, upbeat attitude, **The Rock** shows how a consistent movement routine can power both physical fitness and mental health.

> *"I like to use the hard times in the past to motivate me today."*
> *- Dwayne 'The Rock' Johnson*

Dwayne Johnson
Credit – Wikimedia Commons

SECTION THREE: CONSISTENCY, HABIT STACKING AND ACCOUNTABILITY

7.3.1: THE POWER OF CONSISTENCY

SMALL DAILY WINS

Doing something good for yourself every day—even if it's just for five minutes—can add up to some pretty incredible changes over time.

Research shows that **consistency** is often more important than intensity *(Lally et al., 2010)*. You don't have to do huge things to grow. Whether it's writing a few sentences in your journal, practicing a skill, or simply taking a mindful breath, those small daily wins build real momentum. It's like watering a plant: a little bit each day helps it grow strong and healthy.

HABIT STACKING

One simple trick that really works is called **habit stacking**—linking a new habit to something you already do. For example, if you make coffee every morning, use that moment to read one page from an inspiring book. Since you're already brewing the coffee, adding something positive alongside it feels natural and easy *(Clear, 2018)*. It's a smooth, low-pressure way to weave new behaviors into your life without feeling overwhelmed. The easier it feels, the more likely you are to stick with it!

ACCOUNTABILITY PARTNERS

Sometimes, even the most motivated among us need a little backup. That's where an **accountability partner** comes in—a friend, coworker, or family member who helps you stay on track. Checking in regularly or doing activities together can boost your motivation and make the whole process a lot more fun *(Cohen & Wills, 1985)*. It's like having a built-in cheerleader and teammate rolled into one.

My father leaned heavily on his sponsor when he first worked the steps of *Alcoholics Anonymous*, and it made all the difference. Having someone to confide in and keep you accountable can be a powerful force for change.

7.3.2: HEALING YOUR INNER CHILD THROUGH SUPPORT

A lot of us carry childhood memories where we felt alone, misunderstood, or unsupported. Finding a mentor or a supportive partner later in life can help heal those old wounds. When someone believes in you today, it's like telling your inner child: **It's safe to try, to stumble, and to grow without fear of judgment** (*Worthington & Scherer, 2004*). That emotional safety net builds the confidence you may have missed early on. And once your inner child feels healed and safe, you're free to experience life with more joy, courage, and resilience.

RANDOM ACTS OF KINDNESS AS A ROUTINE

When I first met my **Robin**, I was blown away by how naturally she made kindness part of her daily life. Every single day, she looked for ways to make someone's life better—and then she just showed up and did it. Before meeting her, I'd done thoughtful things here and there, but I wasn't nearly as **proactive**. **Robin**, on the other hand, built a whole world of friendships and goodwill around her because of that daily kindness

Why not **schedule** random acts of kindness into your week? Pick a day—like every Friday—to send a thoughtful text, drop off a little gift, or write a thank-you note to someone. Research backs it up: small acts of generosity lift your mood and help cement positive habits (*Berkeley, 2019*). Kindness, when made a routine, weaves generosity right into the rhythm of your life.

> *"For beautiful eyes, look for the good in others; for beautiful lips, speak only words of kindness; and for poise, walk with the knowledge that you are never alone." – Audrey Hepburn*

CHAPTER EIGHT
NUTRITION, GUT HEALTH, AND EMOTIONAL WELL-BEING

In this section, we'll explore how the food and drinks we consume can affect our body, mind, and emotions. We'll take a closer look at the gut-brain connection, how fasting might help us live longer, and why staying hydrated and getting the right vitamins can boost our mood.

SECTION ONE: THE GUT-BRAIN AXIS
8.1.1: THE "SECOND BRAIN" IN YOUR BELLY

Scientists often call the gut our "second brain," and for good reason. It's packed with its own network of nerves and constantly sends signals up to our main brain (*Mayer, Tillisch, & Gupta, 2015*). This means the food you eat isn't just fueling your muscles—it's influencing your mood, stress levels, and even how optimistic you feel. Your gut and your mind are much more connected than most people realize.

EMOTIONAL HIGHWAY

Picture your gut and brain like two busy cities connected by a superhighway. Messages are constantly traveling back and forth. When your gut is healthy and balanced, it sends positive signals that can lift your mood. But if your gut is upset or out of balance, it can actually contribute to feelings of anxiety, sadness, or mental fog (*Bercik & Collins, 2014*). Keeping that emotional highway clear and flowing in the right direction makes a real difference in how you feel day to day.

FRIENDLY MICROBES

Inside your gut live trillions of tiny organisms called microbes. Many of these are helpful little workers that break down food, support digestion, and even produce important chemicals like serotonin—the "feel good" neurotransmitter that plays a big role in mood regulation. When these friendly microbes are thriving, it can lead to clearer thinking and a much calmer mindset.

8.1.2: EAT FOR EMOTIONAL HEALTH

One of the best ways to support those good gut microbes is through what you eat. Foods rich in fiber—like fruits, veggies, and whole grains—feed the helpful bacteria that keep your gut (and your mind) in a healthy place (Gómez-Pinilla, 2008). On the flip side, diets heavy in sugar and processed foods can throw your gut off balance—and when your gut suffers, your mood often follows. In my book **Vitamins, Supplements, and Herbs for Health and Longevity: Boost Your Immunity, Increase Energy, and Feel Younger in Minutes a Day,** I dive deeper into the best supplements to support a happy, healthy gut.

DOPAMINE BOOSTERS

Certain foods can even give your mood a little extra lift. Nutrients found in things like nuts, seeds, and dark chocolate help support dopamine pathways in the brain (*Cohen, 2018*). Since dopamine is linked to feelings of motivation and pleasure, eating foods that naturally support it can leave you feeling more energized and ready to tackle the day.

HIPPOCRATES

More than 2,000 years ago, Hippocrates said, **"All disease begins in the gut."** Modern science continues to prove how right he was. He encouraged people to focus on eating fresh, whole foods to keep both their bodies and their spirits strong. When you take care of your gut, you're taking care of your entire well-being.

"Let food be thy medicine and medicine be thy food." – Hippocrates

Hippocrates
Credit – Wikimedia Commons

SECTION TWO:
FASTING, CALORIE RESTRICTION AND LONGEVITY
8.2.1: SHORT BURSTS OF CONTROLLED FASTING

GIVE YOUR BODY A BREAK

Fasting doesn't have to mean going days without eating. Even small changes—like skipping breakfast a couple of times a week or spacing your meals farther apart—can give your body a much-needed break from constant digestion (*Longo & Mattson, 2014*). When you do this safely, your cells get time to rest, repair, and recharge, often leaving you feeling more energized overall.

HORMESIS: THE GOOD STRESS

Think of fasting a bit like a short workout. When you run or lift weights, you're stressing your muscles just enough to make them stronger. Fasting can have a similar effect on your cells—introducing a little bit of **"good stress"** called hormesis (*Mattson, 2014*). Over time, your body becomes more resilient and better able to handle challenges.

EMOTIONAL RESET

Some people also notice that fasting doesn't just clear out their bodies—it clears their minds, too. When done carefully, short fasting windows can encourage your body to produce brain-supporting chemicals that help stabilize your mood (*Longo & Mattson, 2014*). It's not just about feeling lighter physically—you may also feel lighter emotionally.

8.2.2: CALORIE RESTRICTION FOR LONGEVITY

Beyond fasting, eating fewer calories overall—while still making sure you get all your essential nutrients—has been linked to longer lifespans in many studies (*Fontana & Partridge, 2015*). Moderate calorie restriction may help support healthier aging, protect against disease, and maintain better energy levels as you get older. If you're curious about how to approach this safely and smartly, I explore it more deeply in my book, **"The Ultimate AI Diet - Consolidating the Best Diets Over the Last 100 Years."**

TIES TO DOPAMINE AND MOOD

Interestingly, both fasting and smart calorie control can influence dopamine, too. By regulating your food intake, you can help steady your energy, balance your appetite, and even experience fewer mood crashes throughout the day (*Cohen, 2018*). It's another way that the mind and body are beautifully, powerfully linked.

DR. DAVID SINCLAIR

David Sinclair, the scientist at *Harvard University* we mentioned a couple other times in the book, studies aging and how to slow it down. He practices intermittent fasting and a low-calorie diet to boost his energy and health. **Sinclair** believes these habits could help people live healthier, longer lives. Controlled calorie intake and fasting aren't just fads—they might be powerful tools for better living. Always remember, anything you do to your body like fasting should be supervised by a licensed medical professional. Everyone has different levels of health and metabolism. I practice intermittent fasting four days a week, eating in a window between 10:00AM and 6:00PM, and I never experience hunger pangs I can't handle. I cover **Dr. Sinclair's** work in detail in my book **Stay Healthy, Stay Youthful: The Science of Living to 150.**

> *"You want to shock the body and not be constant. Intermittent fasting is an increasingly popular way: Skip breakfast, for example. Also, lifting weights, losing your breath from exercise, and alternating between hot and cold temperatures. We think these measures will only get us to 100 to 122 years old. That's our natural lifespan."* - Dr. David Sinclair

SECTION THREE:
HYDRATION, VITAMINS AND SUPPLEMENTS
8.3.1: HYDRATION FOR A HAPPY MIND

DRINK UP FOR MENTAL CLARITY

Our brains comprise a lot of water, so staying hydrated is key for clear thinking and good moods (*Popkin, D'Anci, & Rosenberg, 2010*). Even slight dehydration can lead to crankiness and tiredness. Keep a water bottle close to sip throughout the day. Watch what you're hydrating with, though! A one-liter bottle of *Coke* has roughly **106 grams** of sugar. Choose clean, filtered water first and foremost. And remember... you can actually drink too much water, so stay hydrated but don't drown your system. If you're on a regimen that includes lots of water, pace your intake over the course of the day and evening.

ESSENTIAL VITAMINS FOR EMOTION

Vitamins like B12 and folate can play a significant role in mood regulation. If levels drop too low, you might feel more anxious or sad (*Bottiglieri, 2002*).

Eating leafy greens, beans, and fortified cereals can help maintain a balanced supply.

SUPPLEMENTS AND BRAIN FUNCTION

Supplements like omega-3 fatty acids (found in fish oil) are great for you and might support mental health by improving communication between brain cells. Always check with a doctor to ensure you're taking the right amount and type (*Sublette et al., 2011*). Remember, fish oil is a blood thinner, so if you're on blood thinning drugs, make sure this works for you before you take it. Once again, for a deeper dive into these and other supplements for health and longevity, check out my book **Vitamins, Supplements, and Herbs for Health and Longevity: Boost Your Immunity, Increase Energy, and Feel Younger in Minutes a Day.**

8.3.2: DOPAMINE RECEPTOR SENSITIVITY

Certain minerals—like magnesium—may help fine-tune dopamine receptor function in the brain (*Cohen, 2018*). Getting enough of these nutrients through food or supplements can keep your motivation and mood steady, especially on busy days.

BALANCE, DON'T OVERDO

While vitamins and supplements can help, more isn't always better. Too much of some vitamins can lead to unwanted side effects. Think of supplements as a bridge to fill gaps, not a replacement for a well-rounded diet (*Popkin, D'Anci, & Rosenberg, 2010*). I shouldn't talk. I'm a supplement freak, but I do check to make sure I'm not taking too many of supplements that could harm me in great amounts.

SERENA WILLIAMS

Known for her incredible tennis career, **Serena Williams** pays close attention to hydration and nutrition to keep her energy high and her mind focused. She talks a lot about drinking plenty of water and eating nutrient-dense foods like vegetables and lean proteins. Approaching her nutrition this way supports her intense training schedule and emotional resilience under pressure. **Serena** also keeps a positive attitude, which she developed over a period of time.

> *"I love who I am, and I encourage other people to love and embrace who they are. But it definitely wasn't easy - it took me a while."*
> *- Serena Williams*

Care for your gut, explore safe ways to fast and focus on hydration and key nutrients. In doing so, you can sharpen your mind and lift your spirits. Small daily changes in what you eat or drink can lead to big improvements in how you feel—both physically and emotionally. Remember: a happier, healthier body often starts with the simple choices you make at mealtime, and these choices can make your life fuller of positivity and vitality.

Serena Williams
Credit – Wikimedia Commons

CHAPTER NINE
SPIRITUALITY, PURPOSE, AND THE POWER OF COMMUNITY

In this chapter, we'll explore how having a sense of purpose, embracing comforting traditions, and forming meaningful connections can boost our emotional well-being and even support a longer, happier life. We'll dive into the Japanese idea of **Ikigai,** learn about the Danish concept of **Hygge,** the Indian concept of **Dharma**, the Swedish art of **Lagom**; we'll look at faith and belief systems, and discover how helping our communities can brighten our own spirits.

SECTION ONE:
DISCOVERING YOUR INNER PURPOSE
9.1.1: IKAGAI AND FINDING YOUR "WHY"

WHAT IS IKIGAI?

In Japan, **ikigai** loosely means your "reason for being." It's that special blend of doing what you love, what you're good at, and finding ways to help the world (*García & Miralles, 2017*). When you wake up genuinely excited for the day ahead, that little spark you feel—that's your ikigai in action. You don't need some massive, life-changing goal to feel ikigai. It can be as simple as tending your garden, teaching a friend piano, or doing anything small that brings joy and purpose into your daily life. Little by little, these passions shift your focus toward the positive.

Ikigai also reminds us that what we do matters beyond ourselves. Helping others—whether it's making dinner for someone or lending a hand—can lift your self-esteem and lower stress (*Steptoe & Fancourt, 2019*). Feeling useful gives life a real sense of meaning. A big part of ikigai is staying curious. When you keep learning new skills and exploring new interests, you stay flexible, resilient, and hopeful about what's ahead. Curiosity feeds optimism!

HEALTH BENEFITS

Many Okinawans, famous for living long and healthy lives, say ikigai is one of their secrets (*Buettner, 2010*). Chasing meaningful goals doesn't just make you happier—it can actually lower stress hormones and support longevity.

9.1.2: DHARMA: HOW TO TREAT YOURSELF AND OTHERS

PERSONAL AND UNIVERSAL

Dharma is a little different from strict rules—it's about finding your own personal path. It could mean being a kind neighbor, a loyal friend, or a hardworking student (Klostermaier, 2007). Your unique combination of roles becomes your Dharma.

Living your Dharma means syncing your daily actions with deeper values like compassion, honesty, and service. It's about closing the gap between who you are and how you live. When you're living your Dharma, you feel peaceful inside. It's not about chasing external rewards—it's about knowing deep down you're doing what's right for you (*Vivekananda, 1989*).

ADAPTING THROUGH LIFE STAGES

Your Dharma isn't set in stone. As life changes, so do your roles and responsibilities. Maybe it's learning when you're young, raising a family later, and mentoring others later still. Dharma grows as you do.

STEVE JOBS

Steve Jobs, co-founder of Apple, spoke often about loving what you do. He believed finding personal meaning in your work and life was the key to staying motivated. Although he didn't use the words "ikigai" or "dharma," his idea that you should keep searching until you find your true passion closely matches the spirit of these ancient principles.

"Your work is going to fill a large part of your life, and the only way to be truly satisfied is to do what you believe is great work. And the only way to do great work is to love what you do. If you haven't found it yet, keep looking. Don't settle. As with all matters of the heart, you'll know when you find it." - Steve Jobs

Steve Jobs
Credit – FLICKR / creativecommons.org

SECTION TWO: THE ART OF HAPPINESS
9.2.1: HYGGE - THE DANISH CONCEPT OF HAPPINESS
COZY COMFORT AND SIMPLE PLEASURES

Hygge (pronounced "hoo-gah") is all about creating cozy, warm, content moments (*Wiking, 2016*). Think soft blankets, glowing candles, a good book, or warm drinks shared with friends—anything that feels comforting and safe. You can create hygge at home by dimming the lights, lighting some candles, or playing soft music. And yes, if you've got a significant other, it's pretty romantic, too! Hygge teaches you to savor small pleasures. It's not about having more— it's about enjoying one really good cup of tea or one warm conversation, deeply and fully. Hygge shines brightest when shared. Inviting friends over for a relaxed evening can boost everyone's mood and create lasting, meaningful connections (*Helliwell, Layard, & Sachs, 2021*).

DAILY MOMENTS OF JOY

You don't need a special event to feel hygge. Watching the sunset, pulling on a favorite cozy sweater, or even just breathing deeply in a quiet moment can bring that gentle happiness into your day.

9.2.2: LAGOM - THE SWEDISH ART OF BALANCE, MODERATION, AND CONTENTMENT

Lagom is a Swedish philosophy meaning "not too much, not too little"—just enough (*Dunne, 2017*). This sounds like the **Goldilocks** story to me! But seriously, it's about balance in everything, from work hours to how much stuff you keep around the house. Lagom encourages simpler routines, less clutter, and learning to appreciate what you already have. When you live this way, peace of mind naturally follows.

It's also about being mindful of your community and environment—sharing resources and looking out for each other whenever you can. Lagom teaches that steady happiness—not big highs and crashing lows—comes from small, mindful choices. Even people managing bipolar disorder sometimes practice lagom principles to help balance their lives.

FOSTERING INNER CALM

Lagom isn't about strict rules—it's about feeling your way to balance. Maybe it's trimming down your wardrobe, or taking more breaks during the day. Either way, it's a reminder that happiness often shows up when you know when enough is enough.

MEIK WIKING

Meik Wiking, a Danish happiness researcher, wrote *The Little Book of Hygge*. He popularized this concept worldwide, showing people how small comforts—

like soft lighting, good company, and heartfelt conversations—can lead to lasting happiness. His work reminds us that we can find moments of warmth and peace even in a hectic world.

"Gratitude is more than just a simple "thank you" when you receive a gift. It is about remembering that you live right now, allowing yourself to focus on the moment and appreciate the life you lead, and focusing on all that you do have, not what you don't. Cliches? Totally." - Meik Wiking

SECTION THREE: SERVICE, FAITH, MEDITATION AND BELIEF SYSTEMS
9.3.1: INNER PEACE THROUGH REFLECTION

FAITH AND WELL-BEING
It turns out that having some kind of faith—whether it's through organized religion or a personal belief system—can do wonders for your mental and physical health. Many studies show that spiritual faith is linked to longer lifespans and greater emotional resilience (*Koenig, 2012*). When tough times hit, faith can act like an anchor, giving you hope and comfort when you need it most.

MEDITATION FOR CLARITY
You don't need to be a monk on a mountaintop to meditate. Meditation can be as simple as closing your eyes for a few minutes and focusing on your breath. Even small daily sessions can calm your mind and help you manage stress better (*Creswell, Eisenberger, & Lieberman, 2008*). Think of it as a reset button you can press anytime you feel overwhelmed.

9.3.2: SHARED BELIEF SYSTEMS
Finding a group of people who share your spiritual views can create powerful emotional support. It's not just about the belief itself—it's about the deep friendships and sense of belonging that often come along with it. Feeling connected makes navigating life's ups and downs a whole lot easier.

MINDFUL LIVING
Mindfulness doesn't have to happen only during formal meditation. You can practice mindfulness during the simplest tasks—washing dishes, walking your

dog, sipping your morning coffee. Fully paying attention to the moment invites a sense of calm and lowers everyday anxiety.

HEALTHY DOPAMINE PATHWAYS

Practices like prayer or daily gratitude don't just lift your spirits emotionally—they actually help regulate the dopamine systems in your brain (*Cohen, 2018*). When you focus on hope and gratitude, you naturally strengthen your motivation, emotional balance, and overall outlook on life.

DALAI LAMA

The **Dalai Lama,** a well-known Tibetan spiritual leader, teaches compassion and mindfulness as keys to inner peace. He has shown how daily meditation and positive thinking can help people handle stress and find joy. His life offers a powerful example of how faith and thoughtful habits can bring calm, even in challenging circumstances.

"Happiness is not something ready made. It comes from your own actions." – Dalai Lama

Dalai Lama
Credit – Wikimedia Commons

9.3.3: COMMUNITY ENGAGEMENT AND ACTS OF SERVICE

WHY COMMUNITY MATTERS

We're wired to connect. Feeling part of a community boosts our moods and deepens our sense of purpose (*Van Willigen, 2000*). Getting involved—whether through volunteering or joining a group—can create bonds that keep us resilient and motivated.

ACTS OF SERVICE

Doing small, thoughtful things for others—like delivering groceries to a neighbor—can give you an immediate emotional lift. It's because acts of service activate "feel-good" chemicals in your brain (*Cohen, 2018*). Helping others actually helps you, too!

SHARED GOALS AND GROUP ENERGY

When you team up with others on a project—building a garden, planning a fundraiser—you tap into a special kind of energy. Everyone's strengths feed into the project, and every small success fuels even bigger ones.

I experienced this personally when I started performing at a church in Palm Desert, California in the late 1980s. What began as a simple job turned into a strong community of friends who embraced me and my children. This "village" of loving people became particularly important to me and my kids after my wife passed away. In those moments of grief, the power of community became real to me in a way I'll never forget.

FINDING MENTORS AND ALLIES

Communities aren't just about friendships—they're about finding people to learn from, too. Mentors can share wisdom and help guide you through tough stretches, while allies offer encouragement when doubt sneaks in.

When I was twelve, right after my parents' divorce, my uncle **Guy Weismantel** took the time to visit me. He had a busy life, but he spent that weekend just hanging out with me, showing me I mattered. That simple act of kindness left a lasting impact on a very vulnerable boy.

MAINTAINING YOUR OWN SELF-RELIANCE

Equally as important as the power of community is the need for us to be self-reliant. The strongest communities contain people who can take care of themselves first; they have the strength to take care of others then. Self-reliance, the ability to take charge of your health and well-being, is extremely important for living a longer, healthier life. The simple act of making informed decisions about your diet, exercise, and lifestyle helps you reduce stress, boost confidence, and improve mental health, lowering anxiety levels. Within a community, self-reliance doesn't mean going it alone—it's about knowing when to seek support while maintaining independence. Research, including a 2025 study in *Behavioral Medicine*, shows strong social connections can reduce mortality risk by 30%, enhancing heart health and emotional well-being. When we strike a balance between self-sufficiency and community engagement, we create a supportive network that fosters both individual and collective well-being, paving the way for a vibrant, fulfilling life.

LONG-TERM HEALTH BENEFITS

The perks of community service go far beyond the feel-good moment. Research shows that people who regularly help others tend to have lower stress, stronger mental health, and even longer lives (*Van Willigen, 2000*). Kindness really does come full circle—by lifting others, we lift ourselves.

MOTHER TERESA

Mother Teresa dedicated her entire life to serving the poor and sick in Calcutta, India. Through her organization, the *Missionaries of Charity*, she showed how acts of love and kindness can heal both those in need and the person giving the help. Her compassion and commitment to community engagement remain powerful models for a life focused on service.

"If we have no peace, it is because we have forgotten that we belong to each other." – Mother Teresa

Mother Teresa
Credit – Wikimedia Commons

When you explore your Ikigai or Dharma, embrace warm moments of Hygge and Lagom, find strength in faith and mindfulness, and engage in acts of service, you can nourish your spirit and mind.

These practices lift you up, spark joy, and help you form meaningful bonds that support a fulfilling and possibly longer life. Doing this inner work will help you to stay positive and thrive every season.

CHAPTER TEN
DESIGNING YOUR PERSONAL BLUEPRINT FOR LIFELONG POSITIVE THINKING

Congratulations on reaching the final chapter! By now, you've seen how a positive mindset, daily habits, and emotional well-being can add years to your life. In this chapter, we'll review what we've learned and put all those ideas into practice by creating a roadmap for a long and fulfilling future. Think of this as your personal "blueprint" for continued growth, healing, and happiness. We'll cover how to form a clear vision, develop a solid action plan, keep your energy high, and even use new AI tools to support your journey. Let's dive in!

I WANT TO OFFER YOU A FREE GIFT

I hope you're loving this book so far. In my **HEALTH AND LONGEVITY SERIES,** I address slowing aging, vitamins and supplements for longevity, an excellent AI diet and weight management plan, how positive thinking can add years to your life (this book), and the power of your mind and body. Before we get into crafting your own personalized lifelong positive thinking blueprint, I've also created a **TWELVE-STEP ACTION PLAN FOR LONGEVITY AND HEALTHSPAN**, a roadmap for health and longevity encompassing elements from **all** my books, and I want to share it with you.

If you want a free copy of my plan, email us at…

<<   **modernrenaissancepublishing@gmail.com**   >>

with the subject line **12-STEP ACTION PLAN FOR LONGEVITY,** and I'll email you back a free copy at no obligation whatsoever to you as a heartfelt thanks for reading this book. Or you can access it through our website at **https://www.modernrenaissancepublishing.com**.

In this book, I've outlined how a growing body of research shows that positive thinking truly can boost longevity and vitality (*Levy et al., 2002*). Combine uplifting thoughts with consistent daily habits—like early morning gratitude, physical movement, and acts of kindness—and you'll have a powerful advantage in mental and physical health. It's not just about living longer; it's about feeling more alive every single day.

Imagine plotting a trip on a map. You pick a destination, plan each stop, and pack your essentials. Designing your personal blueprint for lifelong positive thinking is similar. You decide what goals matter most, then schedule small steps to get there—while making room for rest, fun, and self-care. Adding tools like AI apps for tracking mood or suggesting healthy choices allows you to stay on course, even when life gets hectic.

SECTION ONE:
CRAFTING YOUR VISION FOR THE FUTURE
10.1.1: ENVISIONING YOUR LIFE STORY

MAP OUT YOUR GOALS

I once read a story about a man with a magic camera. When he took your picture, the camera would show you what you would look like in five years. He took it to a school, and as he took photos of the children, they squealed with delight and wonder at how they would look in 5 years.

But one child had a blank photo. The child cried with fear and anguish. Did the camera not work for the child, or would the child not be on earth still in five years? This story reminds me first of how precious life is and, next, that we should live each day to its fullest because we all are not guaranteed tomorrow.

"Never leave that till tomorrow which you can do today." – Ben Franklin
Still, it's important to consider where you want to be in five, ten, or even twenty years. Write down your goals—both big and small. According to studies on goal-setting, people who clearly define their objectives are way more likely to achieve them (*Locke & Latham, 2006*). The mystery of tomorrow's story will be written by your thoughts and actions, adding a bit of fate.

Some people find it helpful to create vision boards with pictures or words that represent their dreams. Daily reminders can spark motivation and keep you focused on what truly matters—whatever it takes for you. The main thing is to have a vision.

10.1.2: EMOTIONAL ANCHORS
A future vision isn't just about what you want to do; it's about how you want to feel. Include words like "peaceful," "energetic," or "courageous" to remind you of the emotional states you're aiming for. Google "power words," and you'll find more.

WALT DISNEY
Walt Disney famously said, *"If you can dream it, you can do it."* He started with small sketches of a mouse character and built a worldwide empire of creativity and wonder. His journey reminds us that a big dream can spark endless enthusiasm—and that each of us has the power to design our own magical future.

"All of our dreams can come true if we have the courage to pursue them."
- Walt Disney

Walt Disney
Credit – Wikimedia Commons

HEALING THE INNER CHILD
Take a moment to think about what made you smile as a kid—maybe drawing, dancing, or simply exploring the outdoors. Including those activities in your

present and future plans can help you heal old wounds and stay connected to joy (*Van der Kolk, 2014*).   **Dr. Tom Costa** talked about a revelation he had in his 40s. He said that his parents had both died and yet he was still blaming them for things that happened to him when he was young. He realized how ridiculous that was and immediately went to work on healing his inner child, once and for all.

SECTION TWO: CREATING A PERSONAL ACTION PLAN

This section starts with a caveat. A saying goes something like this: ***If you want to make God laugh, tell Him what you're doing tomorrow.*** Face it: some things are beyond our control. Many times, I've found that although things didn't turn out the way I planned them, some extenuating circumstances actually made the end result more favorable for me. Still, we need to plan ahead. Remember some other old sayings: ***Trust in God but keep your gunpowder dry (or… trust in God, but cut the cards)!***

10.2.1: FROM DREAMS TO DAILY STEPS

BREAK DOWN YOUR GOALS

If you're thinking you want to run a marathon, start by jogging for just five minutes a day. Research on habit formation shows that small, consistent actions build momentum (*Fogg, 2019*).

> *"A journey of a thousand miles begins with a single step."* - Lao Tsu

HABIT STACKING

As I outlined earlier, attach a new, positive habit to something you already do. For instance, if you brew coffee every morning, spend those few minutes writing one sentence in a gratitude journal or mentally going through your blessings one by one (*Clear, 2018*).

PRACTICE KINDNESS REGULARLY

Acts of kindness uplift others and release feel-good chemicals like dopamine in your brain (Cohen, 2018). Schedule **at least one kind act daily**—like sending a cheerful text or helping a neighbor. This is the most fun of all steps because it spreads joy.

REWARD YOURSELF

Celebrate small wins, whether completing a week of daily stretches or tackling that intimidating closet.   Pat yourself on the back with a fun reward—like a bubble bath or a new audiobook—to keep your motivation high.

RICHARD BRANSON

Richard Branson, the founder of the *Virgin Group*, often talks about turning big dreams into bite-sized tasks. He breaks down his visions into clear, daily to-dos. By celebrating small wins—like securing a partnership—he maintains the energy to keep growing. **Branson's** approach shows how chunking your dream into daily steps can lead to extraordinary success. He also emphasizes that we all do things differently, and sometimes we fail, but we must learn the lesson and improve to prepare for the next opportunity.

"You don't learn to walk by following rules. You learn by doing, and by falling over." - Richard Branson

Richard Branson
Credit – Wikimedia Commons

10.2.2: KEEPING YOUR ENERGY HIGH

REFRESH YOUR ENVIRONMENT

Rotate inspiring quotes, rearrange your workspace, or add a new plant. Studies suggest a fresh, engaging environment can lift your mood and help you avoid "goal fatigue" (*Baumeister et al., 2000*). I have a friend who switches around the contents of her socks and underwear drawers in the bedroom to stimulate her mind so as not to become complacent.

MAINTAIN MEANINGFUL CONNECTIONS

Stay close to positive, like-minded friends, mentors, or accountability partners who remind you of your goals. Sharing your wins and struggles can recharge your motivation and deepen your sense of belonging (*Cohen & Wills, 1985*). After my wife died, my four children and I clung to each other. As time progressed, we decided our bond would carry us for life. My kids had to grow up too soon, but our closeness propelled them all to become amazing adults. I know their mother is now their proud angel guardian.

BOOST DOPAMINE NATURALLY

Live with purpose—volunteer, learn new skills, enjoy nature—and your dopamine levels will remain balanced. This neurochemical supports motivation and emotional resilience, making it easier to stick with your plan (*Cohen, 2018*).

KEANU REEVES

Keanu Reeves is widely admired for acting in films like *The Matrix* and *John Wick* and for his genuine kindness and commitment to helping others. **Reeves** has quietly supported cancer charities for years, partly inspired by his sister's battle with leukemia. He even started a private foundation to fund research and children's hospitals, though he rarely takes public credit for it (*Esquire, 2019*).

Reeves gave a large portion of his *Matrix* film earnings to the costume and special effects teams, recognizing their hard work behind the scenes. This rare gesture of gratitude helped those team members financially and boosted morale (*The Guardian, 2001*). Crew members from his projects often mention how **Reeves** regularly treats them to meals or small gifts, demonstrating respect and appreciation for everyone, regardless of their role (*Vanity Fair, 2020*).

Stories abound of **Reeves** offering his seat on the subway, stopping to help strangers with car troubles, and patiently chatting with fans. These everyday acts show that his kindness isn't just for the spotlight—he genuinely cares about the people around him (*People, 2019*). In interviews, he's spoken about the importance of supporting one another in practical ways, reflecting a belief that we can all "pay it forward" with simple, heartfelt actions (*LA Times, 2017*).

> *"The simple act of paying attention can take you a long way."*
> *- Keanu Reeves*

Keanu Reeves
Credit – Wikimedia Commons

REGULARLY PRACTICE KINDNESS

Some people keep a "Kindness Journal" where they note down the acts of kindness they give or receive. Seeing these entries over time can reinforce a bright, hopeful mindset and remind you that goodness often comes full circle. Others make it a point to do at least one kind thing toward another person or even an animal each day.

SECTION THREE:
EMBRACING TECHNOLOGY - HOW AI TOOLS SUPPORT POSITIVE THINKING AND LONGEVITY

Even with the best roadmap, life can get busy. This is where modern AI tools can offer support, guidance, and reminders. Let's explore how technology can help you stick to your positive thinking goals, track your emotional wellness, and stay on a path toward a long, fulfilling life.

10.3.1: AI FOR EMOTIONAL WELL-BEING AND HEALTH

Artificial Intelligence is just computers learning from data—like how a smartphone suggests songs you might like. AI matters because it can analyze patterns in behavior, sleep, or stress to offer personalized tips (*Russell & Norvig, 2010*).

KEVIN LOVE

NBA player **Kevin Love** has publicly shared how using a mental health app helped him track his mood during tough times. While not purely AI-driven, it demonstrates how digital tools can aid emotional wellness in high-pressure settings. **Love** has always been a thoughtful person, on and off the court.

"When you're on the court, there is certain things that you would do that you wouldn't do off the court. When you get off, you obviously have to be gracious and a humble person. When you are on the floor, be a team player. Championships are what you are defined by - legacy. Go about things the right way." - Kevin Love

Kevin Love
Credit – Wikimedia Commons

WHY AI FITS INTO POSITIVE THINKING

Imagine a friendly digital coach sending you encouragement every morning. AI-based apps can do exactly that, offering gentle reminders to stay mindful and upbeat (*Fitzpatrick, Darcy, & Vierhile, 2017*).

DAILY MOOD TRACKING

Many AI apps can note changes in your mood over time, suggesting when you might need more self-care or support from friends. This constant "check-in" can prevent minor issues from becoming big problems. My lovely stepdaughter **Danielle** made it through years of college to become a Physician Assistant. Early on, she had a few meltdowns when assignments became tough or she felt overwhelmed by the pressure of full-time academics. Through time, she learned to recognize the onset of stress and anxiety and became more balanced and nuanced in the way she handled her hectic schedule. AI apps may have helped her if they were available at the time.

PREVENTING BURNOUT

By spotting patterns—like consistent late-night work or lack of exercise—AI can recommend simple fixes to keep you balanced. These might be as small as suggesting a five-minute walk after lunch or a calming breathing exercise before bedtime.

10.3.2: POPULAR TOOLS AND HOW TO USE THEM

APPS AND WEARABLES

Mood-tracking apps like **Wysa** or **Youper** use AI to guide short conversations, while fitness wearables measure heart rate and stress levels. Tracking real-time data can help you see your progress and stay motivated.

CHATBOTS AND VIRTUAL COACHES

AI-based chatbots like **Woebot** use cognitive-behavioral therapy methods to help you handle stress or anxiety (*Fitzpatrick, Darcy, & Vierhile, 2017*). They adapt to your emotional state, offering personalized advice you can access anytime.

RESEARCH-BASED ADVICE

Studies suggest that AI-assisted cognitive behavioral therapy can effectively reduce symptoms of depression or anxiety (*Fitzpatrick, Darcy, & Vierhile, 2017*). This means you can get fundamental science-backed strategies at your fingertips if you're struggling or feeling challenged.

SECURING YOUR PRIVACY

Caveat: If you're using AI-powered apps, make sure to read their privacy policies. Trusted tools clearly explain how they handle your personal data so you can enjoy their benefits with peace of mind.

ARIANA GRANDE

Pop star **Ariana Grande** has spoken about using mental health apps to cope with stress and anxiety. While she hasn't named a specific AI tool, her openness about getting digital support shows how technology can be a lifeline, even for world-famous performers. Over time, **Ariana** has learned to embrace herself precisely how she was made.

"Be happy with being you. Love your flaws. Own your quirks. And know that you are just as perfect as anyone else, exactly as you are."
- Ariana Grande

Ariana Grande
Credit – Store norske leksikon / creativecommons.org

10.3.3: THE FUTURE OF AI IN LONGEVITY AND POSITIVE THINKING

EMERGING TRENDS

AI is making big waves in health and wellness. Today, there are smart nutrition apps that analyze what you eat and give real-time advice on boosting your mood and even extending your longevity. Some even suggest quick recipes based on your daily needs, helping you stay sharp, energized, and thriving.

VIRTUAL REALITY FOR RELAXATION

Technology is also taking relaxation to the next level. Companies are creating VR experiences that let you step into calming nature scenes or peaceful meditations right from your living room. I've always wished I could recreate my trip to Kauai, walking the lush coastlines and waterfalls. Imagine slipping on a headset and being transported back to a place like that—feeling the breeze, hearing the ocean. Virtual reality is making it possible.

ETHICAL AND PRACTICAL CONSIDERATIONS

As exciting as these tools are, it's important to stay grounded. Relying too much on technology—or sharing personal data without caution—can have risks (*Russell & Norvig, 2010*). Use these tools to **enhance** your life, not replace real-world relationships. Balance is the magic word.

FIND THE RIGHT FIT

Always read reviews, check for expert endorsements, and take advantage of free trials. Pay close attention to how the app or device actually makes you feel.

Does it relieve stress—or add to it? Trust your gut—and when needed, talk to a professional for guidance.

HOPEFUL OUTLOOK

Looking ahead, AI and quantum computing will offer even more ways to personalize health strategies. But no matter how advanced tech becomes, your real power still lies in human connection—family, friends, mentors. Use technology as a tool, but keep your heart grounded in the things that truly matter. Building your personal blueprint for a positive, thriving life is an ongoing adventure. Stay connected to your inner child, keep practicing kindness, and lean into every new opportunity to grow—both with your mind and your heart. Here's to a long, meaningful life fueled by optimism and purpose!

CONCLUSION

Right now, you're not just holding a book—you're holding a **compass**— a guide to a new chapter of your life, full of vitality, purpose, and hope. I'm so grateful you took this journey with me. I hope you'll carry gratitude into every day ahead, finding new reasons to appreciate even the smallest blessings. Remember, even when life feels heavy, there's probably someone out there carrying a heavier load. Now, you have the tools to change course, to find hope again—and to be a beacon of strength for others, too.

SECTION ONE: RECAP OF CORE PRINCIPLES
MIND-BODY INTEGRATION

YOUR THOUGHTS AFFECT YOUR CELLS

Every positive or negative thought sends ripples through your body. Studies show that constant stress can actually wear down your DNA, shortening telomeres, while positive emotions help protect them (*Epel et al., 2004*).

POSITIVITY SLOWS AGING

Conscious positivity doesn't just feel good—it helps reduce stress, boosts resilience, and can even slow visible aging (*Fredrickson, 2001*).

ROBERT DOWNEY, JR.

Robert Downey, Jr., famous for his roles in *Iron Man* and *Sherlock Holmes*, once struggled with substance abuse and a crazy lifestyle that took a toll on his body and mind. He wanted to break free from this cycle, so he began exploring mindfulness techniques and dedicated himself to rigorous martial arts training—specifically *Wing Chun*—to regain control of his life (*Men's Health, 2014*). By syncing focused movements with mindful breathing, he built physical strength and found a newfound inner calm. Over time, this combination of physical discipline and mental clarity helped stabilize his emotions and helped him towards a positive outlook on the future.

As he adopted a more optimistic mindset, **Robert** noticed dramatic improvements in his overall well-being. His energy levels rose, and he felt more grounded and confident on and off set. Embracing a kinder attitude toward himself also helped mend strained relationships and spurred healthier life choices. In interviews, he often points to that shift—treating his mind and body as interconnected parts of the same whole—as the way he found a remarkable personal comeback. Through this transformation, **Robert Downey, Jr.** realized that it's never too late to align your thoughts, habits, and body to create a life with hope and resilience.

"I'm coming from a place of total strength and humility now."
— Robert Downey, Jr.

SYNERGY OF MINDFULNESS, GRATITUDE, KINDNESS, AND DAILY HABITS

No single habit creates change—it's the **combination** of small, consistent steps that fuels transformation (*Seligman, 2011*).

DR. CALDWELL ESSELSTYN

Dr. Caldwell Esselstyn is a former surgeon at the *Cleveland Clinic* who gained recognition for his work on preventing and even reversing heart disease through a low-fat, whole-food, plant-based diet (*Esselstyn, 2007*). He emphasizes that emotional support, stress management, and eating healthy foods are key to long-term success. By combining medical expertise with a gentle, encouraging approach, **Dr. Esselstyn** demonstrates how positive thinking, consistent habits, and simple dietary shifts can deliver life-changing results for the heart and beyond.

"Genetics load the gun, lifestyle pulls the trigger."
— Dr. Caldwell Esselstyn

Dr. Caldwell Esselstyn
Credit – Wikimedia Commons

THE ONGOING JOURNEY OF GROWTH

Personal growth isn't a straight line. It's more like learning an instrument—you keep tuning, adjusting, and evolving (*Dweck, 2006*). There's beauty in the practice.

EMBRACING SETBACKS

Bad days aren't failures—they're part of being human. Each tough moment can become a steppingstone toward deeper wisdom.

DREW BARRYMORE

Drew Barrymore found fame as a child star but faced substance misuse and emotional turmoil from a young age. She entered rehab at 13 and struggled with relapses in her teenage years, fueled by negative self-image and industry pressures (*Barrymore, 1990*).

Barrymore decided to step away from toxic influences and rebuild her life through therapy, journaling, and carefully choosing healthier relationships. She re-launched her acting career with a positive outlook, eventually venturing into producing, directing, and even hosting her own talk show with an emphasis on uplifting conversations. She credits her new life balance to acknowledging her past, learning from it, and committing to daily practices that strengthen her emotional well-being.

"Life is very interesting... in the end, some of your greatest pains, become your greatest strengths." – Drew Barrymore

Drew Barrymore
Credit – Wikimedia Commons

SUPPORTIVE COMMUNITIES

You don't have to do this alone. Surround yourself with people who lift you up—and who help you stay accountable (*Cohen & Wills, 1985*).

CALMER EMOTIONAL STORMS

With practice, you'll bounce back faster from setbacks. What once felt overwhelming will someday feel like just another challenge you know how to handle.

BETHANY HAMILTON

Bethany Hamilton was only 13 when a shark attack left her without her left arm. Many feared this injury would end her promising surfing career and derail her dreams (*Hamilton, 2010*).

Instead of giving up, **Hamilton** chose hope and resilience. With the support of her family and a steadfast belief that she could still surf, she learned to adjust her techniques. Within months, she was back in the water. Her powerful story showed the world that a strong mindset and unwavering optimism could transform an impossible situation into a triumphant comeback.

THE COLLECTIVE IMPACT OF POSITIVE THINKING
RIPPLE EFFECT ON LOVED ONES

Your hope doesn't just help you—it lifts up everyone around you. Your positivity might be the spark someone else desperately needs.

RANDOM ACTS OF KINDNESS

Remember, tiny gestures—buying a stranger coffee, sending a kind text—can spark a chain reaction that touches countless lives (*Berkeley, 2019*).

LOVE AND EMPATHY FOR COMMUNITY HEALTH

Empathy strengthens neighborhoods, cities, and even entire countries. Living with kindness improves everyone's health and happiness (*Helliwell et al., 2021*).

MIRACLES BEGIN WITH HOPE

Every great movement, every act of heroism, started with one person daring to hope for something better.

DANNY THOMAS

Danny Thomas was a struggling entertainer in the early years of his career, often worried about how he would support his growing family. In desperation, he prayed for guidance and promised that if he found success, he would use his good fortune to help others. This heartfelt prayer was directed to **St. Jude Thaddeus**, the patron saint of hopeless causes. Shortly thereafter, **Danny's** career took a fortunate turn, and his fame began to rise, confirming that his plea had been heard.

True to his word, **Danny** used his success to found *St. Jude Children's Research Hospital* in 1962. He envisioned a place where children from every walk of life could receive top-tier medical care regardless of their family's ability to pay. The hospital became a beacon of hope for families battling serious childhood diseases and pioneered groundbreaking research that continues to save countless lives worldwide. Through his faith and compassion, **Danny Thomas** showed how one revelation—born in a time of hardship—can grow into a legacy of healing and love.

"Success has nothing to do with what you gain in life or accomplish for yourself. It's what you do for others." – Danny Thomas

Danny Thomas

Credit – UCLA Library Digital Collections (uclalat 1429 b514 221715) / Wikimedia Commons (cropped)

The world needs your hope, your resilience, your compassion—and your unstoppable belief in the goodness that still lies ahead.

SECTION TWO: AN UPLIFTING MESSAGE OF HOPE

EMBRACING THE POWER WITHIN

You hold a remarkable ability to heal, grow, and adapt. Some of the world's most remarkable transformations start with someone saying, *"I can."*

SMALL SHIFTS, BIG RESULTS

Consistent small steps or changes—like a one-minute gratitude check each morning—can have life-altering effects (*Emmons & McCullough, 2003*).

"Too often we underestimate the power of a touch, a smile, a kind word, a listening ear, an honest compliment, or the smallest act of caring, all of which have the potential to turn a life around." - Leo Buscaglia

FRESH STARTS EVERY MORNING

Remember what I said. Every day, you can wake up and reinvent yourself. Each sunrise gives you a blank page. Whether you stumbled yesterday or soared, today offers a new chance to shape your story.

ADVERSITY IS NOT THE FINAL WORD

Challenges appear in every life, but how you respond defines your future. Adversity can become a steppingstone rather than a roadblock. Remember **Dr. Norman Vincent Peale's** philosophy of embracing your problems because the only people without problems are those six feet under.

STEPHEN HAWKING

Despite living with a severe physical condition, **Stephen Hawking** made groundbreaking scientific discoveries. He often spoke about human potential—proving that our minds can explore endless possibilities even in the face of adversity.

"However difficult life may seem, there is always something you can do and succeed at." - Stephen Hawking

Stephen Hawking

Credit – Teoretisk fysiker – Lex / creativecommons.org

A VISION FOR A HEALTHIER, MORE COMPASSIONATE WORLD

When more of us adopt positive thinking, it surely will reduce tension and promote better understanding across communities (*Helliwell et al., 2021*). Remember **Matthew 5:9:** *"Let there be peace on earth, and let it begin with me!"*

SERVICE AND REWARD

Volunteering not only helps who you're helping, but it also gives you an incredible sense of purpose and well-being (*Van Willigen, 2000*).

JON BON JOVI

Jon Bon Jovi founded the *JBJ Soul Kitchen*, a pay-what-you-can community restaurant, in 2011. He volunteered his time and resources to create a dining experience where people could either pay for their meals or offer volunteer services in return. **Bon Jovi** has said that this project reshaped his view on community and kindness, reminding him that fulfilling a simple need like a good meal can create powerful connections and renewed hope.

INVEST IN EMOTIONAL WELLNESS

Societies that support mental health programs—like counseling in schools—reap benefits in lower crime rates and higher productivity (*World Health Organization, 2022*).

YOU'RE PART OF THE SOLUTION

Whenever you choose empathy or lend a helping hand, you are helping to build a culture of compassion. Significant changes often start with one brave person.

OSKAR SCHINDLER

Oskar Schindler was a German industrialist who initially seemed chiefly interested in profiteering from wartime opportunities. Yet, as World War II dragged on, he was deeply moved by the horrific plight of Jewish laborers forced to work in his factory. Unable to stand by while innocent lives were threatened, he began to use his influence, charm, and resources to protect his workers.

Despite great personal risk—including suspicion from the very authorities he once courted—**Schindler** secretly falsified production records and bribed officials to keep as many Jews on his employee list as possible.

In doing so, **Schindler** saved more than a thousand people from near-certain death, proving that empathy and compassion can triumph over brutality even in the darkest chapters of history. His determination to see his workers treated with dignity rather than used as expendable labor has become a profound example of moral courage. Schindler's story reminds us that a single individual, armed with a strong conscience, can make a life-or-death difference—even when danger looms on every side. Check out the movie *Schindler's List*.

Oskar Schindler
Credit – seetheholyland.net / Flickr / creativecommons.org

THE JOURNEY CONTINUES
NEVER STOP LEARNING

New studies, workshops, and mentors can inspire you. Stay curious—like a child in a giant playground of knowledge.

SHARE YOUR STORY

Telling others about your breakthroughs can encourage them to start their own positive transformations. In this journey, you become both a student and a teacher.

CELEBRATE PROGRESS, NOT PERFECTION

No one lives 100% free of negative thoughts. The goal is to keep improving gradually, appreciating each step toward better well-being.

YOUR HEROIC ADVENTURE

Like **Patrick Dempsey** did before surgeries in his role as **Dr. Derek Shephard** on *Grey's Anatomy*, picture and project yourself as the hero of your own story. Heroes grow, evolve, and find new strengths they never knew they had. This is your chance to live boldly and compassionately.

JANE GOODALL

Jane Goodall's journey began with a passion for chimpanzees, but it grew into a global movement for conservation and empathy toward all living things. She continually shares her discoveries, motivating others to protect animals and the environment—an inspiring example of a never-ending mission to do good.

Remember—every moment spent cultivating hope is an investment in your greatest asset: life.

Jane Goodall
Credit – Wikimedia Commons

SECTION THREE:
FINAL WORDS OF ENCOURAGEMENT
SUMMON YOUR INNER STRENGTH

You already have what it takes to shift your mind and body toward greater well-being. Consistent practice unlocks this power.

CONFIDENCE GROWS THROUGH ACTION

Each time you choose optimism over doubt, you strengthen the confidence muscle. Like any exercise, repetition is key (*Bandura, 1977*).

COLONEL HARLAND SANDERS

Colonel Sanders is best known for founding *Kentucky Fried Chicken* (KFC) after years of struggle and multiple career failures. In his 60s, feeling he had little left to lose, he began traveling across the country to sell his fried chicken recipe, offering kindness and free samples to restaurant owners. Through this process, he learned to forgive himself for past shortcomings and began to believe he still had value to share. His positive mindset shift eventually led to a fast-food empire, making him a global hospitality and warmth icon.

"You got to like your work. You have got to like what you are doing, you have got to be doing something worthwhile so you can like it - because it is worthwhile, that it makes a difference, don't you see?" - Colonel Sanders

Colonel Sanders

Credit – Manfred Katz together with Colonel Harland David Sanders / Wikimedia Commons (cropped)

ONE POSITIVE THOUGHT MATTERS

Never underestimate the potential of a single kind or hopeful thought to transform your entire day—or someone else's.

LIFE IS CLOSER TO FULFILLMENT THAN YOU THINK

Often, the biggest challenge is simply believing you deserve joy. Trust that feeling good is not a luxury; it's your birthright. My friend, iconic screen actor **Robert Wagner**, believed this and felt an obligation to make the best of it. He said:

"I've learned one important thing about God's gifts - what we do with them is our gift to Him."

Robert Wagner and Tad Sisler
Source: Tad Sisler's personal collection

STAYING MOTIVATED IN THE LONG TERM
REVISIT AND RECHARGE
Go back to chapters as you evolve. Each reread can offer new insights and fresh motivation based on your current stage of life.

ACCOUNTABILITY AND COMMUNITY
Look for local meetups, online forums, or good friends with similar goals. Encouragement from others lights the path on difficult days (*Cohen & Wills, 1985*).

SUGGESTED READING LIST
I could suggest a hundred books! In addition to the amazing books and authors I've already mentioned in this book, here's a short list of other books from which you may find greater inspiration:

Mindset: The New Psychology of Success by *Carol S. Dweck*
- Examines how believing in your ability to grow can reshape challenges into opportunities.

Learned Optimism by *Martin E. P. Seligman*
- Introduces the concept of optimism as a skill, revealing strategies for defeating pessimism and depression.

The Happiness Advantage by *Shawn Achor*
- Offers practical advice for rewiring your brain toward positivity to improve work performance and relationships.

Flourish by Martin E. P. Seligman
- Expands on positive psychology principles, covering well-being, resilience, and nurturing a fulfilling life.

Ikigai: The Japanese Secret to a Long and Happy Life by *Héctor García and Francesc Miralles*
- Shares how finding your life's purpose and harmony can lead to lasting joy and longevity.

Radical Acceptance by *Tara Brach*
- Encourages embracing every part of yourself with kindness, turning self-judgment into self-compassion.

Dare to Lead by *Brené Brown*
- Explores how vulnerability, courage, and empathy can reshape leadership and boost personal confidence.

The Alchemist by *Paulo Coelho*
- It is a novel about a young shepherd's quest that highlights the importance of holding onto hope and following one's dreams.

Big Magic by *Elizabeth Gilbert*
- Shows how curiosity and creativity flourish when we set aside fear and embrace a more optimistic approach to life's possibilities.

The 7 Habits of Highly Effective People by *Stephen R. Covey*
- Provides foundational principles—like proactive thinking and win-win mindsets—to encourage positive, purposeful living.

Emotional Intelligence by *Daniel Goleman*
- It demonstrates how understanding and managing one's own emotions (and empathizing with others) leads to more harmonious and positive relationships.

Tiny Habits by *BJ Fogg*
- Explains how making small, optimistic shifts in behavior can create big, lasting changes in our mindset and daily routines.

Grit by *Angela Duckworth*
- Emphasizes resilience and long-term passion—powered by a can-do perspective—are often more critical to success than innate talent.

The Book of Hope by *Jane Goodall and Douglas Abrams*
- Chronicles Dr. Goodall's life and advocacy, underscoring how a steadfast belief in the human spirit can drive meaningful change in the world.

Tony Robbins is the greatest motivator of our generation. He constantly updates his seminars, programs, and personal routines. He emphasizes that personal growth is ever-evolving. By staying flexible in his methods, **Tony** keeps his motivation and impact fresh, reinforcing that your tools for positivity can grow right along with you.

Marianne Williamson is also an amazing writer. She grew up as a curious and thoughtful kid, always asking big questions about life. She read many books about spirituality and compassion, inspiring her to believe **love** could solve many of our problems. As she got older, she started giving talks that helped people realize the power of kindness and forgiveness. Eventually, she wrote her own books, like A Return to Love (*Williamson, 1992*), sharing her ideas about how choosing love over fear can create a better world for everyone. Many people liked her words so much that they invited her to speak at large events and on television.

Like a friendly coach who cheered for you, **Marianne** wanted everyone to feel encouraged and hopeful. She often reminded people that if you think good thoughts and show patience toward yourself and others, you can find inner peace and confidence, even when life feels tough. Her message has reached schools, churches, and even national stages, where she has spoken about compassion and honesty. By focusing on love as a guiding force, she believes each person can make a real difference in the world—starting from wherever they are right now.

"The key to abundance is meeting limited circumstances with unlimited thoughts." – Marianne Williamson

Marianne Williamson
Credit – Wikimedia Commons

ADAPT AS LIFE CHANGES
Stressful events or shifts in routine can happen. To stay balanced, be ready to tweak your positivity toolkit—maybe adding a daily breathing exercise or journaling session.

CELEBRATE WINS
Mark each milestone, big or small, as proof of your evolving mindset. Acknowledge how far you've come and get excited about where you're heading.

STEPPING INTO A NEW CHAPTER OF LIFE
A NEW BEGINNING, NOT AN ENDING
This conclusion is simply a doorway to the next phase of your life, which will be filled with greater self-awareness, healthier thoughts, and deeper compassion.

USE OPTIMISM TO ENRICH RELATIONSHIPS
Carry your lessons into your friendships, family life, and community involvement. Watch how positivity shapes stronger, more supportive bonds.

MICHAEL J. FOX

Diagnosed with Parkinson's disease at just 29, actor **Michael J. Fox** initially struggled with the emotional toll of his condition. After a period of denial and fear, he faced his new reality with optimism and a commitment to advocacy.

Fox established the *Michael J. Fox Foundation for Parkinson's Research*, turning his personal challenge into a global mission to fund scientific breakthroughs. His emphasis on humor, gratitude, and public awareness helped redefine Parkinson's not as a defeat but as a catalyst for meaningful change in his life.

> *"Acceptance doesn't mean resignation; it means understanding that something is what it is and that there's got to be a way through it."*
> *- Michael J. Fox*

Michael J. Fox
Credit – Wikimedia Commons

DREAM OF A LONG, PURPOSEFUL FUTURE

By mixing optimism, kindness, and science-backed habits, you can set yourself on a path to a more vibrant and enduring life. In December 1950, **William Faulkner** projected his hope for the future in his *Nobel Prize* acceptance speech when he said:

> *"I believe that man will not merely endure he will prevail. He is immortal not because he alone among creatures has an inexhaustible voice but because he has a soul, a spirit capable of compassion and sacrifice and endurance."*

We will not just survive... we will prevail!

EMBRACE LIFE FULLY

Let gratitude and kindness guide your days. With your mind and heart aligned, every moment can be a step toward lasting fulfillment. May this expanded journey—enriched with wisdom from ancient philosophers to modern thinkers, healing practices for your inner child, and the transformative power of kindness—ignite a radiant spark of positivity within you.

Remember, by nurturing optimism, compassion, and resilience, you can unlock extraordinary well-being and, in turn, share that light with the world.

I sincerely hope your future is filled with hope, love and goodness, deep appreciation for each moment, and the enduring power of a positive mind. You now have the tools, the knowledge, and the heart. I know you can create the life you've envisioned. Just keep the faith and you'll make it!

PLEASE LEAVE A REVIEW

Now that you have everything you need to **work towards a more positive, healthier, and longer life**, it's time to share your newfound knowledge and show other readers where they can find the same support.

By leaving your honest opinion of this book on Amazon or wherever you purchased it, you'll help others discover the guidance they need to elevate their voices and share their passion for **a healthy, meaningful, long life.**

Thank you for your help. The **quest for answers** lives on when we pass on what we've learned, and you're helping **me** to do just that.

REFERENCES

1. LICENSE LINK REFERENCES
• Creative Commons. (n.d.). Attribution-ShareAlike 4.0 International (CC BY-SA 4.0) [License]. Retrieved from https://creativecommons.org/licenses/by/4.0/ or https://creativecommons.org/licenses/by/2.0/

2. WEBSITES / ONLINE REFERENCES
• AZQuotes. (n.d.). Retrieved from https://www.azquotes.com
• AZQuotes (Joe Dispenza). (n.d.). Joe Dispenza Quotes. Retrieved from https://www.azquotes.com/quote/1460333
• BrainyQuote. (n.d.). Retrieved from https://www.brainyquote.com
• CNN. (2010). Larry King Live [TV broadcast]. Dr. Dean Ornish, guest.
• ESPN. (2014). Robert Downey Jr. on Wing Chun and Mind-Body Balance. Retrieved from https://www.menshealth.com
• ESPN. (2018). Tony Hawk discusses the highs and lows of skateboarding. Retrieved from https://www.espn.com
• Goodreads. (n.d.). Quotes. Retrieved from https://www.goodreads.com
• Goodreads. (n.d.). "Whatever we think about and thank about we bring about." [Quote from John F. Demartini]. Retrieved from https://www.goodreads.com/quotes/7257219

- Goodreads. (n.d.). Illusions: The Adventures of a Reluctant Messiah (Quotes) [Richard Bach Quote]. Retrieved from https://www.goodreads.com/work/quotes/30365-illusions-the-adventures-of-a-reluctant-messiah
- Good Housekeeping. (2012). Interview with Kirstie Alley. [Magazine/online interview].
- Good Housekeeping. (2019). Janes, D. "Kelly Clarkson opens up about balancing work and motherhood." Retrieved from https://www.goodhousekeeping.com
- Harper's Bazaar. (2013). Kate Winslet on motherhood and resilience. Retrieved from https://www.harpersbazaar.com
- Interview: Men's Health. (2016). John Goodman on managing wellness and weight. [No direct URL provided.]
- LA Times. (2017). Keanu Reeves on community support and humility. Retrieved from https://www.latimes.com
- Men's Health. (2014). Robert Downey Jr. on Wing Chun and Mind-Body Balance. Retrieved from https://www.menshealth.com
- Mikey O'Connell, Men's Health. (2018). "Chris Pratt on faith, fatherhood, and a new approach to stress." Retrieved from https://www.menshealth.com
- Morgan, S. (1973). "The making of the Jonathan Livingston Seagull soundtrack." Rolling Stone. [No direct URL provided.]
- NPR Staff. (2019). "Shaquille O'Neal on philanthropy and community work." NPR. Retrieved from https://www.npr.org
- Oprah.com. (n.d.). Oprah's Words to Live By: Higher Calling. Retrieved from https://www.oprah.com
- People. (2019). Keanu Reeves' random acts of kindness: A day in the life. Retrieved from https://people.com
- Renker, Greg. Guthy-Renker. (n.d.). OUR STORY. Guthy-Renker. Retrieved April 28, 2025, from https://www.guthy-renker.com/home/our-story/?utm_source=chatgpt.com
- Rolling Stone. (2016). Emma Stone. Retrieved from https://www.rollingstone.com
- Singh, A. (2016, January 18). "Adele overcomes stage fright with help from a hypnotherapist." The Daily Telegraph. Retrieved from https://www.telegraph.co.uk
- Sykes, D. (2013). "Holding on to a Dream" – GWU Professor Reflects on Diversity and MLK, Jr. [PDF]. Retrieved from https://core.ac.uk/download/387859382.pdf
- The Oprah Winfrey Show. (2011). Shania Twain, guest. [TV broadcast]
- The Oprah Winfrey Show (multiple appearances, e.g., 2010). Tyler Perry. [TV broadcast]
- Usadailynews10.com. (n.d.). Oprah Winfrey: A beacon of strength and resilience. Retrieved from https://usadailynews10.com/oprah-winfrey-a-beacon-of-strength-and-resilien/
- Vanity Fair. (2020). Behind the scenes interviews: Keanu Reeves on set etiquette. Retrieved from https://www.vanityfair.com
- Yahoo Entertainment. (n.d.). Sergio Mendes on "The Sound of Joy." Retrieved from https://www.yahoo.com/entertainment/sound-joy-142819675.html

3. BOOKS AND HISTORICAL TEXTS
Modern/Contemporary Books

- Bach, R. (1970). Jonathan Livingston Seagull. Macmillan.
- Bach, R. (1977). Illusions: The adventures of a reluctant messiah. Delacorte Press.
- Barrymore, D. (1990). Little girl lost. Pocket Books.
- Bernstein, G. (2016). The universe has your back: Transform fear to faith. Hay House.
- Bushkin, H. (2013). Johnny Carson. Houghton Mifflin Harcourt.
- Byrne, R. (2006). The secret. Atria Books/Beyond Words.
- Carnegie, D. (1936). How to win friends and influence people. Simon & Schuster.
- Clear, J. (2018). Atomic habits: An easy & proven way to build good habits & break bad ones. Avery.
- Cousins, N. (1979). Anatomy of an illness as perceived by the patient. W. W. Norton.
- Davidson, R. J., & McEwen, B. S. (2012). Social influences on neuroplasticity: Stress and interventions to promote well-being. Nature Neuroscience, 15(5), 689–695.
- Dispenza, J. (2014). You are the placebo: Making your mind matter. Hay House.
- Dyer, W. (1976). Your erroneous zones. Funk & Wagnalls.

- Esselstyn, C. B. (2007). Prevent and reverse heart disease: The revolutionary, scientifically proven, nutrition-based cure. Avery.
- Fredrickson, B. L. (2009). Positivity. Crown.
- Gandhi, M. K. (1927). An autobiography: The story of my experiments with truth. Navajivan Trust. (Also listed under Historical Texts.)
- Harrington, A. (2008). The cure within: A history of mind-body medicine. W.W. Norton.
- Hay, L. (1984). You can heal your life. Hay House.
- Hill, N. (1937). Think and grow rich. The Ralston Society.
- Holiday, R. (2014). The obstacle is the way. Portfolio.
- Holmes, E. (1926). The science of mind. Tarcher.
- Hyman, M. (2012). The blood sugar solution. Little, Brown and Company.
- Kearns Goodwin, D. (2013). Lyndon Johnson and the American dream. Open Road Media.
- Keller, H. (1903). The story of my life. Grosset & Dunlap.
- King, M. L., Jr. (1963). Letter from Birmingham Jail. [Historical Document]
- Krohn, K. (2011). Oprah Winfrey. Twenty-First Century Books.
- Lacey, R. (1986). Ford: The men and the machine. Little, Brown and Company.
- Lash, J. P. (1980). Helen and teacher: The story of Helen Keller and Anne Sullivan Macy. Delacorte Press.
- Lipton, B. H. (2015). The biology of belief: Unleashing the power of consciousness, matter & miracles. Hay House.
- Locke, J. (1689). Two treatises of government. Awnsham Churchill.
- Lovato, D. (2017). Demi Lovato: Simply complicated [Documentary]. YouTube Originals.
- Mandino, O. (1968). The greatest salesman in the world. Frederick Fell.
- McConaughey, M. (2020). Greenlights. Crown.
- Montgomery, T. (2003). Montaigne: Essays. [Edition note not fully specified.]
- Murad, N. (2017). The last girl: My story of captivity, and my fight against the Islamic State. Tim Duggan Books.
- Nhat Hanh, T. (1975). The miracle of mindfulness. Beacon Press.
- Ornish, D. (1998). Dr. Dean Ornish's program for reversing heart disease. Ballantine Books.
- Peale, N. V. (1952). The power of positive thinking. Prentice Hall.
- Perlmutter, D. (2013). Grain brain: The surprising truth about wheat, carbs, and sugar—your brain's silent killers. Little, Brown Spark.
- Peterson, C., & Seligman, M. E. P. (2004). Character strengths and virtues: A handbook and classification. Oxford University Press.
- Phelps, M. (2016). Beneath the surface: My story. RosettaBooks.
- Robbins, A. (1986). Unlimited power. Free Press.
- Robbins, T. (1992). Awaken the giant within. Free Press.
- Ruíz, D. M. (1997). The four agreements: A practical guide to personal freedom. Amber-Allen Publishing.
- Sanford, T. D. (2016). T. Denny Sanford biography. [Website reference, also listed under Websites if needed.]
- Shenk, J. W. (2005). Lincoln's melancholy: How depression challenged a president and fueled his greatness. Houghton Mifflin.
- Sinclair, D. (2019). Lifespan: Why we age—and why we don't have to. Atria Books.
- Somers, S. (2009). Knockout: Interviews with doctors who are curing cancer--and how to prevent getting it in the first place. Harmony Books.
- Thomas, D. (1962). Founding of St. Jude Children's Research Hospital. [Historical Info]
- Turner, T. (2020). Happiness becomes you: A guide to changing your life for good. Atria Books.
- Union, G. (2017). We're going to need more wine: Stories that are funny, complicated, and true. Dey Street Books.
- Weil, A. (2018). Mind over meds: Know when drugs are necessary, when alternatives are better—and when to let your body heal on its own. Little, Brown Spark.
- Williamson, M. (1992). A return to love. [Publisher often cited as HarperCollins or HarperOne.]
- (Historical Document) Jefferson, T., et al. (1776). The Declaration of Independence. Philadelphia.
- (Historical Document) King, M. L., Jr. (1963). Letter from Birmingham Jail.

Classical/Historical Texts

- Aristotle. (1915). Nicomachean ethics (W. D. Ross, Trans.). Clarendon Press.
- Aristotle. (n.d.). Nicomachean ethics. [Various translations available.]
- Dhammapada. (1987). In Carter, J. R., & Palihawadana, M. (Eds.). Oxford University Press.
- Diogenes Laertius. (n.d.). Lives of eminent philosophers. [Various editions.]
- Epictetus. (n.d.). Enchiridion. [Various translations.]
- Emerson, R. W. (1836). Nature. James Munroe and Company.
- Emerson, R. W. (1841). Self-Reliance. J. Munroe and Company.
- Franklin, B. (1791). The autobiography of Benjamin Franklin. J. Parson.
- Gandhi, M. K. (1927). An autobiography: The story of my experiments with truth. Navajivan Trust.
- Holy Bible. (n.d.). 1 Thessalonians 5:18. [Various translations.]
- Holy Bible. (n.d.). Book of Job, New Testament references. [Various editions.]
- Jefferson, T., et al. (1776). The Declaration of Independence. Philadelphia.
- King, M. L., Jr. (1963). Letter from Birmingham Jail. [Historical Document]
- Locke, J. (1689). Two treatises of government. Awnsham Churchill.
- Marcus Aurelius. (n.d.). Meditations. [Various translations.]
- Montaigne, M. (1958). The complete essays of Montaigne (D. M. Frame, Trans.). Stanford University Press.
- Montaigne, M. de. (n.d.). Essays. [Various editions.]
- Plato. (1892). The dialogues of Plato (B. Jowett, Trans.). Oxford University Press.
- Plato. (n.d.). Apology. [Various translations.]
- Prabhavananda, S., & Isherwood, C. (1944). The Song of God: Bhagavad-Gita. Vedanta Press.
- Spinoza, B. (1677). Ethics. [Various translations available.]
- The Vedas. (n.d.). Ancient Indian scriptures.

Other Notable / Documentary Works

- Hamilton, B. (2010). Soul surfer: A true story of faith, family, and fighting to get back on the board. Pocket Books.
- Henson, T. P. (2016). Around the way girl. Atria/37INK.
- King, C. S. (1983). Coretta: The story of Mrs. Martin Luther King, Jr. G.K. Hall & Company.
- Lovato, D. (2017). Demi Lovato: Simply complicated [Documentary]. YouTube Originals.
- Machiavelli, N. (n.d.). The prince. [Various translations.]
- Morgan, S. (1973). "The making of the Jonathan Livingston Seagull soundtrack." Rolling Stone. [Re-listed if considered "Notable" or "Magazine article."]
- Murad, N. (2017). The last girl: My story of captivity, and my fight against the Islamic State. Tim Duggan Books.
- Roy, B. (2012, August 23). Interview with ESPN.
- The Oprah Winfrey Show. (2011). Shania Twain, guest.
- The Oprah Winfrey Show (multiple appearances, e.g., 2010). Tyler Perry.
- Interview: Good Housekeeping, 2012. Kirstie Alley (if you prefer it listed here as well).
- Interview: Men's Health, 2016. John Goodman (sometimes placed under Websites or Notable Works).
- British Vogue. (2020). "Emma Watson on the power of meditation and mindfulness."
- King, M. (2018). The good neighbor: The life and work of Fred Rogers. Abrams Press.

4. JOURNAL ARTICLES

- Allen, A. B., et al. (2018). Associations between trait mindfulness, reappraisal, and the intensity of negative emotions in daily life. Mindfulness, 9(5), 1588–1597.
- American Counseling Association. (2020). Resources for dealing with grief. Retrieved from https://www.counseling.org
- American Psychological Association. (2019). Stress in America: Stress and current events. [Organizational PDF/Report]
- Antoni, M. H., Lehman, J. M., Kilbourn, K. M., et al. (2006). Cognitive-behavioral stress management intervention decreases the prevalence of depression and enhances benefit finding among women under treatment for early-stage breast cancer. Health Psychology, 25(1), 20–27.

• Bandura, A. (1977). Self-efficacy: Toward a unifying theory of behavioral change. Psychological Review, 84(2), 191–215.

• Baumeister, R. F., Bratslavsky, E., Muraven, M., & Tice, D. M. (2000). Ego depletion: Is the active self a limited resource? Journal of Personality and Social Psychology, 74(5), 1252–1265.

• Beecher, H. K. (1955). The powerful placebo. Journal of the American Medical Association, 159(17), 1602–1606.

• Berkeley, A. (2019). The power of kindness for brain health. Journal of Positive Neuroscience, 12(3), 45–57.

• Boehm, J. K., & Kubzansky, L. D. (2012). The heart's content: The association between positive psychological well-being and cardiovascular health. Psychological Bulletin, 138(4), 655–691.

• Bonanno, G. A. (2004). Loss, trauma, and human resilience. American Psychologist, 59(1), 20–28.

• Bottiglieri, T. (2002). Folate, vitamin B12, and homocysteine in depression. Psychiatric Clinics of North America, 25(3), 447–458.

• Bratman, G. N., Hamilton, J. P., & Daily, G. C. (2019). The impacts of nature experience on human cognitive function and mental health. Annals of the New York Academy of Sciences, 1424(1), 1–13.

• Brown, K. W., & Ryan, R. M. (2003). The benefits of being present: Mindfulness and its role in psychological well-being. Journal of Personality and Social Psychology, 84(4), 822–848.

• Carver, C. S., & Scheier, M. F. (2014). Dispositional optimism. Trends in Cognitive Sciences, 18(6), 293–299.

• Chida, Y., & Steptoe, A. (2008). Positive psychological well-being and mortality: a quantitative review of prospective observational studies. Psychosomatic Medicine, 70(7), 741–756.

• Chiesa, A., & Serretti, A. (2009). Mindfulness-based stress reduction for stress management in healthy people: A review and meta-analysis. Journal of Alternative and Complementary Medicine, 15(5), 593–600.

• Cohen, S., & Pressman, S. D. (2006). Positive affect and health. Current Directions in Psychological Science, 15(3), 122–125.

• Cohen, S., & Wills, T. A. (1985). Stress, social support, and the buffering hypothesis. Psychological Bulletin, 98(2), 310–357.

• Corrigan, P. W., & Watson, A. C. (2002). Understanding the impact of stigma on people with mental illness. American Psychologist, 57(6), 765–776.

• Curry, O. S., Rowland, L., Van Lissa, C. J., et al. (2018). Happy to help? A systematic review and meta-analysis of the effects of performing acts of kindness on the well-being of the actor. Journal of Experimental Social Psychology, 76, 320–329.

• Davidson, R. J., & McEwen, B. S. (2012). Social influences on neuroplasticity: Stress and interventions to promote well-being. Nature Neuroscience, 15(5), 689–695.

• Epel, E. S., Blackburn, E. H., Lin, J., Dhabhar, F. S., Adler, N. E., Morrow, J. D., & Cawthon, R. M. (2004). Accelerated telomere shortening in response to life stress. Proceedings of the National Academy of Sciences, 101(49), 17312–17315.

• Evans, G. W. (2003). The built environment and mental health. Journal of Urban Health, 80(4), 536–555.

• Field, T. (2011). Yoga clinical research review. Complementary Therapies in Clinical Practice, 17(1), 1–8.

• Fitzpatrick, K. K., Darcy, A. M., & Vierhile, M. (2017). Delivering cognitive behavior therapy… using a fully automated conversational agent (Woebot). JMIR Mental Health, 4(2), e19.

• Fogg, B. J. (2019). Tiny habits. Houghton Mifflin Harcourt. (Book, but sometimes listed under references for habit research.)

• Fowler, J. H., & Christakis, N. A. (2008). Dynamic spread of happiness in a large social network… BMJ, 337, a2338.

• Fox, K. C. R., Dixon, M. L., Nijeboer, S., Girn, M., Floman, J. L., et al. (2016). Functional neuroanatomy of meditation… Neuroscience & Biobehavioral Reviews, 65, 208–228.

• Fredrickson, B. L. (2001). The role of positive emotions in positive psychology. American Psychologist, 56(3), 218–226.

• Gross, J. J., & Thompson, R. A. (2007). Emotion regulation: Conceptual foundations. In Handbook of emotion regulation (pp. 3–24). The Guilford Press.

• Grumet, J. (2025, February 28). *The hidden key to happiness: Purpose-driven communities*. *Psychology Today*. https://www.psychologytoday.com/us/blog/the-regret-free-life/202502/the-hidden-key-to-happiness-purpose-driven-communities

• Hatch, R. (2005). Abraham Lincoln the writer: A treasury of his greatest speeches and letters. Boyds Mills Press. (Book, referencing historical documents.)

• Heinrichs, M., et al. (2009). Oxytocin and social bonding... Progress in Brain Research, 170, 337–350.

• Helliwell, J. F., Layard, R., Sachs, J., & De Neve, J. (Eds.). (2021). World happiness report. Sustainable Development Solutions Network.

• Holt-Lunstad, J., Smith, T. B., & Layton, J. B. (2015). Social relationships and mortality risk... PLOS Medicine, 7(7), e1000316.

• Holowchak, M. A. (2009). Duty, virtue, and the good society: Thomas Jefferson on education in a republic. Enlightenment and Dissent, 25, 179–203.

• Kabat-Zinn, J. (1990). Full catastrophe living. Delacorte. (Book, but used often in journals referencing mindfulness.)

• Kashdan, T. B., & Silvia, P. J. (2009). Curiosity and interest. Current Directions in Psychological Science, 18(3), 153–156.

• Kazdin, A. E., & Blase, S. L. (2011). Rebooting psychotherapy research... Perspectives on Psychological Science, 6(1), 21–37.

• Kiecolt-Glaser, J. K., McGuire, L., Robles, T. F., & Glaser, R. (2002). Emotions, morbidity, and mortality... Annual Review of Psychology, 53(1), 83–107.

• Kirk, D. (2012). J.K. Rowling's magical impact on literature. Journal of Literary Studies, 28(3), 459–475.

• Kolb, B., & Gibb, R. (2011). Brain plasticity and behaviour... Journal of the Canadian Academy of Child and Adolescent Psychiatry, 20(4), 265–276.

• Lawler, K. A., Younger, J. W., Piferi, R. L., et al. (2005). The unique effects of forgiveness on health... Journal of Behavioral Medicine, 28(2), 157–167.

• Linden, W. (1990). Use of imagery in the treatment of anxiety states. Behaviour Research and Therapy, 28(3), 269–275.

• Linden, W., Vodermaier, A., MacKenzie, R., & Greig, D. (2009). Anxiety and depression after cancer diagnosis... Journal of Affective Disorders, 141(2–3), 343–351.

• Locke, E. A., & Latham, G. P. (2002). Building a practically useful theory of goal setting... American Psychologist, 57(9), 705–717.

• Locke, E. A., & Latham, G. P. (2006). New directions in goal-setting theory. Current Directions in Psychological Science, 15(5), 265–268.

• Loeb, S. J., & AbuDagga, A. (2006). Health-related research on older inmates: An integrative review. Research in Nursing & Health, 29(6), 556–565.

• Longo, V. D., & Mattson, M. P. (2014). Fasting: Molecular mechanisms and clinical applications. Cell Metabolism, 19(2), 181–192.

• Luskin, F. (2002). Forgive for good: A proven prescription for health and happiness. HarperOne. (Book, sometimes cited in academic references.)

• Lyubomirsky, S. (2008). The how of happiness: A new approach to getting the life you want. Penguin Press.

• Martin, A. A., Carver, C. S., & Scheier, M. F. (2017). The role of optimism/pessimism... Psycho-Oncology, 26(10), 1529–1535.

• Martin, R. A. (2001). Humor, laughter, and physical health. Psychological Bulletin, 127(4), 504–519.

• McEwen, B. S. (1998). Stress, adaptation, and disease: Allostasis and allostatic load. Annals of the New York Academy of Sciences, 840, 33–44.

• McGonigal, K. (2015). The upside of stress: Why stress is good for you, and how to get good at it. Avery.

• Miller, G. E., & Siegel, S. D. (2011). Managing stress in cancer survivors. Clinical Advances in Hematology & Oncology, 9(3), 211–213.

• Morgan, B. A. (2021). Implementing gratitude exercises... Journal of Clinical Psychology, 77(8), 1725–1739.

• Morgan, K. (2003). Daytime activity and risk factors for late-life insomnia. Journal of Sleep Research, 12(3), 231–238.

• National Alliance on Mental Illness. (2020). Mental health by the numbers. https://www.nami.org

• National Institutes of Health. (2021). Chronic pain and complementary health approaches. https://www.nih.gov

• Neff, K. D. (2011). Self-compassion, self-esteem, and well-being. Social and Personality Psychology Compass, 5(1), 1–12.

• Park, D. C., & Bischof, G. N. (2013). The aging mind... Dialogues in Clinical Neuroscience, 15(1), 109–119.

• Park, D. C., & Reuter-Lorenz, P. (2009). The adaptive brain... Annual Review of Psychology, 60, 173–196.

• Pennebaker, J. W., & Chung, C. K. (2011). Expressive writing... In The Oxford handbook of health psychology (pp. 417–437). Oxford University Press.

• Pennebaker, J. W., & Seagal, J. D. (1999). Forming a story... Journal of Clinical Psychology, 55(10), 1243–1254.

• Popkin, B. M., D'Anci, K. E., & Rosenberg, I. H. (2010). Water, hydration and health. Nutrition Reviews, 68(8), 439–458.

• Pressman, S. D., & Cohen, S. (2005). Does positive affect influence health? Psychological Bulletin, 131(6), 925–971.

• Putnam, R. D. (2000). Bowling alone: The collapse and revival of American community. Simon & Schuster. (Book, frequently cited in journals.)

• Raposa, E. B., Laws, H. B., & Ansell, E. B. (2016). Prosocial behavior mitigates... Clinical Psychological Science, 4(4), 691–698.

• Rashid, A., & Nasir Abbasi, P. (2025). Gratitude, life satisfaction, and well-being: Unpacking the power of positive emotions and optimism in young adults. *The Critical Review of Social Sciences Studies, 3*(1), 1652–1663. https://doi.org/10.59075/4bcp4x29

• Ridker, P. M., Cushman, M., Stampfer, M. J., et al. (2000). Inflammation, aspirin, and the risk of cardiovascular disease. New England Journal of Medicine, 336(14), 973–979.

• Russell, S. J., & Norvig, P. (2010). Artificial intelligence: A modern approach (3rd ed.). Prentice Hall.

• Ryff, C. D., & Singer, B. (2008). Know thyself and become what you are... Journal of Happiness Studies, 9(1), 13–39.

• Sapolsky, R. M., Romero, L. M., & Munck, A. U. (2000). How do glucocorticoids influence stress responses? Endocrine Reviews, 21(1), 55–89.

• Schutte, N. S., & Malouff, J. M. (2014). A meta-analytic review of the effects of mindfulness... Psychoneuroendocrinology, 42, 45–48.

• Schwartz, K., Ganster, F. M., Voracek, M., & Tran, U. S. (2025). Mindfulness and objective measures of body awareness: A preregistered systematic review and multilevel meta-analysis. BIOPSYCHOSOCIAL SCIENCE AND MEDICINE, 87(4), 235–248. https://journals.lww.com/bsam/pages/default.aspx

• Seligman, M. E. P. (2011). Flourish: A visionary new understanding of happiness and well-being. Free Press. (Book, also cited academically.)

• Seligman, M. E. P., & Csikszentmihalyi, M. (2000). Positive psychology: An introduction. American Psychologist, 55(1), 5–14.

• Sheldon, K. M., & Kasser, T. (1995). Coherence and congruence... Journal of Personality and Social Psychology, 68(3), 531–543.

• Shevchuk, N. A. (2008). Adapted cold shower as a potential treatment for depression. Medical Hypotheses, 70(5), 995–1001.

• Shalev, I., et al. (2013). Exposure to violence during childhood... Molecular Psychiatry, 18(5), 576–581.

• Smith, T. R., Johnson, A. L., & Lee, M. H. (2019). Inner-child therapy combined with mindfulness... Journal of Psychosomatic Research, 120, 13–20.

• Smith, T. W., Glazer, K., Ruiz, J. M., & Gallo, L. C. (2004). Hostility, anger, aggressiveness... Journal of Personality, 72(6), 1217–1270.

• Southwick, S. M., & Charney, D. S. (2012). The science of resilience... Science, 338(6103), 79–82.

• Steidl, L. (2005). Chronický únavový syndrom. Interní Medicína pro Praxi. https://www.solen.cz/pdfs/int/2001/09/02.pdf

• Steptoe, A., Dockray, S., & Wardle, J. (2005). Positive affect and psychobiological processes… Journal of Personality, 73(6), 1367–1396.

• Steptoe, A., Hamer, M., & Chida, Y. (2007). The effects of acute psychological stress… Brain, Behavior, and Immunity, 21(7), 901–912.

• Steptoe, A., & Fancourt, D. (2019). Leading a meaningful life at older ages… Proceedings of the National Academy of Sciences, 116(4), 1207–1212.

• Sudsuang, R., Chentanez, T., & Veluvan, K. (1991). Effect of Buddhist meditation… Physiology & Behavior, 50(3), 543–548.

• Tabatabaei, S. M., Pour Saeid, V., Herfedoost, N., & Hafezi, M. (2024, October 18). *Relationship between attitude of optimism and pessimism with leukocytes telomere length. Journal of Social and Behavioral Sciences, 1*(1). https://doi.org/10.61148/JSBS/004

• Tang, Y. Y., Holzel, B. K., & Posner, M. I. (2015). The neuroscience of mindfulness meditation. Nature Reviews Neuroscience, 16(4), 213–225.

• Toussaint, L., Worthington, E. L., & Williams, D. R. (2015). Forgiveness and health… Annals of Behavioral Medicine, 49(3), 361–375.

• Volkow, N. D., Wang, G.-J., Fowler, J. S., & Telang, F. (2011). Overlapping neuronal circuits in addiction and obesity. NeuroImage, 59(2), 730–737.

• WHO Press. (2021). World report on ageing and health. World Health Organization.

• Wood, A. M., Froh, J. J., & Geraghty, A. W. A. (2010). Gratitude and well-being… Clinical Psychology Review, 30(7), 890–905.

• Worthington, E. L., Witvliet, C. V., Pietrini, P., & Miller, A. J. (2007). Forgiveness, health, and well-being. Journal of Behavioral Medicine, 30(4), 291–302.

• Worthington, E. L., & Scherer, M. (2004). Forgiveness is an emotion-focused coping strategy. Journal of Behavioral Medicine, 27(4), 299–316.

• Young, S. N. (2007). How to increase serotonin in the human brain without drugs. Journal of Psychiatry & Neuroscience, 32(6), 394–399.

5. ADDITIONAL ORGANIZATIONAL / REPORT REFERENCES

• American Counseling Association. (2020). Resources for dealing with grief. Retrieved from https://www.counseling.org

• AMERICAN JOURNAL OF PUBLIC HEALTH. (n.d.). American Public Health Association. Retrieved May 19, 2025, from https://ajph.aphapublications.org/

• American Psychological Association. (2017). Managing stress: Principles and strategies for health and well-being. Retrieved from https://www.apa.org/topics/stress

• American Psychological Association. (2019). Stress in America: Stress and current events. [Organizational PDF/Report]

• FRONTIERS IN PSYCHOLOGY. (n.d.). Retrieved May 19, 2025, from https://www.frontiersin.org/journals/psychology

• JOURNAL OF HEALTH PSYCHOLOGY. (n.d.). SAGE Journals. Retrieved May 19, 2025, from https://journals.sagepub.com/home/hpq

• National Alliance on Mental Illness. (2020). Mental health by the numbers. Retrieved from https://www.nami.org

• National Institutes of Health. (2021). Chronic pain and complementary health approaches. Retrieved from https://www.nih.gov

• NATURE REVIEWS GENETICS. (2025, May 12). EPIGENETICS: ARTICLES WITHIN NATURE REVIEWS GENETICS. Retrieved May 19, 2025, from https://www.nature.com/subjects/epigenetics/nrg

• Optimist International. (n.d.). Optimist Creed. Retrieved from https://www.optimist.org/member/creed.cfm

• THE JOURNAL OF POSITIVE PSYCHOLOGY. (2025). VOLUME 20, ISSUE 3. Taylor & Francis Online. Retrieved May 19, 2025, from https://www.tandfonline.com/toc/rpos20/current

• UC San Diego Health. (2025, May 1). MINDFULNESS CLINICAL TRIALS AT UCSD. Retrieved May 19, 2025, from https://clinicaltrials.ucsd.edu/mindfulness

• World Health Organization. (2021). World report on ageing and health. WHO Press.
• World Health Organization. (2022). Investing in mental health. [WHO Report]

ABOUT THE AUTHOR

Tad Sisler is an American Composer, Author and Producer of feature films and music. More than a thousand of his original works are available through *iTunes, Amazon* and virtually every other major marketplace. Through the years, **Tad** created and released independent feature films and documentaries, television shows, developed a music store and vast collection of music for film and television usages, in addition to published screenplays and books.

Tad is a voting member of *The Academy of Recording Arts & Sciences.* **Tad** invented a wireless karaoke all-in-one microphone that became a best-seller on *Amazon.* A child prodigy, Tad was playing advanced piano pieces at the age of 8, and rating superior in Classical piano competitions at 12. Tad won his first scholarship for singing at 12, attending the Idyllwild School of Music and the Arts, then affiliated with the University of Southern California.

FEATURE FILMS

Tad produced, edited, and released "**The Ghosts of Brewer Town**", a mystery feature film, currently available on *YouTube.*

TELEVISION PROJECTS

Tad launched the **Journey To An Extraordinary Life-Legends Among Us** documentary series, which chronicles the lives and careers of legendary artists, actors, sports figures and heroes of medicine, in a feature-film format.

BOOKS

Books, Audio Books and Podcasts released by **Tad** include "**Reflections in the Key of Life-The Steve Madaio Story**", chronicling the life and times of America's most prolific trumpeter. This book garnered a **Readers' Favorite Book Award** for Tad.

"**Mafia Baby**" is a shocking true story of a woman raped by a Mafioso, who then raised his child alone. Tad's autobiography, "**It's a Long Climb to The Middle**" *is* available currently on *Amazon* and *Barnes & Noble.* Screenplays in development by Tad Sisler include "**The Incredible Spark of Franklin Benjamin**", and "**Please Don't Forget**". Tad's latest **Music Mastery** collection of books is designed to educate and inspire musicians to become masters. His **Health and Longevity Mastery** series of books is crafted to educate on longevity, age reversal, and general wellness.

MUSIC

Tad's production music catalog tripled in size with the addition of thousands of excellent production music tracks, as well as hundreds of sound-alike tracks for the DJ/Karaoke industry, now distributed on **iTunes, Amazon Marketplace, CD Baby, Spotify, Rdio, Xbox Music** and dozens of other outlets Worldwide.

Tad produced and released "The Barcelona Sessions" to 1000 radio stations Worldwide, with never-before-heard original performances by Miles Davis' bassist, Bill Evan's drummer, Frank Sinatra's saxophonist, Maynard Ferguson's guitarist, and Andrae Crouch' flutist/saxophonist, produced by Tad Sisler in his recording studio.

Tad Sisler composed the full score to "**The Encore Of Tony Duran**", an indie feature film starring **Elliott Gould, William Katt, Nicki Ziering and Cody Kasch**, along with his co- composer Andrew Fraga, Jr. After having the distinction of being the first film to sell-out at the prestigious *Palm Springs International Film Festival*, the film won the **Jury Award** for **Best Feature Film** at the *Las Vegas Film Festival* and the *Santa Fe Film Festival*, as well as the **Indie Spirit Award** at the *Fort Lauderdale Film Festival* and the **Audience Favorite Award** at *Tallgrass Film Festival*, in conjunction with a **Lifetime Achievement Award** for **Elliott Gould.** The film is available on *Amazon Prime.*

Tad completed the music and audio editing for the TV Series "**American M.C.**". The first 7 episodes are complete and in the process of distribution through **iTunes**. Tad scored the Main Title theme to **American M.C.** as well as underscore and providing Music Supervision and source music.

PRODUCTION

Tad Sisler has been a valuable member of the team of specialists and project developers for **Yamaha Corporation of America**, delivering hundreds of intricate projects to exact **Yamaha** specifications over a 10-year period.

Tad received accolades in 2011 after being given the honor and challenge of doing the "official" remake of the iconic "**Andy Griffith Theme**" for the estate of the composer **Earle Hagen** as a perfect sound-alike, along with his composing associate Andrew Fraga, Jr.

Following a stint composing for a series entitled "**Famous Families**" on **Foxstar** and working as assistant to composer Jeff Edwards on the television series "**Silk Stalkings**" and "**Renegade**" in the late 1990's, Tad Sisler and founded & developed a production music catalog, containing thousands of high-quality music tracks available for sync licenses in film, television and advertising in more than 150 genres.

In addition to handling Music Supervision on "**The Encore Of Tony Duran**", and on "**American M.C.**", "**The Ghosts of Brewer Town**", "**Tis' The Season**", the "**Journey To an Extraordinary Life**" series, **Tad** placed his original music on **NBC, ABC/Disney, Warner Brothers Television, TNT,** US National Infomercial campaigns through **Guthy/Renker** and **Script To Screen**, as well as custom composing for the TV and Advertising industry.

Tad released contains hundreds of top-quality soundalike tracks produced by **Tad** and his associates, for DJ and Karaoke usages, currently on *ITunes, Amazon Marketplace, Spotify, Rdio, Xbox Music,* and many other outlets.

LIVE PRODUCTION

In the 1980's and 1990's, **Tad** and his team produced a series of live headliner events at multiple venues from the ground up, including sold-out performances by **Kenny Rogers, Earth, Wind & Fire, Los Lobos, Glen Campbell, The Righteous Brothers, Lou Rawls, Tito Puente,** the **Power Jam** featuring **Timmy T, Tara Kemp, Candyman, Soul To Soul** and more.

HISTORY

As a very young man, Tad Sisler worked as a performer for **Frank Sinatra**, studied music in choreography under world-famous Broadway Dancer/Choreographer **Jacque D'Amboise**, received superior ratings in classical piano performance in tough **Joanna Hodges** international competitions, and received private acting lessons from **Richard Burton**, a friend of his family.

Tad attended the prestigious **Idyllwild School of Music and the Arts** on vocal music scholarships during the period when it was affiliated with the **University of Southern California**. In High School, Tad was one of 100 statewide vocalists elected to the prestigious **All-State Choir** in Missouri.

During his storied career, Tad has also had the honor of performing with and working among such greats as **Gladys Knight, Rita Coolidge, B.B. King, Marilyn McCoo, Johnny Mathis, Kenny Rogers, Tito Puente, Sonny and Mary Bono, Gene Barry, Terry Cole-Whittaker, Shecky Greene,**

Peter Marshall, Mary Hart, Blackwell, Herb Jeffries, Trini Lopez, Glen Campbell, Jennifer Hudson and other legends.

Tad Sisler's extensive experience, state of the art facility and history of delivering quality feature films and music on time and on budget, as well as the ability to draw from an extensive catalog of production music, allows his experienced team to offer complete services in custom film and television production as well as in music composition and production efficiently.

Tad is proud and humbled to be a voting member of the **Academy of Recording Arts & Sciences**, which allows him to have a voice to vote for great artists worthy of winning a **Grammy Award**. Many of Tad's works have been placed into Grammy consideration.

In 2023, Tad won a prestigious **Telly Award** for creative excellence in his *Journey to an Extraordinary Life* film series.

Modern Renaissance Publishing is at the forefront of a new intellectual awakening, dedicated to fostering a renaissance of ideas that resonate in today's world. Our mission is to bring cutting-edge concepts and timeless wisdom to the public through a diverse array of publishing formats, including books, eBooks, and audiobooks.

We are proud to launch our **Music Mastery** series, offering comprehensive guides and insights for musicians of all levels. Our **Health and Longevity Mastery** series highlights the latest discoveries and insights into extending the human healthspan and lifespan. In addition to our literary endeavors, we also publish original music, enriching the cultural landscape with creative expressions. Whether you're seeking to expand your knowledge, enhance your skills, or simply be inspired,

Modern Renaissance Publishing provides the resources and content to empower your journey. Join us as we bridge the rich heritage of the past with the innovative spirit of the present to shape a brighter, more enlightened future.

©2025 by Tad Sisler

Publisher: MODERN RENAISSANCE PUBLISHING

IN USA +1 (818) 845-6700

modernrenaissancepublishing.com

Email: modernrenaissancepublishing@gmail.com

ISBN#978-1-966258-20-9

MODERN RENAISSANCE
PUBLISHING